THE
BROKEN ROAD

A. E. W. MASON

The Broken Road

A. E. W. Mason

© 1st World Library, 2007
PO Box 2211
Fairfield, IA 52556
www.1stworldlibrary.com
First Edition

LCCN: 2007934072

Softcover ISBN: 978-1-4218-9603-8
Hardcover ISBN: 978-1-4218-9703-5
eBook ISBN: 978-1-4218-9503-1

Purchase *"The Broken Road"*
as a traditional bound book at:
www.1stWorldLibrary.com/purchase.asp?ISBN=978-1-4218-9603-8

1st World Library is a literary, educational organization
dedicated to:

- Creating a free internet library of downloadable ebooks

- Hosting writing competitions and offering book publishing
  scholarships.

Interested in more 1st World Library books? contact:
literacy@1stworldlibrary.com
Check us out at: www.1stworldlibrary.com

1st World Library Literary Society

Giving Back to the World

"If you want to work on the core problem, it's early school literacy."

- James Barksdale, former CEO of Netscape

"No skill is more crucial to the future of a child, or to a democratic and prosperous society, than literacy."

- Los Angeles Times

"Literacy... means far more than learning how to read and write... The aim is to transmit... knowledge and promote social participation."

- UNESCO

"Literacy is not a luxury, it is a right and a responsibility. If our world is to meet the challenges of the twenty-first century we must harness the energy and creativity of all our citizens."

- President Bill Clinton

"Parents should be encouraged to read to their children, and teachers should be equipped with all available techniques for teaching literacy, so the varying needs and capacities of individual kids can be taken into account."

- Hugh Mackay

CONTENTS

CHAPTER I

THE BREAKING OF THE ROAD

It was the Road which caused the trouble. It usually is the road. That and a reigning prince who was declared by his uncle secretly to have sold his country to the British, and a half-crazed priest from out beyond the borders of Afghanistan, who sat on a slab of stone by the river-bank and preached a *djehad*. But above all it was the road—Linforth's road. It came winding down from the passes, over slopes of shale; it was built with wooden galleries along the precipitous sides of cliffs; it snaked treacherously further and further across the rich valley of Chiltistan towards the Hindu Kush, until the people of that valley could endure it no longer.

Then suddenly from Peshawur the wires began to flash their quiet and ominous messages. The road had been cut behind Linforth and his coolies. No news had come from him. No supplies could reach him. Luffe, who was in the country to the east of Chiltistan, had been informed. He had gathered together what troops he could lay his hands on and had already started over the eastern passes to Linforth's relief. But it was believed that the whole province of Chiltistan had risen. Moreover it was winter-time and the passes were deep in snow. The news was telegraphed to England. Comfortable gentlemen read it in their first-class carriages as they travelled to the City and murmured to each other common-places about the price of empire. And in a house at the foot of the Sussex Downs Linforth's young wife leaned over the cot of her child with the tears streaming from her eyes, and thought of the road with no less horror than the people of Chiltistan. Meanwhile the great men in Calcutta began to mobilise a field force at Nowshera, and all official India said uneasily, "Thank Heaven, Luffe's on the spot."

Charles Luffe had long since abandoned the army for the political service, and, indeed, he was fast approaching the time-limit of his career. He was a man of breadth and height, but rather heavy and dull of feature, with a worn face and a bald forehead. He had made enemies, and still made them, for he had not the art of suffering fools gladly; and, on the other hand, he made no friends. He had no sense of humour and no general information. He was, therefore, of no assistance at a dinner-party, but when there was trouble upon the Frontier, or beyond it, he was usually found to be the chief agent in the settlement.

Luffe alone had foreseen and given warning of the danger. Even Linforth, who was actually superintending the making of the road, had been kept in ignorance. At times, indeed, some spokesman from among the merchants of Kohara, the city of Chiltistan where year by year the caravans from Central Asia met the caravans from Central India, would come to his tent and expostulate.

"We are better without the road, your Excellency. Will you kindly stop it!" the merchant would say; and Linforth would then proceed to demonstrate how extremely valuable to the people of Chiltistan a better road would be:

"Kohara is already a great mart. In your bazaars at summer-time you see traders from Turkestan and Tibet and Siberia, mingling with the Hindoo merchants from Delhi and Lahore. The road will bring you still more trade."

The spokesman went back to the broad street of Kohara seemingly well content, and inch by inch the road crept nearer to the capital.

But Luffe was better acquainted with the Chiltis, a soft-spoken race of men, with musical, smooth voices and polite and pretty ways. But treachery was a point of honour with them and cold-blooded cruelty a habit. There was one particular story which Luffe was accustomed to tell as illustrative of the Chilti character.

"There was a young man who lived with his mother in a little hamlet close to Kohara. His mother continually urged him to marry, but for a long while he would not. He did not wish to marry. Finally, however, he fell in love with a pretty girl, made her his wife, and brought her home, to his mother's delight. But the mother's delight lasted for just five days. She began to complain, she began to quarrel; the young wife replied, and the din of their voices greatly distressed the young man, besides making him an object of ridicule to his neighbours. One evening, in a fit of passion, both women said they would stand it no longer. They ran out of the house and up the hillside, but as there was only one path they ran away together, quarrelling as they went. Then the young Chilti rose, followed them, caught them up, tied them in turn hand and foot, laid them side by side on a slab of stone, and quietly cut their throats.

"'Women talk too much,' he said, as he came back to a house unfamiliarly quiet. 'One had really to put a stop to it.'"

Knowing this and many similar stories, Luffe had been for some while on the alert. Whispers reached him of dangerous talk in the bazaars of Kohara, Peshawur, and even of Benares in India proper. He heard of the growing power of the old Mullah by the river-bank. He was aware of the accusations against the ruling Khan. He knew that after night had fallen Wafadar Nazim, the Khan's uncle, a restless, ambitious, disloyal man, crept down to the river-bank and held converse with the priest. Thus he was ready so far as he could be ready.

The news that the road was broken was flashed to him from the nearest telegraph station, and within twenty-four hours he led out a small force from his Agency—a battalion of Sikhs, a couple of companies of Gurkhas, two guns of a mountain battery, and a troop of irregular levies—and disappeared over the pass, now deep in snow.

"Would he be in time?"

Not only in India was the question asked. It was asked in England, too, in the clubs of Pall Mall, but nowhere with so passionate an outcry as in the house at the foot of the Sussex Downs.

To Sybil Linforth these days were a time of intolerable suspense. The horror of the Road was upon her. She dreamed of it when she slept, so that she came to dread sleep, and tried, as long as she might, to keep her heavy eyelids from closing over her eyes. The nights to her were terrible. Now it was she, with her child in her arms, who walked for ever and ever along that road, toiling through snow or over shale and finding no rest anywhere. Now it was her boy alone, who wandered along one of the wooden galleries high up above the river torrent, until a plank broke and he fell through with a piteous scream. Now it was her husband, who could go neither forward nor backward, since in front and behind a chasm gaped. But most often it was a man—a young

A. E. W. Mason

Englishman, who pursued a young Indian along that road into the mists. Somehow, perhaps because it was inexplicable, perhaps because its details were so clear, this dream terrified her more than all the rest. She could tell the very dress of the Indian who fled—a young man—young as his pursuer. A thick sheepskin coat swung aside as he ran and gave her a glimpse of gay silk; soft leather boots protected his feet; and upon his face there was a look of fury and wild fear. She never woke from this dream but her heart was beating wildly. For a few moments after waking peace would descend upon her.

"It is a dream—all a dream," she would whisper to herself with contentment, and then the truth would break upon her dissociated from the dream. Often she rose from her bed and, kneeling beside the boy's cot, prayed with a passionate heart that the curse of the Road—that road predicted by a Linforth years ago—might overpass this generation.

Meanwhile rumours came—rumours of disaster. Finally a messenger broke through and brought sure tidings. Luffe had marched quickly, had come within thirty miles of Kohara before he was stopped. In a strong fort at a bend of the river the young Khan with his wife and a few adherents had taken refuge. Luffe joined the Khan, sought to push through to Kohara and rescue Linforth, but was driven back. He and his troops and the Khan were now closely besieged by Wafadar Nazim.

The work of mobilisation was pressed on; a great force was gathered at Nowshera; Brigadier Appleton was appointed to command it.

"Luffe will hold out," said official India, trying to be cheerful.

Perhaps the only man who distrusted Luffe's ability to hold out was Brigadier Appleton, who had personal reasons for his views. Brigadier Appleton was no fool, and yet Luffe had not suffered him gladly. All the more, therefore, did he hurry on the preparations. The force marched out on the new road to Chiltistan. But meanwhile the weeks were passing, and up beyond the snow-encumbered hills the beleaguered troops stood cheerfully at bay behind the thick fort-walls.

A. E. W. Mason

CHAPTER II

INSIDE THE FORT

The six English officers made it a practice, so far as they could, to dine together; and during the third week of the siege the conversation happened one evening to take a particular turn. Ever afterwards, during this one hour of the twenty-four, it swerved regularly into the same channel. The restaurants of London were energetically discussed, and their merits urged by each particular partisan with an enthusiasm which would have delighted a shareholder. Where you got the best dinner, where the prettiest women were to be seen, whether a band was a drawback or an advantage—not a point was omitted, although every point had been debated yesterday or the day before. To-night the grave question of the proper number for a supper party was opened by Major Dewes of the 5th Gurkha Regiment.

"Two," said the Political Officer promptly, and he chuckled under his grey moustache. "I remember the last time I was in London I took out to supper—none of the coryphees you boys are so proud of being seen about with, but"—and, pausing impressively, he named a reigning lady of the light-opera stage.

"You did!" exclaimed a subaltern.

"I did," he replied complacently.

"What did you talk about?" asked Major Dewes, and the Political Officer suddenly grew serious.

"I was very interested," he said quietly. "I got knowledge which it was good for me to have. I saw something which it was well for me to see. I wished—I wish now—that some of the rulers and the politicians could have seen what I saw that night."

A brief silence followed upon his words, and during that silence certain sounds became audible—the beating of tom-toms and the cries of men. The dinner-table was set in the verandah of an inner courtyard open to the sky, and the sounds descended into that well quite distinctly, but faintly, as if they were made at a distance in the dark, open country. The six men seated about the table paid no heed to those sounds; they had had them in their ears too long. And five of the six were occupied in wondering what in the world Sir Charles Luffe, K.C.S.I., could have learnt of value to him at a solitary supper party with a lady of comic opera. For it was evident that he had spoken in deadly earnest.

Captain Lynes of the Sikhs broke the silence:

"What's this?" he asked, as an orderly offered to him a dish.

"Let us not inquire too closely," said the Political Officer. "This is the fourth week of the siege."

The rice-fields of the broad and fertile valley were trampled down and built upon with sangars. The siege had cut its scars upon the fort's rough walls of mud and projecting beams. But nowhere were its marks more visible than upon the faces of the Englishmen in the verandah of that courtyard.

A. E. W. Mason

Dissimilar as they were in age and feature, sleepless nights and the unrelieved tension had given to their drawn faces almost a family likeness. They were men tired out, but as yet unaware of their exhaustion, so bright a flame burnt within each one of them. Somewhere amongst the snow-passes on the north-east a relieving force would surely be encamped that night, a day's march nearer than it was yesterday. Somewhere amongst the snow-passes in the south a second force would be surely advancing from Nowshera, probably short of rations, certainly short of baggage, that it might march the lighter. When one of those two forces deployed across the valley and the gates of the fort were again thrown open to the air the weeks of endurance would exact their toll. But that time was not yet come. Meanwhile the six men held on cheerily, inspiring the garrison with their own confidence, while day after day a province in arms flung itself in vain against their blood-stained walls. Luffe, indeed, the Political Officer, fought with disease as well as with the insurgents of Chiltistan; and though he remained the master-mind of the defence, the Doctor never passed him without an anxious glance. For there were the signs of death upon his face.

"The fourth week!" said Lynes. "Is it, by George? Well, the siege won't last much longer now. The Sirkar don't leave its servants in the lurch. That's what these hill-tribes never seem to understand. How is Travers?" he asked of the Doctor.

Travers, a subaltern of the North Surrey Light Infantry, had been shot through the thigh in the covered waterway to the river that morning.

"He's going on all right," replied the Doctor. "Travers had bad luck. It must have been a stray bullet which slipped through that chink in the stones. For he could not have been seen—"

As he spoke a cry rang clearly out. All six men looked upwards through the open roof to the clear dark sky, where the stars shone frostily bright.

"What was that?" asked one of the six.

"Hush," said Luffe, and for a moment they all listened in silence, with expectant faces and their bodies alert to spring from their chairs. Then the cry was heard again. It was a wail more than a cry, and it sounded strangely solitary, strangely sad, as it floated through the still air. There was the East in that cry trembling out of the infinite darkness above their heads. But the six men relaxed their limbs. They had expected the loud note of the Pathan war-cry to swell sonorously, and with intervals shorter and shorter until it became one menacing and continuous roar.

"It is someone close under the walls," said Luffe, and as he ended a Sikh orderly appeared at the entrance of a passage into the courtyard, and, advancing to the table, saluted.

"Sahib, there is a man who claims that he comes with a message from Wafadar Nazim."

"Tell him that we receive no messages at night, as Wafadar Nazim knows well. Let him come in the morning and he shall be admitted. Tell him that if he does not go back at once the sentinels will fire." And Luffe nodded to one of the younger officers. "Do you see to it, Haslewood."

Haslewood rose and went out from the courtyard with the orderly. He returned in a few minutes, saying that the man had returned to Wafadar Nazim's camp. The six men resumed their meal, and just as they ended it a Pathan glided in white flowing garments into the courtyard and bowed low.

A. E. W. Mason

"Huzoor," he said, "His Highness the Khan sends you greeting. God has been very good to him. A son has been born to him this day, and he sends you this present, knowing that you will value it more than all that he has"; and carefully unfolding a napkin, he laid with reverence upon the table a little red cardboard box. The mere look of the box told the six men what the present was even before Luffe lifted the lid. It was a box of fifty gold-tipped cigarettes, and applause greeted their appearance.

"If he could only have a son every day," said Lynes, and in the laugh which followed upon the words Luffe alone did not join. He leaned his forehead upon his hand and sat in a moody silence. Then he turned towards the servant and bade him thank his master.

"I will come myself to offer our congratulations after dinner if his Highness will receive me," said Luffe.

The box of cigarettes went round the table. Each man took one, lighted it, and inhaled the smoke silently and very slowly. The garrison had run out of tobacco a week before. Now it had come to them welcome as a gift from Heaven. The moment was one of which the perfect enjoyment was not to be marred by any speech. Only a grunt of satisfaction or a deep sigh of pleasure was now and then to be heard, as the smoke curled upwards from the little paper sticks. Each man competed with his neighbour in the slowness of his respiration, each man wanted to be the last to lay down his cigarette and go about his work. And then the Doctor said in a whisper to Major Dewes:

"That's bad. Look!"

Luffe, a mighty smoker in his days of health, had let his cigarette go out, had laid it half-consumed upon the edge of his plate. But it seemed that ill-health was not all to blame. He had the look of one who had forgotten his company. He was withdrawn amongst his own speculations, and his eyes looked out beyond that smoke-laden room in a fort amongst the Himalaya mountains into future years dim with peril and trouble.

"There is no moon," he said at length. "We can get some exercise to-night"; and he rose from the table and ascended a little staircase on to the flat roof of the fort. Major Dewes and the three other officers got up and went about their business. Dr. Bodley, the surgeon, alone remained seated. He waited until the tramp of his companions' feet had died away, and then he drew from his pocket a briarwood pipe, which he polished lovingly. He walked round the table and, collecting the ends of the cigarettes, pressed them into the bowl of the pipe.

"Thank Heavens I am not an executive officer," he said, as he lighted his pipe and settled himself again comfortably in his chair. It should be mentioned, perhaps, that he not only doctored and operated on the sick and wounded, but he kept the stores, and when any fighting was to be done, took a rifle and filled any place which might be vacant in the firing-line.

"There are now forty-four cigarettes," he reflected. "At six a day they will last a week. In a week something will have happened. Either the relieving force will be here, or—yes, decidedly something will have happened." And as he blew the smoke out from between his lips he added solemnly: "If not to us, to the Political Officer."

Meanwhile Luffe paced the roof of the fort in the darkness. The fort was built in the bend of a swift, wide river, and so far as three sides were concerned was securely placed. For on three the low precipitous cliffs overhung the tumbling

A. E. W. Mason

water. On the fourth, however, the fertile plain of the valley stretched open and flat up to the very gates.

In front of the forts a line of sangars extended, the position of each being marked even now by a glare of light above it, which struck up from the fire which the insurgents had lit behind the walls of stone. And from one and another of the sangars the monotonous beat of a tom-tom came to Luffe's ears.

Luffe walked up and down for a time upon the roof. There was a new sangar to-night, close to the North Tower, which had not existed yesterday. Moreover, the almond trees in the garden just outside the western wall were in blossom, and the leaves upon the branches were as a screen, where only the bare trunks showed a fortnight ago.

But with these matters Luffe was not at this moment concerned. They helped the enemy, they made the defence more arduous, but they were trivial in his thoughts. Indeed, the siege itself was to him an unimportant thing. Even if the fortress fell, even if every man within perished by the sword—why, as Lynes had said, the Sirkar does not forget its servants. The relieving force might march in too late, but it would march in. Men would die, a few families in England would wear mourning, the Government would lose a handful of faithful servants. England would thrill with pride and anger, and the rebellion would end as rebellions always ended.

Luffe was troubled for quite another cause. He went down from the roof, walked by courtyard and winding passage to the quarters of the Khan. A white-robed servant waited for him at the bottom of a broad staircase in a room given up to lumber. A broken bicycle caught Luffe's eye. On the ledge of a window stood a photographic camera. Luffe mounted the stairs and was ushered into the Khan's presence. He bowed with deference and congratulated the Khan upon the birth of his heir.

"I have been thinking," said the Khan—"ever since my son was born I have been thinking. I have been a good friend to the English. I am their friend and servant. News has come to me of their cities and colleges. I will send my son to England, that he may learn your wisdom, and so return to rule over his kingdom. Much good will come of it." Luffe had expected the words. The young Khan had a passion for things English. The bicycle and the camera were signs of it. Unwise men had applauded his enlightenment. Unwise at all events in Luffe's opinion. It was, indeed, greatly because of his enlightenment that he and a handful of English officers and troops were beleaguered in the fortress.

"He shall go to Eton and to Oxford, and much good for my people will come of it," said the Khan. Luffe listened gravely and politely; but he was thinking of an evening when he had taken out to supper a reigning queen of comic opera. The recollection of that evening remained with him when he ascended once more to the roof of the fort and saw the light of the fires above the sangars. A voice spoke at his elbow. "There is a new sangar being built in the garden. We can hear them at work," said Dewes.

Luffe walked cautiously along the roof to the western end. Quite clearly they could hear the spades at work, very near to the wall, amongst the almond and the mulberry trees.

"Get a fireball," said Luffe in a whisper, "and send up a dozen Sikhs."

On the parapet of the roof a rough palisade of planks had been erected to protect the defenders from the riflemen in the

A. E. W. Mason

valley and across the river. Behind this palisade the Sikhs crept silently to their positions. A ball made of pinewood chips and straw, packed into a covering of canvas, was brought on to the roof and saturated with kerosene oil. "Are you ready?" said Luffe; "then now!" Upon the word the fireball was lit and thrown far out. It circled through the air, dropped, and lay blazing upon the ground. By its light under the branches of the garden trees could be seen the Pathans building a stone sangar, within thirty yards of the fort's walls.

"Fire!" cried Luffe. "Choose your men and fire."

All at once the silence of the night was torn by the rattle of musketry, and afar off the tom-toms beat yet more loudly.

Luffe looked on with every faculty alert. He saw with a smile that the Doctor had joined them and lay behind a plank, firing rapidly and with a most accurate aim. But at the back of his mind all the while that he gave his orders was still the thought, "All this is nothing. The one fateful thing is the birth of a son to the Khan of Chiltistan." The little engagement lasted for about half an hour. The insurgents then drew back from the garden, leaving their dead upon the field. The rattle of the musketry ceased altogether. Behind the parapet one Sikh had been badly wounded by a bullet in the thigh. Already the Doctor was attending to his hurts.

"It is a small thing, Huzoor," said the wounded soldier, looking upwards to Luffe, who stood above him; "a very small thing," but even as he spoke pain cut the words short.

"Yes, a small thing"; Luffe did not speak the words, but he thought them. He turned away and walked back again across the roof. The new sangar would not be built that night. But it was a small thing compared with all that lay hidden in the future.

As he paced that side of the fort which faced the plain there rose through the darkness, almost beneath his feet, once more the cry which had reached his ears while he sat at dinner in the courtyard.

He heard a few paces from him the sharp order to retire given by a sentinel. But the voice rose again, claiming admission to the fort, and this time a name was uttered urgently, an English name.

"Don't fire," cried Luffe to the sentinel, and he leaned over the wall.

"You come from Wafadar Nazim, and alone?"

"Huzoor, my life be on it."

"With news of Sahib Linforth?"

"Yes, news which his Highness Wafadar Nazim thinks it good for you to know"; and the voice in the darkness rose to insolence.

Luffe strained his eyes downwards. He could see nothing. He listened, but he could hear no whispering voices. He hesitated. He was very anxious to hear news of Linforth.

"I will let you in," he cried; "but if there be more than one the lives of all shall be the price."

He went down into the fort. Under his orders Captain Lynes drew up inside the gate a strong guard of Sikhs with their rifles loaded and bayonets fixed. A few lanterns threw a dim light upon the scene, glistening here and there upon the polish of an accoutrement or a rifle-barrel.

"Present," whispered Lynes, and the rifles were raised to the shoulder, with every muzzle pointing towards the gate.

Then Lynes himself went forward, removed the bars, and turned the key in the lock. The gate swung open noiselessly a little way, and a tall man, clad in white flowing robes, with a deeply pock-marked face and a hooked nose, walked majestically in. He stood quite still while the gate was barred again behind him, and looked calmly about him with inquisitive bright eyes.

"Will you follow me?" said Luffe, and he led the way through the rabbit-warren of narrow alleys into the centre of the fort.

CHAPTER III

LINFORTH'S DEATH

Luffe had taken a large bare low-roofed room supported upon pillars for his council-chamber. Thither he conducted his visitor. Camp chairs were placed for himself and Major Dewes and Captain Lynes. Cushions were placed upon the ground for his visitor. Luffe took his seat in the middle, with Dewes upon his right and Lynes upon his left. Dewes expected him at once to press for information as to Linforth. But Luffe knew very well that certain time must first be wasted in ceremonious preliminaries. The news would only be spoken after a time and in a roundabout fashion.

"If we receive you without the distinction which is no doubt your due," said Luffe politely, "you must remember that I make it a rule not to welcome visitors at night."

The visitor smiled and bowed.

"It is a great grief to his Highness Wafadar Nazim that you put so little faith in him," replied the Chilti. "See how he trusts you! He sends me, his Diwan, his Minister of Finance, in the night time to come up to your walls and into your fort, so great is his desire to learn that the Colonel Sahib is well."

A. E. W. Mason

Luffe in his turn bowed with a smile of gratitude. It was not the time to point out that his Highness Wafadar Nazim was hardly taking the course which a genuine solicitude for the Colonel Sahib's health would recommend.

"His Highness has but one desire in his heart. He desires peace—peace so that this country may prosper, and peace because of his great love for the Colonel Sahib."

Again Luffe bowed.

"But to all his letters the Colonel Sahib returns the same answer, and truly his Highness is at a loss what to do in order that he may ensure the safety of the Colonel Sahib and his followers," the Diwan continued pensively. "I will not repeat what has been already said," and at once he began at interminable length to contradict his words. He repeated the proposals of surrender made by Wafadar Nazim from beginning to end. The Colonel Sahib was to march out of the fort with his troops, and his Highness would himself conduct him into British territory.

"If the Colonel Sahib dreads the censure of his own Government, his Highness will take all the responsibility for the Colonel Sahib's departure. But no blame will fall upon the Colonel Sahib. For the British Government, with whom Wafadar Nazim has always desired to live in amity, desires peace too, as it has always said. It is the British Government which has broken its treaties."

"Not so," replied Luffe. "The road was undertaken with the consent of the Khan of Chiltistan, who is the ruler of this country, and Wafadar, his uncle, merely the rebel. Therefore take back my last word to Wafadar Nazim. Let him make submission to me as representative of the Sirkar, and lay down his arms. Then I will intercede for him with the

Government, so that his punishment be light."

The Diwan smiled and his voice changed once more to a note of insolence.

"His Highness Wafadar Nazim is now the Khan of Chiltistan. The other, the deposed, lies cooped up in this fort, a prisoner of the British, whose willing slave he has always been. The British must retire from our country. His Highness Wafadar Nazim desires them no harm. But they must go now!"

Luffe looked sternly at the Diwan.

"Tell Wafadar Nazim to have a care lest they go never, but set their foot firmly upon the neck of this rebellious people."

He rose to signify that the conference was at an end. But the Diwan did not stir. He smiled pensively and played with the tassels of his cushion.

"And yet," he said, "how true it is that his Highness thinks only of the Colonel Sahib's safety."

Some note of satisfaction, not quite perfectly concealed, some sly accent of triumph sounding through the gently modulated words, smote upon Luffe's ears, and warned him that the true meaning of the Diwan's visit was only now to be revealed. All that had gone before was nothing. The polite accusations, the wordy repetitions, the expressions of good will—these were the mere preliminaries, the long salute before the combat. Luffe steeled himself against a blow, controlling his face and his limbs lest a look or a gesture should betray the hurt. And it was well that he did, for the next moment the blow fell.

A. E. W. Mason

"For bad news has come to us. Sahib Linforth met his death two days ago, fifty miles from here, in the camp of his Excellency Abdulla Mahommed, the Commander-in-Chief to his Highness. Abdulla Mahommed is greatly grieved, knowing well that this violent act will raise up a prejudice against him and his Highness. Moreover, he too would live in friendship with the British. But his soldiers are justly provoked by the violation of treaties by the British, and it is impossible to stay their hands. Therefore, before Abdulla Mahommed joins hands with my master, Wafadar Nazim, before this fort, it will be well for the Colonel Sahib and his troops to be safely out of reach."

Luffe was doubtful whether to believe the words or no. The story might be a lie to frighten him and to discourage the garrison. On the other hand, it was likely enough to be true. And if true, it was the worst news which Luffe had heard for many a long day.

"Let me hear how the accident—occurred," he said, smiling grimly at the euphemism he used.

"Sahib Linforth was in the tent set apart for him by Abdulla Mahommed. There were guards to protect him, but it seems they did not watch well. Huzoor, all have been punished, but punishment will not bring Sahib Linforth to life again. Therefore hear the words of Wafadar Nazim, spoken now for the last time. He himself will escort you and your soldiers and officers to the borders of British territory, so that he may rejoice to know that you are safe. You will leave his Highness Mir Ali behind, who will resign his throne in favour of his uncle Wafadar, and so there will be peace."

"And what will happen to Mir Ali, whom we have promised to protect?"

The Diwan shrugged his shoulders in a gentle, deprecatory fashion and smiled his melancholy smile. His gesture and his attitude suggested that it was not in the best of taste to raise so unpleasant a question. But he did not reply in words.

"You will tell Wafadar Nazim that we will know how to protect his Highness the Khan, and that we will teach Abdulla Mahommed a lesson in that respect before many moons have passed," Luffe said sternly. "As for this story of Sahib Linforth, I do not believe a word of it."

The Diwan nodded his head.

"It was believed that you would reply in this way."

"Therefore here are proofs." He drew from his dress a silver watch upon a leather watch-guard, a letter-case, and to these he added a letter in Linforth's own hand. He handed them to Luffe.

Luffe handed the watch and chain to Dewes, and opened the letter-case. There was a letter in it, written in a woman's handwriting, and besides the letter the portrait of a girl. He glanced at the letter and glanced at the portrait. Then he passed them on to Dewes.

Dewes looked at the portrait with a greater care. The face was winning rather than pretty. It seemed to him that it was one of those faces which might become beautiful at many moments through the spirit of the woman, rather than from any grace of feature. If she loved, for instance, she would be really beautiful for the man she loved.

"I wonder who she is," he said thoughtfully.

"I know," replied Luffe, almost carelessly. He was immersed

in the second letter which the Diwan had handed to him.

"Who is it?" asked Dewes.

"Linforth's wife."

"His wife!" exclaimed Dewes, and, looking at the photograph again, he said in a low voice which was gentle with compassion, "Poor woman!"

"Yes, yes. Poor woman!" said Luffe, and he went on reading his letter.

It was characteristic of Luffe that he should feel so little concern in the domestic side of Linforth's life. He was not very human in his outlook on the world. Questions of high policy interested and engrossed his mind; he lived for the Frontier, not so much subduing a man's natural emotions as unaware of them. Men figured in his thoughts as the instruments of policy; their womenfolk as so many hindrances or aids to the fulfilment of their allotted tasks. Thus Linforth's death troubled him greatly, since Linforth was greatly concerned in one great undertaking. Moreover, the scheme had been very close to Linforth's heart, even as it was to Luffe's. But Linforth's wife was in England, and thus, as it seemed to him, neither aid nor impediment. But in that he was wrong. She had been the mainspring of Linforth's energy, and so much was evident in the letter which Luffe read slowly to the end.

"Yes, Linforth's dead," said he, with a momentary discouragement. "There are many whom we could more easily have spared. Of course the thing will go on. That's certain," he said, nodding his head. A cold satisfaction shone in his eyes. "But Linforth was part of the Thing."

He passed the second letter to Dewes, who read it; and for a while both men remained thoughtful and, as it seemed, unaware for the moment of the Diwan's presence. There was this difference, however. Luffe was thinking of "the Thing"; Dewes was pondering on the grim little tragedy which these letters revealed, and thanking Heaven in all simplicity of heart that there was no woman waiting in fear because of him and trembling at sight of each telegraph boy she met upon the road.

The grim little tragedy was not altogether uncommon upon the Indian frontier, but it gained vividness from the brevity of the letters which related it. The first one, that in the woman's hand, written from a house under the Downs of Sussex, told of the birth of a boy in words at once sacred and simple. They were written for the eyes of one man, and Major Dewes had a feeling that his own, however respect-fully, violated their sanctity. The second letter was an unfinished one written by the husband to the wife from his tent amongst the rabble of Abdulla Mahommed. Linforth clearly understood that this was the last letter he would write. "I am sitting writing this by the light of a candle. The tent door is open. In front of me I can see the great snow-mountains. All the ugliness of the lower shale slopes is hidden. By such a moonlight, my dear, may you always look back upon my memory. For it is over, Sybil. They are waiting until I fall asleep. I have been warned of it. But I shall fall asleep to-night. I have kept awake for two nights. I am very tired."

He had fallen asleep even before the letter was completed. There was a message for the boy and a wish:

"May he meet a woman like you, my dear, when his time comes, and love her as I love you," and again came the phrase, "I am very tired." It spoke of the boy's school, and

A. E. W. Mason

continued: "Whether he will come out here it is too early to think about. But the road will not be finished—and I wonder. If he wants to, let him! We Linforths belong to the road," and for the third time the phrase recurred, "I am very tired," and upon the phrase the letter broke off.

Dewes could imagine Linforth falling forward with his head upon his hands, his eyes heavy with sleep, while from without the tent the patient Chiltis watched until he slept.

"How did it happen?" he asked.

"They cast a noose over his head," replied the Diwan, "dragged him from the tent and stabbed him."

Dewes nodded and turned to Luffe.

"These letters and things must go home to his wife. It's hard on her, with a boy only a few months old."

"A boy?" said Luffe, rousing himself from his thoughts. "Oh! there's a boy? I had not noticed that. I wonder how far the road will have gone when he comes out." There was no doubt in Luffe's mind, at all events, as to the boy's destiny. He turned to the Diwan.

"Tell Wafadar Nazim that I will open the gates of this fort and march down to British territory after he has made submission," he said.

The Diwan smiled in a melancholy way. He had done his best, but the British were, of course, all mad. He bowed himself out of the room and stalked through the alleys to the gates.

"Wafadar Nazim must be very sure of victory," said Luffe.

"He would hardly have given us that unfinished letter had he a fear we should escape him in the end."

"He could not read what was written," said Dewes.

"But he could fear what was written," replied Luffe.

As he walked across the courtyard he heard the crack of a rifle. The sound came from across the river. The truce was over, the siege was already renewed.

CHAPTER IV

LUFFE LOOKS FORWARD

It was the mine underneath the North Tower which brought the career of Luffe to an end. The garrison, indeed, had lived in fear of this peril ever since the siege began. But inasmuch as no attempt to mine had been made during the first month, the fear had grown dim. It was revived during the fifth week. The officers were at mess at nine o'clock in the evening, when a havildar of Sikhs burst into the courtyard with the news that the sound of a pick could be heard from the chamber of the tower.

"At last!" cried Dewes, springing to his feet. The six men hurried to the tower. A long loophole had been fashioned in the thick wall on a downward slant, so that a marksman might command anyone who crept forward to fire the fort. Against this loophole Luffe leaned his ear.

"Do you hear anything, sir?" asked a subaltern of the Sappers who was attached to the force.

"Hush!" said Luffe.

He listened, and he heard quite clearly underneath the ground below him the dull shock of a pickaxe. The noise came almost from beneath his feet; so near the mine had been already driven to the walls. The strokes fell with the regularity of the ticking of a clock. But at times the sound changed in character. The muffled thud of the pick upon earth became a clang as it struck upon stone.

"Do you listen!" said Luffe, giving way to Dewes, and Dewes in his turn leaned his ear against the loophole.

"What do you think?" asked Luffe.

Dewes stood up straight again.

"I'll tell you what I am thinking. I am thinking it sounds like the beating of a clock in a room where a man lies dying," he said.

Luffe nodded his head. But images and romantic sayings struck no response from him. He turned to the young Sapper.

"Can we countermine?"

The young Engineer took the place of Major Dewes.

"We can try, but we are late," said he.

"It must be a sortie then," said Luffe.

"Yes," exclaimed Lynes eagerly. "Let me go, Sir Charles!"

Luffe smiled at his enthusiasm.

"How many men will you require?" he asked. "Sixty?"

"A hundred," replied Dewes promptly.

All that night Luffe superintended the digging of the countermine, while Dewes made ready for the sortie. By daybreak the arrangements were completed. The gunpowder bags, with their fuses attached, were distributed, the gates were suddenly flung open, and Lynes raced out with a hundred Ghurkhas and Sikhs across the fifty yards of open ground to the sangar behind which the mine shaft had been opened. The work of the hundred men was quick and complete. Within half an hour, Lynes, himself wounded, had brought back his force, and left the mine destroyed. But during that half-hour disaster had fallen upon the garrison. Luffe had dropped as he was walking back across the courtyard to his office. For a few minutes he lay unnoticed in the empty square, his face upturned to the sky, and then a clamorous sound of lamentation was heard and an orderly came running through the alleys of the Fort, crying out that the Colonel Sahib was dead.

He was not dead, however. He recovered conciousness that night, and early in the morning Dewes was roused from his sleep. He woke to find the Doctor shaking him by the shoulder.

"Luffe wants you. He has not got very long now. He has something to say."

Dewes slipped on his clothes, and hurried down the stairs. He followed the Doctor through the little winding alleys which gave to the Fort the appearance of a tiny village. It was broad daylight, but the fortress was strangely silent. The people whom he passed either spoke not at all or spoke only in low tones. They sat huddled in groups, waiting. Fear was abroad that morning. It was known that the brain of the defence was dying. It was known, too, what cruel fate awaited those within the Fort, if those without ever forced the gates and burst in upon their victims.

Dewes found the Political Officer propped up on pillows on his camp-bed. The door from the courtyard was open, and the morning light poured brightly into the room.

"Sit here, close to me, Dewes," said Luffe in a whisper, "and listen, for I am very tired." A smile came upon his face. "Do you remember Linforth's letters? How that phrase came again and again: 'I am very tired.'"

The Doctor arranged the pillows underneath his shoulders, and then Luffe said:

"All right. I shall do now."

He waited until the Doctor had gone from the room and continued:

"I am not going to talk to you about the Fort. The defence is safe in your hands, so long as defence is possible. Besides, if it falls it's not a great thing. The troops will come up and trample down Wafadar Nazim and Abdulla Mahommed. They are not the danger. The road will go on again, even though Linforth's dead. No, the man whom I am afraid of is—the son of the Khan."

Dewes stared, and then said in a soothing voice:

"He will be looked after."

"You think my mind's wandering," continued Luffe. "It never was clearer in my life. The Khan's son is a boy a week old. Nevertheless I tell you that boy is the danger in Chiltistan. The father—we know him. A good fellow who has lost all the confidence of his people. There is hardly an adherent of his who genuinely likes him; there's hardly a man in this Fort who doesn't believe that he wished to sell

A. E. W. Mason

his country to the British. I should think he is impossible here in the future. And everyone in Government House knows it. We shall do the usual thing, I have no doubt—pension him off, settle him down comfortably outside the borders of Chiltistan, and rule the country as trustee for his son—until the son comes of age."

Dewes realised surely enough that Luffe was in possession of his faculties, but he thought his anxiety exaggerated.

"You are looking rather far ahead, aren't you, sir?" he asked.

Luffe smiled.

"Twenty-one years. What are twenty-one years to India? My dear Dewes!"

He was silent. It seemed as though he were hesitating whether he would say a word more to this Major who in India talked of twenty-one years as a long span of time. But there was no one else to whom he could confide his fears. If Dewes was not brilliant, he was at all events all that there was.

"I wish I was going to live," he cried in a low voice of exasperation. "I wish I could last just long enough to travel down to Calcutta and *make* them listen to me. But there's no hope of it. You must do what you can, Dewes, but very likely they won't pay any attention to you. Very likely you'll believe me wrong yourself, eh? Poor old Luffe, a man with a bee in his bonnet, eh?" he whispered savagely.

"No, sir," replied Dewes. "You know the Frontier. I know that."

"And even there you are wrong. No man knows the Frontier.

We are all stumbling in the dark among these peoples, with their gentle voices and their cut-throat ways. The most that you can know is that you are stumbling in the dark. Well, let's get back to the boy here. This country will be kept for him, for twenty-one years. Where is he going to be during those twenty-one years?"

Dewes caught at the question as an opportunity for reassuring the Political Officer.

"Why, sir, the Khan told us. Have you forgotten? He is to go to Eton and Oxford. He'll see something of England. He will learn—" and Major Dewes stopped short, baffled by the look of hopelessness upon the Political Officer's face.

"I think you are all mad," said Luffe, and he suddenly started up in his bed and cried with vehemence, "You take these boys to England. You train them in the ways of the West, the ideas of the West, and then you send them back again to the East, to rule over Eastern people, according to Eastern ideas, and you think all is well. I tell you, Dewes, it's sheer lunacy. Of course it's true—this boy won't perhaps suffer in esteem among his people quite as much as others have done. He belongs and his people belong to the Maulai sect. The laws of religion are not strict among them. They drink wine, they eat what they will, they do not lose caste so easily. But you have to look at the man as he will be, the hybrid mixture of East and West."

He sank back among his pillows, exhausted by the violence of his outcry, and for a little while he was silent. Then he began again, but this time in a low, pleading voice, which was very unusual in him, and which kept the words he spoke vivid and fresh in Dewes' memory for many years to come. Indeed, Dewes would not have believed that Luffe could have spoken on any subject with so much wistfulness.

A. E. W. Mason

"Listen to me, Dewes. I have lived for the Frontier. I have had no other interest, almost no other ties. I am not a man of friends. I believed at one time Linforth was my friend. I believed I liked him very much. But I think now that it was only because he was bound up with the Frontier. The Frontier has been my wife, my children, my home, my one long and lasting passion. And I am very well content that it has been so. I don't regret missed opportunities of happiness. What I regret is that I shall not be alive in twenty-one years to avert the danger I foresee, or to laugh at my fears if I am wrong. They can do what they like in Rajputana and Bengal and Bombay. But on the Frontier I want things to go well. Oh, how I want them to go well!"

Luffe had grown very pale, and the sweat glistened upon his forehead. Dewes held to his lips a glass of brandy which stood upon a table beside the bed.

"What danger do you foresee?" asked Dewes. "I will remember what you say."

"Yes, remember it; write it out, so that you may remember it, and din it into their ears at Government House," said Luffe. "You take these boys, you give them Oxford, a season in London—did you ever have a season in London when you were twenty-one, Dewes? You show them Paris. You give them opportunities of enjoyment, such as no other age, no other place affords—has ever afforded. You give them, for a short while, a life of colour, of swift crowding hours of pleasure, and then you send them back—to settle down in their native States, and obey the orders of the Resident. Do you think they will be content? Do you think they will have their heart in their work, in their humdrum life, in their elaborate ceremonies? Oh, there are instances enough to convince if only people would listen. There's a youth now in the South, the heir of an Indian throne—he has six weeks' holiday. How does he use it, do you think? He travels hard to England, spends a week there, and travels back again. In England he is treated as an *equal*; here, in spite of his ceremonies, he is an *inferior*, and will and must be so. The best you can hope is that he will be merely unhappy. You pray that he won't take to drink and make his friends among the jockeys and the trainers. He has lost the taste for the native life, and nevertheless he has got to live it. Besides— besides—I haven't told you the worst of it."

Dewes leaned forward. The sincerity of Luffe had gained upon him. "Let me hear all," he said.

"There is the white woman," continued Luffe. "The English woman, the English girl, with her daintiness, her pretty frocks, her good looks, her delicate charm. Very likely she only thinks of him as a picturesque figure; she dances with him, but she does not take him seriously. Yes, but he may take her seriously, and often does. What then? When he is told to go back to his State and settle down, what then? Will he be content with a wife of his own people? He is already a stranger among his own folk. He will eat out his heart with bitterness and jealousy. And, mind you, I am speaking of the best—the best of the Princes and the best of the English women. What of the others? The English women who take his pearls, and the Princes who come back and boast of their success. Do you think that is good for British rule in India? Give me something to drink!"

Luffe poured out his vehement convictions to his companion, wishing with all his heart that he had one of the great ones of the Viceroy's Council at his side, instead of this zealous but somewhat commonplace Major of a Sikh regiment. All the more, therefore, must he husband his strength, so that all that he had in mind might be remembered. There would be little chance, perhaps, of it bearing fruit. Still, even that little

A. E. W. Mason

chance must be grasped. And so in that high castle beneath the Himalayas, besieged by insurgent tribes, a dying Political Officer discoursed upon this question of high policy.

"I told you of a supper I had one night at the Savoy—do you remember? You all looked sufficiently astonished when I told you to bear it in mind."

"Yes, I remember," said Dewes.

"Very well. I told you I learned something from the lady who was with me which it was good for me to know. I saw something which it was good for me to see. Good—yes, but not pleasant either to know or see. There was a young Prince in England then. He dined in high places and afterwards supped at the Savoy with the *coryphees;* and both in the high places and among the *coryphees* his jewels had made him welcome. This is truth I am telling you. He was a boaster. Well, after supper that night he threw a girl down the stairs. Never mind what she was—she was of the white ruling race, she was of the race that rules in India, he comes back to India and insolently boasts. Do you approve? Do you think that good?"

"I think it's horrible," exclaimed Dewes.

"Well, I have done," said Luffe. "This youngster is to go to Oxford. Unhappiness and the distrust of his own people will be the best that can come of it, while ruin and disasters very well may. There are many ways of disaster. Suppose, for instance, this boy were to turn out a strong man. Do you see?"

Dewes nodded his head.

"Yes, I see," he answered, and he answered so because he

saw that Luffe had come to the end of his strength. His voice had weakened, he lay with his eyes sunk deep in his head and a leaden pallor upon his face, and his breath laboured as he spoke.

"I am glad," replied Luffe, "that you understand."

But it was not until many years had passed that Dewes saw and understood the trouble which was then stirring in Luffe's mind. And even then, when he did see and understand, he wondered how much Luffe really had foreseen. Enough, at all events, to justify his reputation for sagacity. Dewes went out from the bedroom and climbed up on to the roof of the Fort. The sun was up, the day already hot, and would have been hotter, but that a light wind stirred among the almond trees in the garden. The leaves of those trees now actually brushed against the Fort walls. Five weeks ago there had been bare stems and branches. Suddenly a rifle cracked, a little puff of smoke rose close to a boulder on the far side of the river, a bullet sang in the air past Dewes' head. He ducked behind the palisade of boards. Another day had come. For another day the flag, manufactured out of some red cloth, a blue turban and some white cotton, floated overhead. Meanwhile, somewhere among the passes, the relieving force was already on the march.

Late that afternoon Luffe died, and his body was buried in the Fort. He had done his work. For two days afterwards the sound of a battle was heard to the south, the siege was raised, and in the evening the Brigadier-General in Command rode up to the gates and found a tired and haggard group of officers awaiting him. They received him without cheers or indeed any outward sign of rejoicing. They waited in a dead silence, like beaten and dispirited men. They were beginning to pay the price of their five weeks' siege.

The Brigadier looked at the group.

"What of Luffe?" he asked.

"Dead, sir," replied Dewes.

"A great loss," said Brigadier Appleton solemnly. But he was paying his tribute rather to the class to which Luffe belonged than to the man himself. Luffe was a man of independent views, Brigadier Appleton a soldier clinging to tradition. Moreover, there had been an encounter between the two in which Luffe had prevailed.

The Brigadier paid a ceremonious visit to the Khan on the following morning, and once more the Khan expounded his views as to the education of his son. But he expounded them now to sympathetic ears.

"I think that his Excellency disapproved of my plan," said the Khan.

"Did he?" cried Brigadier Appleton. "On some points I am inclined to think that Luffe's views were not always sound. Certainly let the boy go to Eton and Oxford. A fine idea, your Highness. The training will widen his mind, enlarge his ideas, and all that sort of thing. I will myself urge upon the Government's advisers the wisdom of your Highness' proposal."

Moreover Dewes failed to carry Luffe's dying message to Calcutta. For on one point—a point of fact—Luffe was immediately proved wrong. Mir Ali, the Khan of Chiltistan, was retained upon his throne. Dewes turned the matter over in his slow mind. Wrong definitely, undeniably wrong on the point of fact, was it not likely that Luffe was wrong too on the point of theory? Dewes had six months furlong too, besides, and was anxious to go home. It would be a bore to travel to Bombay by way of Calcutta. "Let the boy go to Eton and Oxford!" he said. "Why not?" and the years answered him.

CHAPTER V

A MAGAZINE ARTICLE

The little war of Chiltistan was soon forgotten by the world. But it lived vividly enough in the memories of a few people to whom it had brought either suffering or fresh honours. But most of all it was remembered by Sybil Linforth, so that even after fourteen years a chance word, or a trivial coincidence, would bring back to her the horror and the misery of that time as freshly as if only a single day had intervened. Such a coincidence happened on this morning of August.

She was in the garden with her back to the Downs which rose high from close behind the house, and she was looking across the fields rich with orchards and yellow crops. She saw a small figure climb a stile and come towards the house along a footpath, increasing in stature as it approached. It was Colonel Dewes, and her thoughts went back to the day when first, with reluctant steps, he had walked along that path, carrying with him a battered silver watch and chain and a little black leather letter-case. Because of that memory she advanced slowly towards him now.

"I did not know that you were home," she said, as they shook hands. "When did you land?"

"Yesterday. I am home for good now. My time is up." Sybil Linforth looked quickly at his face and turned away.

"You are sorry?" she said gently.

"Yes. I don't feel old, you see. I feel as if I had many years' good work in me yet. But there! That's the trouble with the mediocre men. They are shelved before they are old. I am one of them."

He laughed as he spoke, and looked at his companion.

Sybil Linforth was now thirty-eight years old, but the fourteen years had not set upon her the marks of their passage as they had upon Dewes. Indeed, she still retained a look of youth, and all the slenderness of her figure.

Dewes grumbled to her with a smile upon his face.

"I wonder how in the world you do it. Here am I white-haired and creased like a dry pippin. There are you—" and he broke off. "I suppose it's the boy who keeps you young. How is he?"

A look of anxiety troubled Mrs. Linforth's face; into her eyes there came a glint of fear. Colonel Dewes' voice became gentle with concern.

"What's the matter, Sybil?" he said. "Is he ill?"

"No, he is quite well."

"Then what is it?"

Sybil Linforth looked down for a moment at the gravel of the garden-path. Then, without raising her eyes, she said in a low voice:

"I am afraid."

"Ah," said Dewes, as he rubbed his chin, "I see."

It was his usual remark when he came against anything which he did not understand.

"You must let me have him for a week or two sometimes, Sybil. Boys will get into trouble, you know. It is their nature to. And sometimes a man may be of use in putting things straight."

The hint of a smile glimmered about Sybil Linforth's mouth, but she repressed it. She would not for worlds have let her friend see it, lest he might be hurt.

"No," she replied, "Dick is not in any trouble. But—" and she struggled for a moment with a feeling that she ought not to say what she greatly desired to say; that speech would be disloyal. But the need to speak was too strong within her, her heart too heavily charged with fear.

"I will tell you," she said, and, with a glance towards the open windows of the house, she led Colonel Dewes to a corner of the garden where, upon a grass mound, there was a garden seat. From this seat one overlooked the garden hedge. To the left, the little village of Poynings with its grey church and tall tapering spire, lay at the foot of the gap in the Downs where runs the Brighton road. Behind them the Downs ran like a rampart to right and left, their steep green sides scarred here and there by landslips and showing the white chalk. Far away the high trees of Chanctonbury Ring stood out against the sky.

"Dick has secrets," Sybil said, "secrets from me. It used not to be so. I have always known how a want of sympathy makes a child hide what he feels and thinks, and drives him in upon himself, to feed his thoughts with imaginings and dreams. I have seen it. I don't believe that anything but harm ever comes of it. It builds up a barrier which will last for life. I did not want that barrier to rise between Dick and me—I—" and her voice shook a little—"I should be very unhappy if it were to rise. So I have always tried to be his friend and comrade, rather than his mother."

"Yes," said Colonel Dewes, wisely nodding his head. "I have seen you playing cricket with him."

Colonel Dewes had frequently been puzzled by a peculiar change of manner in his friends. When he made a remark which showed how clearly he understood their point of view and how closely he was in agreement with it, they had a way of becoming reticent in the very moment of expansion. The current of sympathy was broken, and as often as not they turned the conversation altogether into a conventional and less interesting channel. That change of manner became apparent now. Sybil Linforth leaned back and abruptly ceased to speak.

"Please go on," said Dewes, turning towards her.

She hesitated, and then with a touch of reluctance continued:

"I succeeded until a month or so ago. But a month or so ago the secrets came. Oh, I know him so well. He is trying to hide that there are any secrets lest his reticence should hurt me. But we have been so much together, so much to each other—how should I not know?" And again she leaned forward with her hands clasped tightly together upon her knees and a look of great distress lying like a shadow upon

A. E. W. Mason

her face. "The first secrets," she continued, and her voice trembled, "I suppose they are always bitter to a mother. But since I have nothing but Dick they hurt me more deeply than is perhaps reasonable"; and she turned towards her companion with a poor attempt at a smile.

"What sort of secrets?" asked Dewes. "What is he hiding?"

"I don't know," she replied, and she repeated the words, adding to them slowly others. "I don't know—and I am a little afraid to guess. But I know that something is stirring in his mind, something is—" and she paused, and into her eyes there came a look of actual terror—"something is calling him. He goes alone up on to the top of the Downs, and stays there alone for hours. I have seen him. I have come upon him unawares lying on the grass with his face towards the sea, his lips parted, and his eyes strained, his face absorbed. He has been so lost in dreams that I have come close to him through the grass and stood beside him and spoken to him before he grew aware that anyone was near."

"Perhaps he wants to be a sailor," suggested Dewes.

"No, I do not think it is that," Sybil answered quietly. "If it were so, he would have told me."

"Yes," Dewes admitted. "Yes, he would have told you. I was wrong."

"You see," Mrs. Linforth continued, as though Dewes had not interrupted, "it is not natural for a boy at his age to want to be alone, is it? I don't think it is good either. It is not natural for a boy of his age to be thoughtful. I am not sure that that is good. I am, to tell you the truth, very troubled."

Dewes looked at her sharply. Something, not so much in her

words as in the careful, slow manner of her speech, warned him that she was not telling him all of the trouble which oppressed her. Her fears were more definite than she had given him as yet reason to understand. There was not enough in what she had said to account for the tense clasp of her hands, and the glint of terror in her eyes.

"Anyhow, he's going to the big school next term," he said; "that is, if you haven't changed your mind since you last wrote to me, and I hope you haven't changed your mind. All that he wants really," the Colonel added with unconscious cruelty, "is companions of his own age. He passed in well, didn't he?"

Sybil Linforth's face lost for the moment all its apprehension. A smile of pride made her face very tender, and as she turned to Dewes he thought to himself that really her eyes were beautiful.

"Yes, he passed in very high," she said.

"Eton, isn't it?" said Dewes. "Whose house?"

She mentioned the name and added: "His father was there before him." Then she rose from her seat. "Would you like to see Dick? I will show you him. Come quietly."

She led the way across the lawn towards an open window. It was a day of sunshine; the garden was bright with flowers, and about the windows rose-trees climbed the house-walls. It was a house of red brick, darkened by age, and with a roof of tiles. To Dewes' eyes, nestling as it did beneath the great grass Downs, it had a most homelike look of comfort. Sybil turned with a finger on her lips.

"Keep this side of the window," she whispered, "or your

A. E. W. Mason

shadow will fall across the floor."

Standing aside as she bade him, he looked into the room. He saw a boy seated at a table with his head between his hands, immersed in a book which lay before him. He was seated with his side towards the window and his hands concealed his face. But in a moment he removed one hand and turned the page. Colonel Dewes could now see the profile of his face. A firm chin, a beauty of outline not very common, a certain delicacy of feature and colour gave to him a distinction of which Sybil Linforth might well be proud.

"He'll be a dangerous fellow among the girls in a few years' time," said Dewes, turning to the mother. But Sybil did not hear the words. She was standing with her head thrust forward. Her face was white, her whole aspect one of dismay. Dewes could not understand the change in her. A moment ago she had been laughing playfully as she led him towards the window. Now it seemed as though a sudden disaster had turned her to stone. Yet there was nothing visible to suggest disaster. Dewes looked from Sybil to the boy and back again. Then he noticed that her eyes were riveted, not on Dick's face, but on the book which he was reading.

"What is the matter?" he asked.

"Hush!" said Sybil, but at that moment Dick lifted his head, recognised the visitor, and came forward to the window with a smile of welcome. There was no embarrassment in his manner, no air of being surprised. He had not the look of one who nurses secrets. A broad open forehead surmounted a pair of steady clear grey eyes.

"Well, Dick, I hear you have done well in your examination," said the Colonel, as he shook hands. "If you keep it up I will leave you all I save out of my pension."

"Thank you, sir," said Dick with a laugh. "How long have you been back, Colonel Dewes?"

"I left India a fortnight ago."

"A fortnight ago." Dick leaned his arms upon the sill and with his eyes on the Colonel's face asked quietly: "How far does the Road reach now?"

At the side of Colonel Dewes Sybil Linforth flinched as though she had been struck. But it did not need that movement to explain to the Colonel the perplexing problem of her fears. He understood now. The Linforths belonged to the Road. The Road had slain her husband. No wonder she lived in terror lest it should claim her son. And apparently it did claim him.

"The road through Chiltistan?" he said slowly.

"Of course," answered Dick. "Of what other could I be thinking?"

"They have stopped it," said the Colonel, and at his side he was aware that Sybil Linforth drew a deep breath. "The road reaches Kohara. It does not go beyond. It will not go beyond."

Dick's eyes steadily looked into the Colonel's face; and the Colonel had some trouble to meet their look with the same frankness. He turned aside and Mrs. Linforth said,

"Come and see my roses."

Dick went back to his book. The man and woman passed on

round the corner of the house to a little rose-garden with a stone sun-dial in the middle, surrounded by low red brick walls. Here it was very quiet. Only the bees among the flowers filled the air with a pleasant murmur.

"They are doing well—your roses," said Dewes.

"Yes. These Queen Mabs are good. Don't you think so? I am rather proud of them," said Sybil; and then she broke off suddenly and faced him.

"Is it true?" she whispered in a low passionate voice. "Is the road stopped? Will it not go beyond Kohara?"

Colonel Dewes attempted no evasion with Mrs. Linforth.

"It is true that it is stopped. It is also true that for the moment there is no intention to carry it further. But—but—"

And as he paused Sybil took up the sentence.

"But it will go on, I know. Sooner or later." And there was almost a note of hopelessness in her voice. "The Power of the Road is beyond the Power of Governments," she added with the air of one quoting a sentence.

They walked on between the alleys of rose-trees and she asked:

"Did you notice the book which Dick was reading?"

"It looked like a bound volume of magazines."

Sybil nodded her head.

"It was a volume of the 'Fortnightly.' He was reading an

article written forty years ago by Andrew Linforth—" and she suddenly cried out, "Oh, how I wish he had never lived. He was an uncle of Harry's—my husband. He predicted it. He was in the old Company, then he became a servant of the Government, and he was the first to begin the road. You know his history?"

"No."

"It is a curious one. When it was his time to retire, he sent his money to England, he made all his arrangements to come home, and then one night he walked out of the hotel in Bombay, a couple of days before the ship sailed, and disappeared. He has never been heard of since."

"Had he no wife?" asked Dewes.

"No," replied Sybil. "Do you know what I think? I think he went back to the north, back to his Road. I think it called him. I think he could not keep away."

"But we should have come across him," cried Dewes, "or across news of him. Surely we should!"

Sybil shrugged her shoulders.

"In that article which Dick was reading, the road was first proposed. Listen to this," and she began to recite:

"The road will reach northwards, through Chiltistan, to the foot of the Baroghil Pass, in the mountains of the Hindu Kush. Not yet, but it will. Many men will die in the building of it from cold and dysentery, and even hunger—Englishmen and coolies from Baltistan. Many men will die fighting over it, Englishmen and Chiltis, and Gurkhas and Sikhs. It will cost millions of money, and from policy or economy successive Governments will try to stop it; but the power of the Road will be greater than the power of any Government. It will wind through valleys so deep that the day's sunshine is gone within the hour. It will be carried in galleries along the faces of mountains, and for eight months of the year sections of it will be buried deep in snow. Yet it will be finished. It will go on to the foot of the Hindu Kush, and then only the British rule in India will be safe."

She finished the quotation.

"That is what Andrew Linforth prophesied. Much of it has already been justified. I have no doubt the rest will be in time. I think he went north when he disappeared. I think the Road called him, as it is now calling Dick."

She made the admission at last quite simply and quietly. Yet it was evident to Dewes that it cost her much to make it.

"Yes," he said. "That is what you fear."

She nodded her head and let him understand something of the terror with which the Road inspired her.

"When the trouble began fourteen years ago, when the road was cut and day after day no news came of whether Harry lived or, if he died, how he died—I dreamed of it—I used to see horrible things happening on that road—night after night I saw them. Dreadful things happening to Dick and his father while I stood by and could do nothing. Oh, it seems to me a living thing greedy for blood—our blood."

She turned to him a haggard face. Dewes sought to reassure her.

"But there is peace now in Chiltistan. We keep a close watch on that country, I can tell you. I don't think we shall be caught napping there again."

But these arguments had little weight with Sybil Linforth. The tragedy of fourteen years ago had beaten her down with too strong a hand. She could not reason about the road. She only felt, and she felt with all the passion of her nature.

"What will you do, then?" asked Dewes.

She walked a little further on before she answered.

"I shall do nothing. If, when the time comes, Dick feels that work upon that road is his heritage, if he wants to follow in his father's steps, I shall say not a single word to dissuade him."

Dewes stared at her. This half-hour of conversation had made real to him at all events the great strength of her hostility. Yet she would put the hostility aside and say not a word.

"That's more than I could do," he said, "if I felt as you do. By George it is!"

Sybil smiled at him with friendliness.

"It's not bravery. Do you remember the unfinished letter which you brought home to me from Harry? There were three sentences in that which I cannot pretend to have forgotten," and she repeated the sentences:

"'Whether he will come out here, it is too early to think about. But the road will not be finished—and I wonder. If he wants to, let him.' It is quite clear—isn't it?—that Harry wanted him to take up the work. You can read that in the words. I can imagine him speaking them and hear the tone he would use. Besides—I have still a greater fear than the one of which you know. I don't want Dick, when he grows up, ever to think that I have been cowardly, and, because I was cowardly, disloyal to his father."

"Yes, I see," said Colonel Dewes.

And this time he really did understand.

"We will go in and lunch," said Sybil, and they walked back to the house.

CHAPTER VI

A LONG WALK

The footsteps sounded overhead with a singular regularity. From the fireplace to the door, and back again from the door to the fireplace. At each turn there was a short pause, and each pause was of the same duration. The footsteps were very light; it was almost as though an animal, a caged animal, padded from the bars at one end to the bars at the other. There was something stealthy in the footsteps too.

In the room below a man of forty-five sat writing at a desk— a very tall, broad-shouldered man, in clerical dress. Twenty-five years before he had rowed as number seven in the Oxford Eight, with an eye all the while upon a mastership at his old school. He had taken a first in Greats; he had obtained his mastership; for the last two years he had had a House. As he had been at the beginning, so he was now, a man without theories but with an instinctive comprehension of boys. In consequence there were no vacancies in his house, and the Headmaster had grown accustomed to recommend the Rev. Mr. Arthur Pollard when boys who needed any special care came to the school.

He was now so engrossed with the preparations for the term which was to begin to-morrow that for some while the

A. E. W. Mason

footsteps overhead did not attract his attention. When he did hear them he just lifted his head, listened for a moment or two, lit his pipe and went on with his work.

But the sounds continued. Backwards and forwards from the fireplace to the door, the footsteps came and went—without haste and without cessation; stealthily regular; inhumanly light. Their very monotony helped them to pass as unnoticed as the ticking of a clock. Mr. Pollard continued the preparation of his class-work for a full hour, and only when the dusk was falling, and it was becoming difficult for him to see what he was writing, did he lean back in his chair and stretch his arms above his head with a sigh of relief.

Then once more he became aware of the footsteps overhead. He rose and rang the bell.

"Who is that walking up and down the drawingroom, Evans?" he asked of the butler.

The butler threw back his head and listened.

"I don't know, sir," he replied.

"Those footsteps have been sounding like that for more than an hour."

"For more than an hour?" Evans repeated. "Then I am afraid, sir, it's the new young gentleman from India."

Arthur Pollard started.

"Has he been waiting up there alone all this time?" he exclaimed. "Why in the world wasn't I told?"

"You were told, sir," said Evans firmly but respectfully. "I came into the study here and told you, and you answered 'All right, Evans.' But I had my doubts, sir, whether you really heard or not."

Mr. Pollard hardly waited for the end of the explanation. He hurried out of the room and sprang up the stairs. He had arranged purposely for the young Prince to come to the house a day before term began. He was likely to be shy, ill-at-ease and homesick, among so many strange faces and unfamiliar ways. Moreover, Mr. Pollard wished to become better acquainted with the boy than would be easily possible once the term was in full swing. For he was something more of an experiment than the ordinary Indian princeling from a State well under the thumb of the Viceroy and the Indian Council. This boy came of the fighting stock in the north. To leave him tramping about a strange drawing-room alone for over an hour was not the best possible introduction to English ways and English life. Mr. Pollard opened the door and saw a slim, tall boy, with his hands behind his back and his eyes fixed on the floor, walking up and down in the gloom.

"Shere Ali," he said, and he held out his hand. The boy took it shyly.

"You have been waiting here for some time," Mr. Pollard continued, "I am sorry. I did not know that you had come. You should have rung the bell."

"I was not lonely," Shere Ali replied. "I was taking a walk."

"Yes, so I gathered," said the master with a smile. "Rather a long walk."

"Yes, sir," the boy answered seriously. "I was walking from Kohara up the valley, and remembering the landmarks as I went. I had walked a long way. I had come to the fort where my father was besieged."

"Yes, that reminds me," said Pollard, "you won't feel so lonely to-morrow as you do to-day. There is a new boy joining whose father was a great friend of your father's. Richard Linforth is his name. Very likely your father has mentioned that name to you."

Mr. Pollard switched on the light as he spoke and saw Shere All's face flash with eagerness.

"Oh yes!" he answered, "I know. He was killed upon the road by my uncle's people."

"I have put you into the next room to his. If you will come with me I will show you."

Mr. Pollard led the way along a passage into the boys' quarters.

"This is your room. There's your bed. Here's your 'burry,'" pointing to a bureau with a bookcase on the top. He threw open the next door. "This is Linforth's room. By the way, you speak English very well."

"Yes," said Shere Ali. "I was taught it in Lahore first of all. My father is very fond of the English."

"Well, come along," said Mr. Pollard. "I expect my wife has come back and she shall give us some tea. You will dine with us to-night, and we will try to make you as fond of the English as your father is."

The next day the rest of the boys arrived, and Mr. Pollard took the occasion to speak a word or two to young Linforth.

"You are both new boys," he said, "but you will fit into the scheme of things quickly enough. He won't. He's in a strange land, among strange people. So just do what you can to help him."

Dick Linforth was curious enough to see the son of the Khan of Chiltistan. But not for anything would he have talked to him of his father who had died upon the road, or of the road itself. These things were sacred. He greeted his companion in quite another way.

"What's your name?" he asked.

"Shere Ali," replied the young Prince.

"That won't do," said Linforth, and he contemplated the boy solemnly. "I shall call you Sherry-Face," he said.

And "Sherry-Face" the heir to Chiltistan remained; and in due time the name followed him to College.

CHAPTER VII

IN THE DAUPHINE

The day broke tardily among the mountains of Dauphine. At half-past three on a morning of early August light should be already stealing through the little window and the chinks into the hut upon the Meije. But the four men who lay wrapped in blankets on the long broad shelf still slept in darkness. And when the darkness was broken it was by the sudden spit of a match. The tiny blue flame spluttered for a few seconds and then burned bright and yellow. It lit up the face of a man bending over the dial of a watch and above him and about him the wooden rafters and walls came dimly into view. The face was stout and burned by the sun to the colour of a ripe apple, and in spite of a black heavy moustache had a merry and good-humoured look. Little gold earrings twinkled in his ears by the light of the match. Annoyance clouded his face as he remarked the time.

"Verdammt! Verdammt!" he muttered.

The match burned out, and for a while he listened to the wind wailing about the hut, plucking at the door and the shutters of the window. He climbed down from the shelf with a rustle of straw, walked lightly for a moment or two about the hut, and then pulled open the door quickly. As quickly he shut it again.

From the shelf Linforth spoke:

"It is bad, Peter?"

"It is impossible," replied Peter in English with a strong German accent. For the last three years he and his brother had acted as guides to the same two men who were now in the Meije hut. "We are a strong party, but it is impossible. Before I could walk a yard from the door, I would have to lend a lantern. And it is after four o'clock! The water is frozen in the pail, and I have never known that before in August."

"Very well," said Linforth, turning over in his blankets. It was warm among the blankets and the straw, and he spoke with contentment. Later in the day he might rail against the weather. But for the moment he was very clear that there were worse things in the world than to lie snug and hear the wind tearing about the cliffs and know that there was no chance of facing it.

"We will not go back to La Berarde," he said. "The storm may clear. We will wait in the hut until tomorrow."

And from a third figure on the shelf there came in guttural English:

"Yes, yes. Of course."

The fourth man had not wakened from his sleep, and it was not until he was shaken by the shoulder at ten o'clock in the morning that he sat up and rubbed his eyes.

The fourth man was Shere Ali.

A. E. W. Mason

"Get up and come outside," said Linforth.

Ten years had passed since Shere Ali had taken his long walk from Kohara up the valley in the drawing-room of his house-master at Eton. And those ten years had had their due effect. He betrayed his race nowadays by little more than his colour, a certain high-pitched intonation of his voice and an extraordinary skill in the game of polo. There had been a time of revolt against discipline, of inability to understand the points of view of his masters and their companions, and of difficulty to discover much sense in their institutions.

It is to be remembered that he came from the hill-country, not from the plains of India. That honour was a principle, not a matter of circumstance, and that treachery was in itself disgraceful, whether it was profitable or not—here were hard sayings for a native of Chiltistan. He could look back upon the day when he had thought a public-house with a great gilt sign or the picture of an animal over the door a temple for some particular sect of worshippers.

"And, indeed, you are far from wrong," his tutor had replied to him. "But since we do not worship at that fiery shrine such holy places are forbidden us."

Gradually, however, his own character was overlaid; he was quick to learn, and in games quick to excel. He made friends amongst his schoolmates, he carried with him to Oxford the charm of manner which is Eton's particular gift, and from Oxford he passed to London. He was rich, he was liked, and he found a ready welcome, which did not spoil him. Luffe would undoubtedly have classed him amongst the best of the native Princes who go to England for their training, and on that very account, would have feared the more for his future. Shere Ali was now just twenty-four, he was tall, spare of body and wonderfully supple of limbs, and but for a fulness of the lower lip, which was characteristic of his family, would have been reckoned more than usually handsome.

He came out of the door of the hut and stood by the side of Linforth. They looked up towards the Meije, but little of that majestic mass of rock was visible. The clouds hung low; the glacier below them upon their left had a dull and unillumined look, and over the top of the Breche de la Meije, the pass to the left of their mountain, the snow whirled up from the further side like smoke. The hut is built upon a great spur of the mountain which runs down into the desolate valley des Etancons, and at its upper end melts into the great precipitous rock-wall which forms one of the main difficulties of the ascent. Against this wall the clouds were massed. Snow lay where yesterday the rocks had shone grey and ruddy brown in the sunlight, and against the great wall here and there icicles were hung.

"It looks unpromising," said Linforth. "But Peter says that the mountain is in good condition. To-morrow it may be possible. It is worth while waiting. We shall get down to La Grave to-morrow instead of to-day. That is all."

"Yes. It will make no difference to our plans," said Shere Ali; and so far as their immediate plans were concerned Shere Ali was right. But these two men had other and wider plans which embraced not a summer's holiday but a lifetime, plans which they jealously kept secret; and these plans, as it happened, the delay of a day in the hut upon the Meije was deeply to affect.

They turned back into the room and breakfasted. Then Linforth lit his pipe and once more curled himself up in his rug upon the straw. Shere Ali followed his example. And it was of the wider plans that they at once began to talk.

A. E. W. Mason

"But heaven only knows when I shall get out to India," cried Linforth after a while. "There am I at Chatham and not a chance, so far as I can see, of getting away. You will go back first."

It was significant that Linforth, who had never been in India, none the less spoke habitually of going back to it, as though that country in truth was his native soil. Shere Ali shook his head.

"I shall wait for you," he said. "You will come out there." He raised himself upon his elbow and glanced at his friend's face. Linforth had retained the delicacy of feature, the fineness of outline which ten years before had called forth the admiration of Colonel Dewes. But the ten years had also added a look of quiet strength. A man can hardly live with a definite purpose very near to his heart without gaining some reward from the labour of his thoughts. Though he speak never so little, people will be aware of him as they are not aware of the loudest chatterer in the room. Thus it was with Linforth. He talked with no greater wit than his companions, he made no greater display of ability, he never outshone, and yet not a few men were conscious of a force underlying his quietude of manner. Those men were the old and the experienced; the unobservant overlooked him altogether.

"Yes," said Shere Ali, "since you want to come you will come."

"I shall try to come," said Linforth, simply. "We belong to the Road," and for a little while he lay silent. Then in a low voice he spoke, quoting from that page which was as a picture in his thoughts.

"Over the passes! Over the snow passes to the foot of the Hindu Kush!"

"Then and then only India will be safe," the young Prince of Chiltistan added, speaking solemnly, so that the words seemed a kind of ritual.

And to both they were no less. Long before, when Shere Ali was first brought into his room, on his first day at Eton, Linforth had seen his opportunity, and seized it. Shere Ali's father retained his kingdom with an English Resident at his elbow. Shere Ali would in due time succeed. Linforth had quietly put forth his powers to make Shere Ali his friend, to force him to see with his eyes, and to believe what he believed. And Shere Ali had been easily persuaded. He had become one of the white men, he proudly told himself. Here was a proof, the surest of proofs. The belief in the Road— that was one of the beliefs of the white men, one of the beliefs which marked him off from the native, not merely in Chiltistan, but throughout the East. To the white man, the Road was the beginning of things, to the Oriental the shadow of the end. Shere Ali sided with the white men. He too had faith in the Road and he was proud of his faith because he shared it with the white men.

"We shall be very glad of these expeditions, some day, in Chiltistan," said Linforth.

Shere Ali stared.

"It was for that reason—?" he asked.

"Yes."

Shere Ali was silent for a while. Then he said, and with some regret:

"There is a great difference between us. You can wait and wait. I want everything done within the year."

A. E. W. Mason

Linforth laughed. He knew very well the impulsiveness of his friend.

"If a few miles, or even a few furlongs, stand to my credit at the end, I shall not think that I have failed."

They were both young, and they talked with the bright and simple faith in their ideals which is the great gift of youth. An older man might have laughed if he had heard, but had there been an older man in the hut to overhear them, he would have heard nothing. They were alone, save for their guides, and the single purpose for which—as they then thought—their lives were to be lived out made that long day short as a summer's night.

"The Government will thank us when the work is done," said Shere Ali enthusiastically.

"The Government will be in no hurry to let us begin," replied Linforth drily. "There is a Resident at your father's court. Your father is willing, and yet there's not a coolie on the road."

"Yes, but you will get your way," and again confidence rang in the voice of the Chilti prince.

"It will not be I," answered Linforth. "It will be the Road. The power of the Road is beyond the power of any Government."

"Yes, I remember and I understand." Shere Ali lit his pipe and lay back among the straw. "At first I did not understand what the words meant. Now I know. The power of the Road is great, because it inspires men to strive for its completion."

"Or its mastery," said Linforth slowly. "Perhaps one day on the other side of the Hindu Kush, the Russians may covet it—and then the Road will go on to meet them."

"Something will happen," said Shere Ali. "At all events something will happen."

The shadows of the evening found them still debating what complication might force the hand of those in authority. But always they came back to the Russians and a movement of troops in the Pamirs. Yet unknown to both of them the something else had already happened, though its consequences were not yet to be foreseen. A storm had delayed them for a day in a hut upon the Meije. They went out of the hut. The sky had cleared; and in the sunset the steep buttress of the Promontoire ran sharply up to the Great Wall; above the wall the small square patch of ice sloped to the base of the Grand Pic and beyond the deep gap behind that pinnacle the long serrated ridge ran out to the right, rising and falling, to the Doight de Dieu.

There were some heavy icicles overhanging the Great Wall, and Linforth looked at them anxiously. There was also still a little snow upon the rocks.

"It will be possible," said Peter, cheerily. "Tomorrow night we shall sleep in La Grave."

"Yes, yes, of course," said his brother.

They walked round the hut, looked for a little while down the stony valley des Etancons, with its one green patch up which they had toiled from La Berarde the day before, and returned to watch the purple flush of the sunset die off the crags of the Meije. But the future they had planned was as a vision before their eyes, and even along the high cliffs of the Dauphine the road they were to make seemed to wind and climb.

"It would be strange," said Linforth, "if old Andrew Linforth were still alive. Somewhere in your country, perhaps in Kohara, waiting for the thing he dreamed to come to pass. He would be an old man now, but he might still be alive."

"I wonder," said Shere Ali absently, and he suddenly turned to Linforth. "Nothing must come between us," he cried almost fiercely. "Nothing to hinder what we shall do together."

He was the more emotional of the two. The dreams to which they had given utterance had uplifted him.

"That's all right," said Linforth, and he turned back into the hut. But he remembered afterwards that it was Shere Ali who had protested against the possibility of their association being broken.

They came out from the hut again at half-past three in the morning and looked up to a cloudless starlit sky which faded in the east to the colour of pearl. Above their heads some knobs of rock stood out upon the thin crest of the buttress against the sky. In the darkness of a small couloir underneath the knobs Peter was already ascending. The traverse of the Meije even for an experienced mountaineer is a long day's climb. They reached the summit of the Grand Pic in seven hours, descended into the Breche Zsigmondy, climbed up the precipice on the further side of that gap, and reached the Pic Central by two o'clock in the afternoon. There they rested for an hour, and looked far down to the village of La Grave among the cornfields of the valley. There was no reason for any hurry.

"We shall reach La Grave by eight," said Peter, but he was wrong, as they soon discovered. A slope which should have been soft snow down which they could plunge was hard ice, in which a ladder of steps must be cut before the glacier could be reached. The glacier itself was crevassed so that many a devour was necessary, and occasionally a jump; and evening came upon them while they were on the Rocher de L'Aigle. It was quite dark when at last they reached the grass slopes, and still far below them the lights were gleaming in La Grave. To both men those grass slopes seemed interminable. The lights of La Grave seemed never to come nearer, never to grow larger. Little points of fire very far away—as they had been at first, so they remained. But for the slope of ground beneath his feet and the aching of his knees, Linforth could almost have believed that they were not descending at all. He struck a match and looked at his watch and saw that it was after nine; and a little while after they had come to water and taken their fill of it, that it was nearly ten, but now the low thunder of the river in the valley was louder in his ears, and then suddenly he saw that the lights of La Grave were bright and near at hand.

Linforth flung himself down upon the grass, and clasping his hands behind his head, gave himself up to the cool of the night and the stars overhead.

"I could sleep here," he said. "Why should we go down to La Grave to-night?"

"There is a dew falling. It will be cold when the morning breaks. And La Grave is very near. It is better to go," said Peter.

The question was still in debate when above the roar of the river there came to their ears a faint throbbing sound from across the valley. It grew louder and suddenly two blinding lights flashed along the hill-side opposite.

"A motor-car," said Shere Ali, and as he spoke the lights ceased to travel.

A. E. W. Mason

"It's stopping at the hotel," said Linforth carelessly.

"No," said Peter. "It has not reached the hotel. Look, not by a hundred yards. It has broken down."

Linforth discussed the point at length, not because he was at all interested at the moment in the movements of that or of any other motor-car, but because he wished to stay where he was. Peter, however, was obdurate. It was his pride to get his patron indoors each night.

"Let us go on," he said, and Linforth wearily rose to his feet.

"We are making a big mistake," he grumbled, and he spoke with more truth than he was aware.

They reached the hotel at eleven, ordered their supper and bathed. It was half-past eleven before Linforth and Shere Ali entered the long dining-room, and they found another party already supping there. Linforth heard himself greeted by name, and turned in surprise. It was a party of four—two ladies and two men. One of the men had called to him, an elderly man with a bald forehead, a grizzled moustache, and a shrewd kindly face.

"I remember you, though you can't say as much of me," he said. "I came down to Chatham a year ago and dined at your mess as the guest of your Colonel."

Linforth came forward with a smile of recognition.

"I beg your pardon for not recognising you at once. I remember you, of course, quite well," he said.

"Who am I, then?"

"Sir John Casson, late Lieutenant-Governor of the United Provinces," said Linforth promptly.

"And now nothing but a bore at my club," replied Sir John cheerfully. "We were motoring through to Grenoble, but the car has broken down. You are mountain-climbing, I suppose. Phyllis," and he turned to the younger of the two ladies, "this is Mr. Linforth of the Royal Engineers. My daughter, Linforth!" He introduced the second lady.

"Mrs. Oliver," he said, and Linforth turning, saw that the eyes of Mrs. Oliver were already fixed upon him. He returned the look, and his eyes frankly showed her that he thought her beautiful.

"And what are you going to do with yourself?" said Sir John.

"Go to the country from which you have just come, as soon as I can," said Linforth with a smile. At this moment the fourth of the party, a stout, red-faced, plethoric gentleman, broke in.

"India!" he exclaimed indignantly. "Bless my soul, what on earth sends all you young fellows racing out to India? A great mistake! I once went to India myself—to shoot a tiger. I stayed there for months and never saw one. Not a tiger, sir!"

But Linforth was paying very little attention to the plethoric gentleman. Sir John introduced him as Colonel Fitzwarren, and Linforth bowed politely. Then he asked of Sir John:

"Your car was not seriously damaged, I suppose?"

"Keep us here two days," said Sir John. "The chauffeur will have to go on by diligence to-morrow to get a new sparking plug. Perhaps we shall see more of you in consequence."

Linforth's eyes travelled back to Mrs. Oliver.

"We are in no hurry," he said slowly. "We shall rest here probably for a day or so. May I introduce my friend?"

He introduced him as the son of the Khan of Chiltistan, and Mrs. Oliver's eyes, which had been quietly resting upon Linforth's face, turned towards Shere Ali, and as quietly rested upon his.

"Then, perhaps, you can tell me," said Colonel Fitzwarren, "how it was I never saw a tiger in India, though I stayed there four months. A most disappointing country, I call it. I looked for a tiger everywhere and I never saw one—no, not one."

The Colonel's one idea of the Indian Peninsula was a huge tiger waiting somewhere in a jungle to be shot.

But Shere Ali was paying no more attention to the Colonel's disparagements than Linforth had done.

"Will you join us at supper?" said Sir John, and both young men replied simultaneously, "We shall be very pleased."

Sir John Casson smiled. He could never quite be sure whether it was or was not to Mrs. Oliver's credit that her looks made so powerful an appeal to the chivalry of young men. "All young men immediately want to protect her," he was wont to say, "and their trouble is that they can't find anyone to protect her from."

He watched Shere Ali and Dick Linforth with a sly amusement, and as a result of his watching promised himself yet more amusement during the next two days. He was roused from this pleasing anticipation by his irascible friend, Colonel Fitzwarren, who, without the slightest warning, flung a loud and defiant challenge across the table to Shere Ali.

"I don't believe there is one," he cried, and breathed heavily.

Shere Ali interrupted his conversation with Mrs. Oliver. "One what?" he asked with a smile.

"Tiger, sir, tiger," said the Colonel, rapping with his knuckles upon the table. "Of what else should I be speaking? I don't believe there's a tiger in India outside the Zoo. Otherwise, why didn't I see one?"

Colonel Fitzwarren glared at Shere Ali as though he held him personally responsible for that unhappy omission. Sir John, however, intervened with smooth speeches and for the rest of supper the conversation was kept to less painful topics. But the Colonel had not said his last word. As they went upstairs to their rooms he turned to Shere Ali, who was just behind him, and sighed heavily.

"If I had shot a tiger in India," he said, with an indescribable look of pathos upon his big red face, "it would have made a great difference to my life."

A. E. W. Mason

CHAPTER VIII

A STRING OF PEARLS

"So you go to parties nowadays," said Mrs. Linforth, and Sir John Casson, leaning his back against the wall of the ballroom, puzzled his brains for the name of the lady with the pleasant winning face to whom he had just been introduced. At first it had seemed to him merely that her hearing was better than his. The "nowadays," however, showed that it was her memory which had the advantage. They were apparently old acquaintances; and Sir John belonged to an old-fashioned school which thought it discourtesy to forget even the least memorable of his acquaintances.

"You were not so easily persuaded to decorate a ball-room at Mussoorie," Mrs. Linforth continued.

Sir John smiled, and there was a little bitterness in the smile.

"Ah!" he said, and there was a hint, too, of bitterness in his voice, "I was wanted to decorate ball-rooms then. So I didn't go. Now I am not wanted. So I do."

"That's not the true explanation," Mrs. Linforth said gently, and she shook her head. She spoke so gently and with so clear a note of sympathy and comprehension that Sir John was at more pains than ever to discover who she was. To hardly anyone would it naturally have occurred that Sir John Casson, with a tail of letters to his name, and a handsome pension, enjoyed at an age when his faculties were alert and his bodily strength not yet diminished, could stand in need of sympathy. But that precisely was the fact, as the woman at his side understood. A great ruler yesterday, with a council and an organized Government, subordinated to his leadership, he now merely lived at Camberley, and as he had confessed, was a bore at his club. And life at Camberley was dull.

He looked closely at Mrs. Linforth. She was a woman of forty, or perhaps a year or two more. On the other hand, she might be a year or two less. She had the figure of a young woman, and though her dark hair was flecked with grey, he knew that was not to be accounted as a sign of either age or trouble. Yet she looked as if trouble had been no stranger to her. There were little lines about the eyes which told their tale to a shrewd observer, though the face smiled never so pleasantly. In what summer, he wondered, had she come up to the hill station of Mussoorie.

"No," he said. "I did not give you the real explanation. Now I will."

He nodded towards a girl who was at that moment crossing the ball-room towards the door, upon the arm of a young man.

"That's the explanation."

Mrs. Linforth looked at the girl and smiled.

"The explanation seems to be enjoying itself," she said. "Yours?"

A. E. W. Mason

"Mine," replied Sir John with evident pride.

"She is very pretty," said Mrs. Linforth, and the sincerity of her admiration made the father glow with satisfaction. Phyllis Casson was a girl of eighteen, with the fresh looks and the clear eyes of her years. A bright colour graced her cheeks, where, when she laughed, the dimples played, and the white dress she wore was matched by the whiteness of her throat. She was talking gaily with the youth on whose arm her hand lightly rested.

"Who is he?" asked Mrs. Linforth.

Sir John raised his shoulders.

"I am not concerned," he replied. "The explanation is amusing itself, as it ought to do, being only eighteen. The explanation wants everyone to love her at the present moment. When she wants only one, then it will be time for me to begin to get flurried." He turned abruptly to his companion. "I would like you to know her."

"Thank you," said Mrs. Linforth, as she bowed to an acquaintance.

"Would you like to dance?" asked Sir John. "If so, I'll stand aside."

"No. I came here to look on," she explained.

"Lady Marfield," and she nodded towards their hostess, "is my cousin, and—well, I don't want to grow rusty. You see I have an explanation too—oh, not here! He's at Chatham, and it's as well to keep up with the world—" She broke off abruptly, and with a perceptible start of surprise. She was looking towards the door. Casson followed the direction of her eyes, and saw young Linforth in the doorway.

At last he remembered. There had been one hot weather, years ago, when this boy's father and his newly-married wife had come up to the hill-station of Mussoorie. He remembered that Linforth had sent his wife back to England, when he went North into Chiltistan on that work from which he was never to return. It was the wife who was now at his side.

"I thought you said he was at Chatham," said Sir John, as Dick Linforth advanced into the room.

"So I believed he was. He must have changed his mind at the last moment." Then she looked with a little surprise at her companion. "You know him?"

"Yes," said Sir John, "I will tell you how it happened. I was dining eighteen months ago at the Sappers' mess at Chatham. And that boy's face came out of the crowd and took my eyes and my imagination too. You know, perhaps, how that happens at times. There seems to be no particular reason why it should happen at the moment. Afterwards you realise that there was very good reason. A great career, perhaps, perhaps only some one signal act, an act typical of a whole unknown life, leaps to light and justifies the claim the young face made upon your sympathy. Anyhow, I noticed young Linforth. It was not his good looks which attracted me. There was something else. I made inquiries. The Colonel was not a very observant man. Linforth was one of the subalterns—a good bat and a good change bowler. That was all. Only I happened to look round the walls of the Sappers' mess. There are portraits hung there of famous members of that mess who were thought of no particular account when they were subalterns at Chatham. There's one alive to-day. Another died at Khartoum."

A. E. W. Mason

"Yes," said Mrs. Linforth.

"Well, I made the acquaintance of your son that night," said Sir John.

Mrs. Linforth stood for a moment silent, her face for the moment quite beautiful. Then she broke into a laugh.

"I am glad I scratched your back first," she said. "And as for the cricket, it's quite true. I taught him to keep a straight bat myself."

Meanwhile, Dick Linforth was walking across the floor of the ball-room, quite unconscious of the two who talked of him. He was not, indeed, looking about him at all. It seemed to both his mother and Sir John, as they watched him steadily moving in and out amongst the throng—for it was the height of the season, and Lady Marfield's big drawing-room in Chesterfield Gardens was crowded—that he was making his way to a definite spot, as though just at this moment he had a definite appointment.

"He changed his mind at the last moment," said Sir John with a laugh, which gave to him the look of a boy. "Let us see who it is that has brought him up from Chatham to London at the last moment!"

"Would it be fair?" asked Mrs. Linforth reluctantly. She was, indeed, no less curious upon the point than her companion, and while she asked the question, her eyes followed her son's movements. He was tall, and though he moved quickly and easily, it was possible to keep him in view.

A gap in the crowd opened before them, making a lane—and at the end of the lane they saw Linforth approach a lady and receive the welcome of her smile. For a moment the gap remained open, and then the bright frocks and black coats swept across the space. But both had seen, and Mrs. Linforth, in addition, was aware of a barely perceptible start made by Sir John at her side.

She looked at him sharply. His face had grown grave.

"You know her?" asked Mrs. Linforth. There was anxiety in her voice. There was also a note of jealousy.

"Yes."

"Who is she?"

"Mrs. Oliver. Violet Oliver."

"Married!"

"A widow. I introduced her to your son at La Grave in the Dauphine country last summer. Our motor-car had broken down. We all stayed for a couple of days together in the same hotel. Mrs. Oliver is a friend of my daughter's. Phyllis admires her very much, and in most instances I am prepared to trust Phyllis' instincts."

"But not in this instance," said Mrs. Linforth quietly. She had been quick to note a very slight embarrassment in Sir John Casson's manner.

"I don't say that," he replied quickly—a little too quickly.

"Will you find me a chair?" said Mrs. Linforth, looking about her. "There are two over here." She led the way to the chairs which were placed in a nook of the room not very far from the door by which Linforth had entered. She took her seat, and when Sir John had seated himself beside her, she said:

"Please tell me what you know of her."

Sir John spread out his hands in protest.

"Certainly, I will. But there is nothing to her discredit, so far as I know, Mrs. Linforth—nothing at all. Beyond that she is beautiful—really beautiful, as few women are. That, no doubt, will be looked upon as a crime by many, though you and I will not be of that number."

Sybil Linforth maintained a determined silence—not for anything would she admit, even to herself, that Violet Oliver was beautiful.

"You are telling me nothing," she said.

"There is so little to tell," replied Sir John. "Violet Oliver comes of a family which is known, though it is not rich. She studied music with a view to making her living as a singer. For she has a very sweet voice, though its want of power forbade grand opera. Her studies were interrupted by the appearance of a cavalry captain, who made love to her. She liked it, whereas she did not like studying music. Very naturally she married the cavalry officer. Captain Oliver took her with him abroad, and, I believe, brought her to India. At all events she knows something of India, and has friends there. She is going back there this winter. Captain Oliver was killed in a hill campaign two years ago. Mrs. Oliver is now twenty-three years old. That is all."

Mrs. Linforth, however, was not satisfied.

"Was Captain Oliver rich?" she asked.

"Not that I know of," said Sir John. "His widow lives in a little house at the wrong end of Curzon Street."

"But she is wearing to-night very beautiful pearls," said Sybil Linforth quietly.

Sir John Casson moved suddenly in his chair. Moreover, Sybil Linforth's eyes were at that moment resting with a quiet scrutiny upon his face.

"It was difficult to see exactly what she was wearing," he said. "The gap in the crowd filled up so quickly."

"There was time enough for any woman," said Mrs. Linforth with a smile. "And more than time enough for any mother."

"Mrs. Oliver is always, I believe, exquisitely dressed," said Sir John with an assumption of carelessness. "I am not much of a judge myself."

But his carelessness did not deceive his companion. Sybil Linforth was certain, absolutely certain, that the cause of the constraint and embarrassment which had been audible in Sir John's voice, and noticeable in his very manner, was that double string of big pearls of perfect colour which adorned Violet Oliver's white throat.

She looked Sir John straight in the face.

"Would you introduce Dick to Mrs. Oliver now, if you had not done it before?" she asked.

"My dear lady," protested Sir John, "if I met Dick at a little hotel in the Dauphine, and did not introduce him to the ladies who were travelling with me, it would surely reflect upon Dick, not upon the ladies"; and with that subtle evasion Sir John escaped from the fire of questions. He turned the conversation into another channel, pluming himself upon his cleverness. But he forgot that the subtlest evasions of the male mind are clumsy and obvious to a woman, especially if the woman be on the alert. Sybil Linforth did not think Sir John had showed any cleverness whatever. She let him turn the conversation, because she knew what she had set out to know. That string of pearls had made the difference between Sir John's estimate of Violet Oliver last year and his estimate of her this season.

CHAPTER IX

LUFFE IS REMEMBERED

Violet Oliver took a quick step forward when she caught sight of Linforth's tall and well-knit figure coming towards her; and the smile with which she welcomed him was a warm smile of genuine pleasure. There were people who called Violet Oliver affected—chiefly ladies. But Phyllis Casson was not one of them.

"There is no one more natural in the room," she was in the habit of stoutly declaring when she heard the gossips at work, and we know, on her father's authority, that Phyllis Casson's judgments were in most instances to be respected. Certainly it was not Violet Oliver's fault that her face in repose took on a wistful and pathetic look, and that her dark quiet eyes, even when her thoughts were absent—and her thoughts were often absent—rested pensively upon you with an unconscious flattery. It appeared that she was pondering deeply who and what you were; whereas she was probably debating whether she should or should not powder her nose before she went in to supper. Nor was she to blame because at the approach of a friend that sweet and thoughtful face would twinkle suddenly into mischief and amusement. "She is as God made her," Phyllis Casson protested, "and He made her beautiful."

It will be recognised, therefore, that there was truth in Sir John's observation that young men wanted to protect her. But the bald statement is not sufficient. Whether that quick transition from pensiveness to a dancing gaiety was the cause, or whether it only helped her beauty, this is certain. Young men went down before her like ninepins in a bowling alley. There was something singularly virginal about her. She had, too, quite naturally, an affectionate manner which it was difficult to resist; and above all she made no effort ever. What she said and what she did seemed always purely spontaneous. For the rest, she was a little over the general height of women, and even looked a little taller. For she was very fragile, and dainty, like an exquisite piece of china. Her head was small, and, poised as it was upon a slender throat, looked almost overweighted by the wealth of her dark hair. Her features were finely chiselled from the nose to the oval of her chin, and the red bow of her lips; and, with all her fragility, a delicate colour in her cheeks spoke of health.

"You have come!" she said.

Linforth took her little white-gloved hand in his.

"You knew I should," he answered.

"Yes, I knew that. But I didn't know that I should have to wait," she replied reproachfully. "I was here, in this corner, at the moment."

"I couldn't catch an earlier train. I only got your telegram saying you would be at the dance late in the afternoon."

"I did not know that I should be coming until this morning," she said.

"Then it was very kind of you to send the telegram at all."

"Yes, it was," said Violet Oliver simply, and Linforth laughed.

"Shall we dance?" he asked.

Mrs. Oliver nodded.

"Round the room as far as the door. I am hungry. We will go downstairs and have supper."

Linforth could have wished for nothing better. But the moment that his arm was about her waist and they had started for the door, Violet Oliver realised that her partner was the lightest dancer in the room. She herself loved dancing, and for once in a way to be steered in and out amongst the couples without a bump or even a single entanglement of her satin train was a pleasure not to be foregone. She gave herself up to it.

"Let us go on," she said. "I did not know. You see, we have never danced together before. I had not thought of you in that way."

She ceased to speak, being content to dance. Linforth for his part was content to watch her, to hold her as something very precious, and to evoke a smile upon her lips when her eyes met his. "I had not thought of you in that way!" she had said. Did not that mean that she had at all events been thinking of him in some way? And with that flattery still sweet in his thoughts, he was aware that her feet suddenly faltered. He looked at her face. It had changed. Yet so swiftly did it recover its composure that Linforth had not even the time to understand what the change implied. Annoyance, surprise, fear! One of these feelings, certainly, or perhaps a trifle of each. Linforth could not make sure. There had been a flash of some sudden emotion. That at all events was certain. But

A. E. W. Mason

in guessing fear, he argued, his wits must surely have gone far astray; though fear was the first guess which he had made.

"What was the matter?"

Violet Oliver answered readily.

"A big man was jigging down upon us. I saw him over your shoulder. I dislike being bumped by big men," she said, with a little easy laugh. "And still more I hate having a new frock torn."

Dick Linforth was content with the answer. But it happened that Sybil Linforth was looking on from her chair in the corner, and the corner was very close to the spot where for a moment Violet Oliver had lost countenance. She looked sharply at Sir John Casson, who might have noticed or might not. His face betrayed nothing whatever. He went on talking placidly, but Mrs. Linforth ceased to listen to him.

Violet Oliver waltzed with her partner once more round the room. Then she said:

"Let us stop!" and in almost the same breath she added, "Oh, there's your friend."

Linforth turned and saw standing just within the doorway his friend Shere Ali.

"You could hardly tell that he was not English," she went on; and indeed, with his straight features, his supple figure, and a colour no darker than many a sunburnt Englishman wears every August, Shere Ali might have passed unnoticed by a stranger. It seemed that he had been watching for the couple to stop dancing. For no sooner had they stopped than he advanced quickly towards them.

Linforth, however, had not as yet noticed him.

"It can't be Shere Ali," he said. "He is in the country. I heard from him only to-day."

"Yet it is he," said Mrs. Oliver, and then Linforth saw him.

"Hallo!" he said softly to himself, and as Shere Ali joined them he added aloud, "something has happened."

"Yes, I have news," said Shere Ali. But he was looking at Mrs. Oliver, and spoke as though the news had been pushed for a moment into the back of his mind.

"What is it?" asked Linforth.

Shere Ali turned to Linforth.

"I go back to Chiltistan."

"When?" asked Linforth, and a note of envy was audible in his voice. Mrs. Oliver heard it and understood it. She shrugged her shoulders impatiently.

"By the first boat to Bombay."

"In a week's time, then?" said Mrs. Oliver, quickly.

Shere Ali glanced swiftly at her, seeking the meaning of that question. Did regret prompt it? Or, on the other hand, was she glad?

"Yes, in a week's time," he replied slowly.

"Why?" asked Linforth. "Is there trouble in Chiltistan?" He spoke regretfully. It would be hard luck if that uneasy State were to wake again into turmoil while he was kept kicking his heels at Chatham.

"Yes, there is trouble," Shere Ali replied. "But it is not the kind of trouble which will help you forward with the Road."

The trouble, indeed, was of quite another kind. The Russians were not stirring behind the Hindu Kush or on the Pamirs. The turbulent people of Chiltistan were making trouble, and profit out of the trouble, it is true. That they would be sure to do somewhere, and, moreover, they would do it with a sense of humour more common upon the Frontier than in the Provinces of India. But they were not at the moment making trouble in their own country. They were heard of in Masulipatam and other cities of Madras, where they were badly wanted by the police and not often caught. The quarrel in Chiltistan lay between the British Raj, as represented by the Resident, and the Khan, who was spending the revenue of his State chiefly upon his own amusements. It was claimed that the Resident should henceforth supervise the disposition of the revenue, and it had been suggested to the Khan that unless he consented to the proposal he would have to retire into private life in some other quarter of the Indian Peninsula. To give to the suggestion the necessary persuasive power, the young Prince was to be brought back at once, so that he might be ready at a moment's notice to succeed. This reason, however, was not given to Shere Ali. He was merely informed by the Indian Government that he must return to his country at once.

Shere Ali stood before Mrs. Oliver.

"You will give me a dance?" he said.

"After supper," she replied, and she laid her hand within Linforth's arm. But Shere Ali did not give way.

"Where shall I find you?" he asked.

"By the door, here."

And upon that Shere Ali's voice changed to one of appeal. There came a note of longing into his voice. He looked at Violet Oliver with burning eyes. He seemed unaware Linforth was standing by.

"You will not fail me?" he said; and Linforth moved impatiently.

"No. I shall be there," said Violet Oliver, and she spoke hurriedly and moved by through the doorway. Beneath her eyelids she stole a glance at her companion. His face was clouded. The scene which he had witnessed had jarred upon him, and still jarred. When he spoke to her his voice had a sternness which Violet Oliver had not heard before. But she had always been aware that it might be heard, if at any time he disapproved.

"'Your friend,' you called him, speaking to me," he said. "It seems that he is your friend too."

"He was with you at La Grave. I met him there."

"He comes to your house?"

"He has called once or twice," said Mrs. Oliver submissively. It was by no wish of hers that Shere Ali had appeared at this dance. She had, on the contrary, been at some pains to assure herself that he would not be there. And while she answered Linforth she was turning over in her mind a difficulty which

A. E. W. Mason

had freshly arisen. Shere Ali was returning to India. In some respects that was awkward. But Linforth's ill-humour promised her a way of escape. He was rather silent during the earlier part of their supper. They had a little table to themselves, and while she talked, and talked with now and then an anxious glance at Linforth, he was content to listen or to answer shortly. Finally she said:

"I suppose you will not see your friend again before he starts?"

"Yes, I shall," replied Linforth, and the frown gathered afresh upon his forehead. "He dines to-morrow night with me at Chatham."

"Then I want to ask you something," she continued. "I want you not to mention to him that I am paying a visit to India in the cold weather."

Linforth's face cleared in an instant.

"I am glad that you have made that request," he said frankly. "I have no right to say it, perhaps. But I think you are wise."

"Things are possible here," she agreed, "which are impossible there."

"Friendship, for instance."

"Some friendships," said Mrs. Oliver; and the rest of their supper they ate cheerily enough. Violet Oliver was genuinely interested in her partner. She was not very familiar with the large view and the definite purpose. Those who gathered within her tiny drawing-room, who sought her out at balls and parties, were, as a rule, the younger men of the day, and Linforth, though like them in age and like them, too, in his capacity for enjoyment, was different in most other ways. For the large view and the definite purpose coloured all his life, and, though he spoke little of either, set him apart.

Mrs. Oliver did not cultivate many illusions about herself. She saw very clearly what manner of men they were to whom her beauty made its chief appeal—lean-minded youths for the most part not remarkable for brains—and she was sincerely proud that Linforth sought her out no less than they did. She could imagine herself afraid of Linforth, and that fancy gave her a little thrill of pleasure. She understood that he could easily be lost altogether, that if once he went away he would not return; and that knowledge made her careful not to lose him. Moreover, she had brains herself. She led him on that evening, and he spoke with greater freedom than he had used with her before—greater freedom, she hoped, than he had used with anyone. The lighted supper-room grew dim before his eyes, the noise and the laughter and the passing figures of the other guests ceased to be noticed. He talked in a low voice, and with his keen face pushed a trifle forward as though, while he spoke, he listened. He was listening to the call of the Road.

He stopped abruptly and looked anxiously at Violet.

"Have I bored you?" he asked. "Generally I watch you," he added with a smile, "lest I should bore you. To-night I haven't watched."

"For that reason I have been interested to-night more than I have been before."

She gathered up her fan with a little sigh. "I must go upstairs again," she said, and she rose from her chair. "I am sorry. But I have promised dances."

A. E. W. Mason

"I will take you up. Then I shall go."

"You will dance no more?"

"No," he said with a smile. "I'll not spoil a perfect evening."
Violet Oliver was not given to tricks or any play of the
eyelids. She looked at him directly, and she said simply
"Thank you."

He took her up to the landing, and came down stairs again
for his hat and coat. But, as he passed with them along the
passage door he turned, and looking up the stairs, saw Violet
Oliver watching him. She waved her hand lightly and smiled.
As the door closed behind him she returned to the ball-room.
Linforth went away with no suspicion in his mind that she
had stayed her feet upon the landing merely to make very
sure that he went. He had left his mother behind, however,
and she was all suspicion. She had remarked the little scene
when Shere Ali had unexpectedly appeared. She had noticed
the embarrassment of Violet Oliver and the anger of Shere
Ali. It was possible that Sir John Casson had also not been
blind to it. For, a little time afterwards, he nodded towards
Shere Ali.

"Do you know that boy?" he asked.

"Yes. He is Dick's great friend. They have much in common.
His father was my husband's friend."

"And both believed in the new Road, I know," said Sir John. He
pulled at his grey moustache thoughtfully, and asked: "Have the
sons the Road in common, too?" A shadow darkened Sybil
Linforth's face. She sat silent for some seconds, and when she
answered, it was with a great reluctance.

"I believe so," she said in a low voice, and she shivered. She turned her face towards Casson. It was troubled, fear-stricken, and in that assembly of laughing and light-hearted people it roused him with a shock. "I wish, with all my heart, that they had not," she added, and her voice shook and trembled as she spoke.

The terrible story of Linforth's end, long since dim in Sir John Casson's recollections, came back in vivid detail. He said no more upon that point. He took Mrs. Linforth down to supper, and bringing her back again, led her round the ball-room. An open archway upon one side led into a conservatory, where only fairy lights glowed amongst the plants and flowers. As the couple passed this archway, Sir John looked in. He did not stop, but, after they had walked a few yards further, he said:

"Was it pale blue that Violet Oliver was wearing? I am not clever at noticing these things."

"Yes, pale blue and—pearls," said Sybil Linforth.

"There is no need that we should walk any further. Here are two chairs," said Sir John. There was in truth no need. He had ascertained something about which, in spite of his outward placidity, he had been very curious.

"Did you ever hear of a man named Luffe?" he asked.

Sybil Linforth started. It had been Luffe whose continual arguments, entreaties, threats, and persuasions had caused the Road long ago to be carried forward. But she answered quietly, "Yes."

"Of course you and I remember him," said Sir John. "But how many others? That's the penalty of Indian service. You are soon forgotten, in India as quickly as here. In most cases,

A. E. W. Mason

no doubt, it doesn't matter. Men just as good and younger stand waiting at the milestones to carry on the torch. But in some cases I think it's a pity."

"In Mr. Luffe's case?" asked Sybil Linforth.

"Particularly in Luffe's case," said Sir John.

CHAPTER X

AN UNANSWERED QUESTION

Sir John had guessed aright. Shere Ali was in the conservatory, and Violet Oliver sat by his side.

"I did not expect you to-night," she said lightly, as she opened and shut her fan.

"Nor did I mean to come," he answered. "I had arranged to stay in the country until to-morrow. But I got my letter from the India Office this morning. It left me—restless." He uttered the word with reluctance, and almost with an air of shame. Then he clasped his hands together, and blurted out violently: "It left me miserable. I could not stay away," and he turned to his companion. "I wanted to see you, if only for five minutes." It was Violet Oliver's instinct to be kind. She fitted herself naturally to the words of her companions, sympathised with them in their troubles, laughed with them when they were at the top of their spirits. So now her natural kindness made her eyes gentle. She leaned forward.

"Did you?" she asked softly. "And yet you are going home!"

"I am going back to Chiltistan," said Shere Ali.

A. E. W. Mason

"Home!" Violet Oliver repeated, dwelling upon the word with a friendly insistence.

But the young prince did not assent; he remained silent—so long silent that Violet Oliver moved uneasily. She was conscious of suspense; she began to dread his answer. He turned to her quickly as she moved.

"You say that I am going home. That's the whole question," he said. "I am trying to answer it—and I can't. Listen!"

Into the quiet and dimly lit place of flowers the music of the violins floated with a note of wistfulness in the melody they played—a suggestion of regret. Through a doorway at the end of the conservatory Shere Ali could see the dancers swing by in the lighted ball-room, the women in their bright frocks and glancing jewels, some of whom had flattered him, a few of whom had been his friends, and all of whom had treated him as one of their own folk and their equal.

"I have heard the tune, which they are playing, before," he said slowly. "I heard it one summer night in Geneva. Linforth and I had come down from the mountains. We were dining with a party on the balcony of a restaurant over the lake. A boat passed hidden by the darkness. We could hear the splash of the oars. There were musicians in the boat playing this melody. We were all very happy that night. And I hear it again now—when I am with you. I think that I shall remember it very often in Chiltistan."

There was so unmistakable a misery in his manner, in his voice, in his dejected looks, that Violet was moved to a deep sympathy. He was only a boy, of course, but he was a boy sunk in distress.

"But there are your plans," she urged. "Have you forgotten

them? You were going to do so much. There was so much to do. So many changes, so many reforms which must be made. You used to talk to me so eagerly. No more of your people were to be sold into slavery. You were going to stop all that. You were going to silence the mullahs when they preached sedition and to free Chiltistan from their tyranny."

Violet remembered with a whimsical little smile how Shere All's enthusiasm had wearied her, but she checked the smile and continued:

"Are all those plans mere dreams and fancies?"

"No," replied Shere Ali, lifting his head. "No," he said again with something of violence in the emphasis; and for a moment he sat erect, with his shoulders squared, fronting his destiny. Almost for a moment he recaptured that for which he had been seeking—his identity with his own race. But the moment passed. His attitude relaxed. He turned to Violet with troubled eyes. "No, they are not dreams; they are things which need to be done. But I can't realise them now, with you sitting here, any more than I can realise, with this music in my ears, that it is my home to which I am going back."

"Oh, but you will!" cried Violet. "When you are out there you will. There's the road, too, the road which you and Mr. Linforth—"

She did not complete the sentence. With a low cry Shere All broke in upon her words. He leaned forward, with his hands covering his face.

"Yes," he whispered, "there's the road—there's the road." A passion of self-reproach shook him. Not for nothing had Linforth been his friend. "I feel a traitor," he cried. "For ten years we have talked of that road, planned it, and made it in

A. E. W. Mason

thought, poring over the maps. Yes, for even at the beginning, in our first term at Eton, we began. Over the passes to the foot of the Hindu Kush! Only a year ago I was eager, really, honestly eager," and he paused for a moment, wondering at that picture of himself which his words evoked, wondering whether it was indeed he—he who sat in the conservatory—who had cherished those bright dreams of a great life in Chiltistan. "Yes, it is true. I was honestly eager to go back."

"Less than a year ago," said Violet Oliver quickly. "Less than a week ago. When did I see you last? On Sunday, wasn't it?"

"But was I honest then?" exclaimed Shere Ali. "I don't know. I thought I was—right up to to-day, right up to this morning when the letter came. And then—" He made a despairing gesture, as of a man crumbling dust between his fingers.

"I will tell you," he said, turning towards her. "I believe that the last time I was really honest was in August of last year. Linforth and I talked of the Road through a long day in the hut upon the Meije. I was keen then—honestly keen. But the next evening we came down to La Grave, and—I met you."

"No," Violet Oliver protested. "That's not the reason."

"I think it is," said Shere Ali quietly; and Violet was silent.

In spite of her pity, which was genuine enough, her thoughts went out towards Shere Ali's friend. With what words and in what spirit would he have received Shere Ali's summons to Chiltistan? She asked herself the question, knowing well the answer. There would have been no lamentations—a little regret, perhaps, perhaps indeed a longing to take her with him. But there would have been not a thought of abandoning the work. She recognised that truth with a sudden spasm of anger, but yet admiration strove with the anger and mastered it.

"If what you say is true," she said to Shere Ali gently, "I am very sorry. But I hope it is not true. You have been ten years here; you have made many friends. Just for the moment the thought of leaving them behind troubles you. But that will pass."

"Will it?" he asked quietly. Then a smile came upon his face. "There's one thing of which I am glad," he whispered.

"Yes."

"You are wearing my pearls to-night."

Violet Oliver smiled, and with a tender caressing movement her fingers touched and felt the rope of pearls about her neck. Both the smile and the movement revealed Violet Oliver. She had a love of beautiful things, but, above all, of jewels. It was a passion with her deeper than any she had ever known. Beautiful stones, and pearls more than any other stones, made an appeal to her which she could not resist.

"They are very lovely," she said softly.

"I shall be glad to remember that you wore them to-night," said Shere Ali; "for, as you know, I love you."

"Hush!" said Mrs. Oliver; and she rose with a start from her chair. Shere Ali did the same.

"It's true," he said sullenly; and then, with a swift step, he placed himself in her way. Violet Oliver drew back quietly. Her heart beat quickly. She looked into Shere Ali's face and was afraid. He was quite still; even the expression of his face was set, but his eyes burned upon her. There was a fierceness in his manner which was new to her.

His hand darted out quickly towards her. But Violet Oliver was no less quick. She drew back yet another step. "I didn't understand," she said, and her lips shook, so that the words were blurred. She raised her hands to her neck and loosened the coils of pearls about it as though she meant to lift them off and return them to the giver.

"Oh, don't do that, please," said Shere Ali; and already his voice and his manner had changed. The sullenness had gone. Now he besought. His English training came to his aid. He had learned reverence for women, acquiring it gradually and almost unconsciously rather than from any direct teaching. He had spent one summer's holidays with Mrs. Linforth for his hostess in the house under the Sussex Downs, and from her and from Dick's manner towards her he had begun to acquire it. He had become conscious of that reverence, and proudly conscious. He had fostered it. It was one of the qualities, one of the essential qualities, of the white people. It marked the sahibs off from the Eastern races. To possess that reverence, to be influenced and moved and guided by it— that made him one with them. He called upon it to help him now. Almost he had forgotten it.

"Please don't take them off," he implored. "There was nothing to understand."

And perhaps there was not, except this—that Violet Oliver was of those who take but do not give. She removed her hands from her throat. The moment of danger had passed, as she very well knew.

"There is one thing I should be very grateful for," he said humbly. "It would not cause you very much trouble, and it would mean a great deal to me. I would like you to write to me now and then."

"Why, of course I will," said Mrs. Oliver, with a smile.

"You promise?"

"Yes. But you will come back to England."

"I shall try to come next summer, if it's only for a week," said Shere Ali; and he made way for Violet.

She moved a few yards across the conservatory, and then stopped for Shere Ali to come level with her. "I shall write, of course, to Chiltistan," she said carelessly.

"Yes," he replied, "I go northwards from Bombay. I travel straight to Kohara."

"Very well. I will write to you there," said Violet Oliver; but it seemed that she was not satisfied. She walked slowly towards the door, with Shere Ali at her side.

"And you will stay in Chiltistan until you come back to us?" she asked. "You won't go down to Calcutta at Christmas, for instance? Calcutta is the place to which people go at Christmas, isn't it? I think you are right. You have a career in your own country, amongst your own people."

She spoke urgently. And Shere Ali, thinking that thus she spoke in concern for his future, drew some pride from her encouragement. He also drew some shame; for she might have been speaking, too, in pity for his distress.

"Mrs. Oliver," he said, with hesitation; and she stopped and turned to him. "Perhaps I said more than I meant to say a few minutes ago. I have not forgotten really that there is much for me to do in my own country; I have not forgotten that I can thank all of you here who have shown me so much kindness by more than mere words. For I can help in Chiltistan—I can really help."

Then came a smile upon Violet Oliver's face, and her eyes shone.

"That is how I would have you speak," she cried. "I am glad. Oh, I am glad!" and her voice rang with the fulness of her pleasure. She had been greatly distressed by the unhappiness of her friend, and in that distress compunction had played its part. There was no hardness in Violet Oliver's character. To give pain flattered no vanity in her. She understood that Shere Ali would suffer because of her, and she longed that he should find his compensation in the opportunities of rulership.

"Let us say good-bye here," he said. "We may not be alone again before I go."

She gave him her hand, and he held it for a little while, and then reluctantly let it go.

"That must last me until the summer of next year," he said with a smile.

"Until the summer," said Violet Oliver; and she passed out from the doorway into the ball-room. But as she entered the room and came once more amongst the lights and the noise, and the familiar groups of her friends, she uttered a little sigh of relief. The summer of next year was a long way off; and meanwhile here was an episode in her life ended as she wished it to end; for in these last minutes it had begun to disquiet her.

Shere Ali remained behind in the conservatory. His eyes wandered about it. He was impressing upon his memory every detail of the place, the colours of the flowers and their very perfumes. He looked through the doorway into the ball-room whence the music swelled. The note of regret was louder than ever in his ears, and dominated the melody. To-morrow the lights, the delicate frocks, the laughing voices and bright eyes would be gone. The violins spoke to him of that morrow of blank emptiness softly and languorously like one making a luxury of grief. In a week's time he would be setting his face towards Chiltistan; and, in spite of the brave words he had used to Violet Oliver, once more the question forced itself into his mind.

"Do I belong here?" he asked. "Or do I belong to Chiltistan?"

On the one side was all that during ten years he had gradually learned to love and enjoy; on the other side was his race and the land of his birth. He could not answer the question; for there was a third possibility which had not yet entered into his speculations, and in that third possibility alone was the answer to be found.

A. E. W. Mason

CHAPTER XI

AT THE GATE OF LAHORE

Shere Ali, accordingly, travelled with reluctance to Bombay, and at that port an anonymous letter with the postmark of Calcutta was brought to him on board the steamer. Shere Ali glanced through it, and laughed, knowing well his country-men's passion for mysteries and intrigues. He put the letter in his pocket and took the northward mail. These were the days before the North-West Province had been severed from the Punjab, and instructions had been given to Shere Ali to break his journey at Lahore. He left the train, therefore, at that station, on a morning when the thermometer stood at over a hundred in the shade, and was carried in a barouche drawn by camels to Government House. There a haggard and heat-worn Commissioner received him, and in the cool of the evening took him for a ride, giving him sage advice with the accent of authority.

"His Excellency would have liked to have seen you himself," said the Commissioner. "But he is in the Hills and he did not think it necessary to take you so far out of your way. It is as well that you should get to Kohara as soon as possible, and on particular subjects the Resident, Captain Phillips, will be able and glad to advise you."

The Commissioner spoke politely enough, but the accent of authority was there. Shere Ali's ears were quick to notice and resent it. Some years had passed since commands had been laid upon him.

"I shall always be glad to hear what Captain Phillips has to say," he replied stiffly.

"Yes, yes, of course," said the Commissioner, taking that for granted. "Captain Phillips has our views."

He did not seem to notice the stiffness of Shere Ali's tone. He was tired with the strain of the hot weather, as his drawn face and hollow eyes showed clearly.

"On general lines," he continued, "his Excellency would like you to understand that the Government has no intention and no wish to interfere with the customs and laws of Chiltistan. In fact it is at this moment particularly desirable that you should throw your influence on the side of the native observances."

"Indeed," said Shere Ali, as he rode along the Mall by the Commissioner's side. "Then why was I sent to Oxford?"

The Commissioner was not surprised by the question, though it was abruptly put.

"Surely that is a question to ask of his Highness, your father," he replied. "No doubt all you learnt and saw there will be extremely valuable. What I am saying now is that the Government wishes to give no pretext whatever to those who would disturb Chiltistan, and it looks to you with every confidence for help and support."

"And the road?" asked Shere Ali.

A. E. W. Mason

"It is not proposed to carry on the road. The merchants in Kohara think that by bringing more trade, their profits would become less, while the country people look upon it as a deliberate attack upon their independence. The Government has no desire to force it upon the people against their wish."

Shere Ali made no reply, but his heart grew bitter within him. He had come out to India sore and distressed at parting from his friends, from the life he had grown to love. All the way down the Red Sea and across the Indian Ocean, the pangs of regret had been growing keener with each new mile which was gathered in behind the screw. He had lain awake listening to the throb of the engine with an aching heart, and with every longing for the country he had left behind growing stronger, every recollection growing more vivid and intense. There was just one consolation which he had. Violet Oliver had enheartened him to make the most of it, and calling up the image of her face before him, he had striven so to do. There were his plans for the regeneration of his country. And lo! here at Lahore, three days after he had set foot on land, they were shattered—before they were begun. He had been trained and educated in the West according to Western notions and he was now bidden to go and rule in the East according to the ideals of the East. Bidden! For the quiet accent of authority in the words of the unobservant man who rode beside him rankled deeply. He had it in his thoughts to cry out: "Then what place have I in Chiltistan?"

But though he never uttered the question, it was none the less answered.

"Economy and quiet are the two things which Chiltistan needs," said the Commissioner. Then he looked carelessly at Shere Ali.

"It is hoped that you will marry and settle down as soon as

possible," he said.

Shere Ali reined in his horse, stared for a moment at his companion and then began quietly to laugh. The laughter was not pleasant to listen to, and it grew harsher and louder. But it brought no change to the tired face of the Commissioner, who had stopped his horse beside Shere Ali's and was busy with the buckle of his stirrup leather. He raised his head when the laughter stopped. And it stopped as abruptly as it had begun.

"You were saying—" he remarked politely.

"That I would like, if there is time, to ride through the Bazaar."

"Certainly," said the Commissioner. "This way," and he turned at right angles out of the Mall and its avenue of great trees and led the way towards the native city. Short of it, however, he stopped.

"You won't mind if I leave you here," he said. "There is some work to be done. You can make no mistake. You can see the Gate from here."

"Is that the Delhi Gate?" asked Shere Ali.

"Yes. You can find your own way back, no doubt"; and the unobservant Commissioner rode away at a trot.

Shere Ali went forward alone down the narrowing street towards the Gate. He was aflame with indignation. So he was to be nothing, he was to do nothing, except to practice economy and marry—a *nigger*. The contemptuous word rose to his mind. Long ago it had been applied to him more than once during his early school-days, until desperate battles and black eyes had won him immunity. Now he used it savagely himself to stigmatise his own people. He was of the White People, he declared. He felt it, he looked it. Even at that moment a portly gentleman of Lahore in a coloured turban and patent-leather shoes salaamed to him as he passed upon his horse. "Surely," he thought, "I am one of the Sahibs. This fool of a Commissioner does not understand."

A woman passed him carrying a babe poised upon her head, with silver anklets upon her bare ankles and heavy silver rings upon her toes. She turned her face, which was overshadowed by a hood, to look at Shere Ali as he rode by. He saw the heavy stud of silver and enamel in her nostril, the withered brown face. He turned and looked at her, as she walked flat-footed and ungainly, her pyjamas of pink cotton showing beneath her cloak. He had no part or lot with any of these people of the East. The face of Violet Oliver shone before his eyes. There was his mate. He recalled the exquisite daintiness of her appearance, her ruffles of lace, the winning sweetness of her eyes. Not in Chiltistan would he find a woman to drive that image from his thoughts.

Meanwhile he drew nearer to the Delhi Gate. A stream of people flowed out from it towards him. Over their heads he looked through the archway down the narrow street, where between the booths and under the carved overhanging balconies the brown people robed and turbaned, in saffron and blue, pink and white, thronged and chattered and jostled, a kaleidoscope of colour. Shere Ali turned his eyes to the right and the left as he went. It was not merely to rid himself of the Commissioner that he had proposed to ride on to the bazaars by way of the Delhi Gate. The anonymous letter bearing the postmark of Calcutta, which had been placed in his hand when the steamer reached Bombay, besought him to pass by the Delhi Gate at Lahore and do certain things by which means he would hear much to his advantage. He had no thought at the moment to do the particular things, but he was sufficiently curious to pass by the Delhi Gate. Some intrigue was on hand into which it was sought to lure him. He had not forgotten that his countrymen were born intriguers.

Slowly he rode along. Here and there a group of people were squatting on the ground, talking noisily. Here and there a beggar stretched out a maimed limb and sought for alms. Then close to the gate he saw that for which he searched: a man sitting apart with a blanket over his head. No one spoke to the man, and for his part he never moved. He sat erect with his legs crossed in front of him and his hands resting idly on his knees, a strange and rather grim figure; so motionless, so utterly lifeless he seemed. The blanket reached almost to the ground behind and hung down to his lap in front, and Shere Ali noticed that a leathern begging-bowl at his side was well filled with coins. So he must have sat just in that attitude, with that thick covering stifling him, all through the fiery heat of that long day. As Shere Ali looked, he saw a poor bent man in rags, with yellow caste marks on his forehead, add a copper pi to the collection in the bowl. Shere Ali stopped the giver.

"Who is he?" he asked, pointing to the draped figure.

The old Hindu raised his hand and bowed his forehead into the palm.

"Huzoor, he is a holy man, a stranger who has lately come to Lahore, but the holiest of all the holy men who have ever sat by the Delhi Gate. His fame is already great."

"But why does he sit covered with the blanket?" asked Shere Ali.

A. E. W. Mason

"Huzoor, because of his holiness. He is so holy that his face must not be seen."

Shere Ali laughed.

"He told you that himself, I suppose," he said.

"Huzoor, it is well known," said the old man. "He sits by the road all day until the darkness comes—"

"Yes," said Shere Ali, bethinking him of the recommendations in his letter, "until the darkness comes—and then?"

"Then he goes away into the city and no one sees him until the morning"; and the old man passed on.

Shere Ali chuckled and rode by the hooded man. His curiosity increased. It was quite likely that the blanket hid a Mohammedan Pathan from beyond the hills. To come down into the plains and mulct the pious Hindu by some such ingenious practice would appeal to the Pathan's sense of humour almost as much as to his pocket. Shere Ali drew the letter from his pocket, and in the waning light read it through again. True, the postmark showed that the letter had been posted in Calcutta, but more than one native of Chiltistan had come south and set up as a money-lender in that city on the proceeds of a successful burglary. He replaced the letter in his pocket, and rode on at a walk through the throng. The darkness came quickly; oil lamps were lighted in the booths and shone though the unglazed window-spaces overhead. A refreshing coolness fell upon the town, the short, welcome interval between the heat of the day and the suffocating heat of the night. Shere Ali turned his horse and rode back again to the gate. The hooded beggar still sat upon the ground, but he was alone. The others, the blind and the maimed, had crawled away to their dens. Except this grim motionless man, there was no one squatting upon the ground.

Shere Ali reined in beside him, and bending forward in his saddle spoke in a low voice a few words of Pushtu. The hooded figure did not move, but from behind the blanket there issued a muffled voice.

"If your Highness will ride slowly on, your servant will follow and come to his side."

Shere Ali went on, and in a few moments he heard the soft patter of a man running barefoot along the dusty road. He stopped his horse and the patter of feet ceased, but a moment after, silent as a shadow, the man was at his side.

"You are of my country?" said Shere Ali.

"I am of Kohara," returned the man. "Safdar Khan of Kohara. May God keep your Highness in health. We have waited long for your presence."

"What are you doing in Lahore?" asked Shere Ali.

In the darkness he saw a flash of white as Safdar Khan smiled.

"There was a little trouble, your Highness, with one Ishak Mohammed and—Ishak Mohammed's son is still alive. He is a boy of eight, it is true, and could not hold a rifle to his shoulder. But the trouble took place near the road."

Shere Ali nodded his head in comprehension. Safdar Khan had shot his enemy on the road, which is a holy place, and therefore he came within the law.

"Blood-money was offered," continued Safdar Khan, "but

the boy would not consent, and claims my life. His mother would hold the rifle for him while he pulled the trigger. So I am better in Lahore. Moreover, your Highness, for a poor man life is difficult in Kohara. Taxes are high. So I came down to this gate and sat with a cloak over my head."

"And you have found it profitable," said Shere Ali.

Again the teeth flashed in the darkness and Safdar Khan laughed.

"For two days I sat by the Delhi Gate and no one spoke to me or dropped a single coin in my bowl. But on the third day a good man, may God preserve him, passed by when I was nearly stifled and asked me why I sat in the heat of the sun under a blanket. Thereupon I told him, what doubtless your Highness knows, that my face is much too holy to be looked upon, and since then your Highness' servant has prospered exceedingly. The device is a good one."

Suddenly Safdar Khan stumbled as he walked and lurched against the horse and its rider. He recovered himself in a moment, with prayers for forgiveness and curses upon his stupidity for setting his foot upon a sharp stone. But he had put out his hand as he stumbled and that hand had run lightly down Shere Ali's coat and had felt the texture of his clothes.

"I had a letter from Calcutta," said the Prince, "which besought me to speak to you, for you had something for my ear. Therefore speak, and speak quickly."

But a change had come over Safdar Khan. Certainly Shere Ali was wearing the dress of one of the Sahibs. A man passed carrying a lantern, and the light, feeble though it was, threw into outline against the darkness a pith helmet and a very English figure. Certainly, too, Shere Ali spoke the

Pushtu tongue with a slight hesitation, and an unfamiliar accent. He seemed to grope for words.

"A letter?" he cried. "From Calcutta? Nay, how can that be? Some foolish fellow has dared to play a trick," and in a few short, effective sentences Safdar Khan expressed his opinion of the foolish fellow and of his ancestry distant and immediate.

"Yet the letter bade me seek you by the Delhi Gate of Lahore," continued Shere Ali calmly, "and by the Delhi Gate of Lahore I found you."

"My fame is great," replied Safdar Khan bombastically. "Far and wide it has spread like the boughs of a gigantic tree."

"Rubbish," said Shere Ali curtly, breaking in upon Safdar's vehemence. "I am not one of the Hindu fools who fill your begging-bowl," and he laughed.

In the darkness he heard Safdar Khan laugh too.

"You expected me," continued Shere Ali. "You looked for my coming. Your ears were listening for the few words of Pushtu. Why else should you say, 'Ride forward and I will follow'?"

Safdar Khan walked for a little while in silence. Then in a voice of humility, he said:

"I will tell my lord the truth. Yes, some foolish talk has passed from one man to another, and has been thrown back again like a ball. I too," he admitted, "have been without wisdom. But I have seen how vain such talk is. The Mullahs in the Hills speak only ignorance and folly."

A. E. W. Mason

"Ah!" said Shere Ali. He took the letter from his pocket and tore it into fragments and scattered the fragments upon the Road. "So I thought. The letter is of their prompting."

"My lord, it may be so," replied Safdar Khan. "For my part I have no lot or share in any of these things. For I am now of Lahore."

"Aye," said Shere Ali. "The begging-bowl is filled to overflowing at the Delhi Gate. So you are of Lahore, though your name is Safdar Khan and you were born at Kohara," and suddenly he leaned down and asked in a wistful voice with a great curiosity, "Are you content? Have you forgotten the hills and valleys? Is Lahore more to you than Chiltistan?"

So perpetually had Shere All's mind run of late upon his isolation that it crept into all his thoughts. So now it seemed to him that there was some vague parallel between his mental state and that of Safdar Khan. But Safdar Khan's next words disabused him:

"Nay, nay," he said. "But the widow of a rich merchant in the city here, a devout and holy woman, has been greatly moved by my piety. She seeks my hand in marriage and—" here Safdar Khan laughed pleasantly—"I shall marry her. Already she has given me a necklace of price which I have had weighed and tested to prove that she does not play me false. She is very rich, and it is too hot to sit in the sun under a blanket. So I will be a merchant of Lahore instead, and live at my ease on the upper balcony of my house."

Shere Ali laughed and answered, "It is well." Then he added shrewdly: "But it is possible that you may yet at some time meet the man in Calcutta who wrote the letter to me. If so, tell him what I did with it," and Shere Ali's voice became hard and stern. "Tell him that I tore it up and scattered it in the dust. And let him send the news to the Mullahs in the Hills. I know that soft-handed brood with their well-fed bodies and their treacherous mouths. If only they would let me carry on the road!" he cried passionately, "I would drag them out of the houses where they batten on poor men's families and set them to work till the palms of their hands were honestly blistered. Let the Mullahs have a care, Safdar Khan. I go North to-morrow to Kohara."

He spoke with a greater vehemence than perhaps he had meant to show. But he was carried along by his own words, and sought always a stronger epithet than that which he had used. He was sore and indignant, and he vented his anger on the first object which served him as an opportunity. Safdar Khan bowed his head in the darkness. Safe though he might be in Lahore, he was still afraid of the Mullahs, afraid of their curses, and mindful of their power to ruin the venturesome man who dared to stand against them.

"It shall be as your Highness wishes," he said in a low voice, and he hurried away from Shere Ali's side. Abuse of the Mullahs was dangerous—as dangerous to listen to as to speak. Who knew but what the very leaves of the neem trees might whisper the words and bear witness against him? Moreover, it was clear that the Prince of Chiltistan was a Sahib. Shere Ali rode back to Government House. He understood clearly why Safdar Khan had so unceremoniously fled; and he was glad. If the fool of a Commissioner did not know him for what he was, at all events Safdar Khan did. He was one of the White People. For who else would dare to speak as he had spoken of the Mullahs? The Mullahs would hear what he had said. That was certain. They would hear it with additions. They would try to make things unpleasant for him in Chiltistan in consequence. But Shere Ali was glad. For their very opposition—in so loverlike a way did every thought somehow reach out to Violet Oliver—brought him a little nearer to the lady who held his heart. He found the Commissioner sealing up his letters in his office.

That unobservant man had just written at length, privately and confidentially, both to the Lieutenant-Governor of the Punjab at the hill-station and to the Resident at Kohara. And to both he had written to the one effect:

"We must expect trouble in Chiltistan."

He based his conclusions upon the glimpse which he had obtained into the troubled feelings of Shere Ali. The next morning Shere Ali travelled northwards and forty-eight hours later from the top of the Malakand Pass he saw winding across the Swat valley past Chakdara the road which reached to Kohara and there stopped.

CHAPTER XII

ON THE POLO-GROUND

Violet Oliver travelled to India in the late autumn of that year, free from apprehension. Somewhere beyond the high snow-passes Shere Ali would be working out his destiny among his own people. She was not of those who seek publicity either for themselves or for their gowns in the daily papers. Shere Ali would never hear of her visit; she was safe. She spent her Christmas in Calcutta, saw the race for the Viceroy's Cup run without a fear that on that crowded racecourse the importunate figure of the young Prince of Chiltistan might emerge to reproach her, and a week later went northwards into the United Provinces. It was a year, now some while past, when a royal visitor came from a neighbouring country into India. And in his honour at one great city in those Provinces the troops gathered and the tents went up. Little towns of canvas, gay with bordered walks and flowers, were dotted on the dusty plains about and within the city. Great ministers and functionaries came with their retinues and their guests. Native princes from Rajputana brought their elephants and their escorts. Thither also came Violet Oliver. It was, indeed, to attend this Durbar that she had been invited out from England. She stayed in a small camp on the great Parade Ground where the tents faced one another in a single street, each with its little garden of grass

A. E. W. Mason

and flowers before the door. The ends of the street were closed in by posts, and outside the posts sentries were placed.

It was a week of bright, sunlit, rainless days, and of starry nights. It was a week of reviews and State functions. But it was also a week during which the best polo to be seen in India drew the visitors each afternoon to the club-ground. There was no more constant attendant than Violet Oliver. She understood the game and followed it with a nice appreciation of the player's skill. The first round of the competition had been played off on the third day, but a native team organised by the ruler of a Mohammedan State in Central India had drawn a by and did not appear in the contest until the fourth day. Mrs. Oliver took her seat in the front row of the stand, as the opposing teams cantered into the field upon their ponies. A programme was handed to her, but she did not open it. For already one of the umpires had tossed the ball into the middle of the ground. The game had begun.

The native team was matched against a regiment of Dragoons, and from the beginning it was plain that the four English players were the stronger team. But on the other side there was one who in point of skill outstripped them all. He was stationed on the outside of the field farthest away from Violet Oliver. He was a young man, almost a boy, she judged; he was beautifully mounted, and he sat his pony as though he and it were one. He was quick to turn, quick to pass the ball; and he never played a dangerous game. A desire that the native team should win woke in her and grew strong just because of that slim youth's extraordinary skill. Time after time he relieved his side, and once, as it seemed to her, he picked the ball out of the very goalposts. The bugle, she remembered afterwards, had just sounded. He drove the ball out from the press, leaned over until it seemed he must fall to resist an opponent who tried to ride him off, and then somehow he shook himself free from the tangle of polo-sticks and ponies.

"Oh, well done! well done!" cried Violet Oliver, clenching her hands in her enthusiasm. A roar of applause went up. He came racing down the very centre of the ground, the long ends of his white turban streaming out behind him like a pennant. The seven other players followed upon his heels outpaced and outplayed. He rode swinging his polo-stick for the stroke, and then with clean hard blows sent the ball skimming through the air like a bird. Violet Oliver watched him in suspense, dreading lest he should override the ball, or that his stroke should glance. But he made no mistake. The sound of the strokes rose clear and sharp; the ball flew straight. He drove it between the posts, and the players streamed in behind as though through the gateway of a beleaguered town. He had scored the first goal of the game at the end of the first chukkur. He cantered back to change his pony. But this time he rode along the edge of the stand, since on this side the ponies waited with their blankets thrown over their saddles and the syces at their heads. He ran his eyes along the row of onlookers as he cantered by, and suddenly Violet Oliver leaned forward. She had been interested merely in the player. Now she was interested in the man who played. She was more than interested. For she felt a tightening of the heart and she caught her breath. "It could not be," she said to herself. She could see his face clearly, however, now; and as suddenly as she had leaned forward she drew back. She lowered her head, until her broad hat-brim hid her face. She opened her programme, looked for and found the names of the players. Shere Ali's stared her in the face.

"He has broken his word," she said angrily to herself, quite forgetting that he had given no word, and that she had asked

A. E. W. Mason

for none. Then she fell to wondering whether or no he had recognised her as he rode past the stand. She stole a glance as he cantered back, but Shere Ali was not looking towards her. She debated whether she should make an excuse and go back to her camp. But if he had thought he had seen her, he would look again, and her empty place would be convincing evidence. Moreover, the teams had changed goals. Shere Ali would be playing on this side of the ground during the next chukkur unless the Dragoons scored quickly. Violet Oliver kept her place, but she saw little of the game. She watched Shere Ali's play furtively, however, hoping thereby to learn whether he had noticed her. And in a little while she knew. He played wildly, his strokes had lost their precision, he was less quick to follow the twists of the ball. Shere Ali had seen her. At the end of the game he galloped quickly to the corner, and when Violet Oliver came out of the enclosure she saw him standing, with his long overcoat already on his shoulders, waiting for her.

Violet Oliver separated herself from her friends and went forward towards him. She held out her hand. Shere Ali hesitated and then took it. All through the game, pride had been urging him to hold his head high and seek not so much as a single word with her. But he had been alone for six months in Chiltistan and he was young.

"You might have let me know," he said, in a troubled voice.

Violet Oliver faltered out some beginnings of an excuse. She did not want to bring him away from his work in Chiltistan. But Shere Ali was not listening to the excuses.

"I must see you again," he said. "I must."

"No doubt we shall meet," replied Violet Oliver.

"To-morrow," continued Shere Ali. "To-morrow evening. You will be going to the Fort."

There was to be an investiture, and after the investiture a great reception in the Fort on the evening of the next day. It would be as good a place as any, thought Violet Oliver— nay, a better place. There would be crowds of people wandering about the Fort. Since they must meet, let it be there and soon.

"Very well," she said. "To-morrow evening," and she passed on and rejoined her friends.

A. E. W. Mason

CHAPTER XIII

THE INVIDIOUS BAR

Violet Oliver drove back to her camp in the company of her friends and they remarked upon her silence.

"You are tired, Violet?" her hostess asked of her.

"A little, perhaps," Violet admitted, and, urging fatigue as her excuse, she escaped to her tent. There she took counsel of her looking-glass.

"I couldn't possibly have foreseen that he would be here," she pleaded to her reflection. "He was to have stayed in Chiltistan. I asked him and he told me that he meant to stay. If he had stayed there, he would never have known that I was in India," and she added and repeated, "It's really not my fault."

In a word she was distressed and sincerely distressed. But it was not upon her own account. She was not thinking of the awkwardness to her of this unexpected encounter. But she realised that she had given pain where she had meant not to give pain. Shere Ali had seen her. He had been assured that she sought to avoid him. And this was not the end. She must go on and give more pain.

Violet Oliver had hoped and believed that her friendship with the young Prince was something which had gone quite out of her life. She had closed it and put it away, as you put away upon an upper shelf a book which you do not mean to read again. The last word had been spoken eight months ago in the conservatory of Lady Marfield's house. And behold they had met again. There must be yet another meeting, yet another last interview. And from that last interview nothing but pain could come to Shere Ali. Therefore she anticipated it with a great reluctance. Violet Oliver did not live among illusions. She was no sentimentalist. She never made up and rehearsed in imagination little scenes of a melting pathos where eternal adieux were spoken amid tears. She had no appreciation of the woeful luxury of last interviews. On the contrary, she hated to confront distress or pain. It was in her character always to take the easier way when trouble threatened. She would have avoided altogether this meeting with Shere Ali, had it been possible.

"It's a pity," she said, and that was all. She was reluctant, but she had no misgiving. Shere Ali was to her still the youth to whom she had said good-bye in Lady Marfield's conservatory. She had seen him in the flush of victory after a close-fought game, and thus she had seen him often enough before. It was not to be wondered at that she noted no difference at that moment.

But the difference was there for the few who had eyes to see. He had journeyed up the broken road into Chiltistan. At the Fort of Chakdara, in the rice fields on the banks of the Swat river, he had taken his luncheon one day with the English commandant and the English doctor, and there he had parted with the ways of life which had become to him the only ways. He had travelled thence for a few hundred yards along a straight strip of road running over level ground, and so with the levies of Dir to escort him he swung round to the

A. E. W. Mason

left. A screen of hillside and grey rock moved across the face of the country behind him. The last outpost was left behind. The Fort and the Signal Tower on the pinnacle opposite and the English flag flying over all were hidden from his sight. Wretched as any exile from his native land, Shere Ali went up into the lower passes of the Himalayas. Days were to pass and still the high snow-peaks which glittered in the sky, gold in the noonday, silver in the night time, above the valleys of Chiltistan were to be hidden in the far North. But already the words began to be spoken and the little incidents to occur which were to ripen him for his destiny. They were garnered into his memories as separate and unrelated events. It was not until afterwards that he came to know how deeply they had left their marks, or that he set them in an ordered sequence and gave to them a particular significance. Even at the Fort of Chakdara a beginning had been made.

Shere Ali was standing in the little battery on the very summit of the Fort. Below him was the oblong enclosure of the men's barracks, the stone landings and steps, the iron railings, the numbered doors. He looked down into the enclosure as into a well. It might almost have been a section of the barracks at Chatham. But Shere Ali raised his head, and, over against him, on the opposite side of a natural gateway in the hills, rose the steep slope and the Signal Tower.

"I was here," said the Doctor, who stood behind him, "during the Malakand campaign. You remember it, no doubt?"

"I was at Oxford. I remember it well," said Shere Ali.

"We were hard pressed here, but the handful of men in the Signal Tower had the worst of it," continued the Doctor in a matter-of-fact voice. "It was reckoned that there were fourteen thousand men from the Swat Valley besieging us, and as they did not mind how many they lost, even with the

Maxims and our wire defences it was difficult to keep them off. We had to hold on to the Signal Tower because we could communicate with the people on the Malakand from there, while we couldn't from the Fort itself. The Amandara ridge, on the other side of the valley, as you can see, just hides the Pass from us. Well, the handful of men in the tower managed to keep in communication with the main force, and this is how it was done. A Sepoy called Prem Singh used to come out into full view of the enemy through a porthole of the tower, deliberately set up his apparatus, and heliograph away to the main force in the Malakand Camp, with the Swatis firing at him from short range. How it was he was not hit, I could never understand. He did it day after day. It was the bravest and coolest thing I ever saw done or ever heard of, with one exception, perhaps. Prem Singh would have got the Victoria Cross—" and the Doctor stopped suddenly and his face flushed.

Shere Ali, however, was too keenly interested in the incident itself to take any note of the narrator's confusion. Baldly though it was told, there was the square, strong tower with its door six feet from the ground, its machicoulis, its narrow portholes over against him, to give life and vividness to the story. Here that brave deed had been done and daily repeated. Shere Ali peopled the empty slopes which ran down from the tower to the river and the high crags beyond the tower with the hordes of white-clad Swatis, all in their finest robes, like men who have just reached the goal of a holy pilgrimage, as indeed they had. He saw their standards, he heard the din of their firearms, and high above them on the wall of the tower he saw the khaki-clad figure of a single Sepoy calmly flashing across the valley news of the defenders' plight.

"Didn't he get the Victoria Cross?" he asked.

A. E. W. Mason

"No," returned the Doctor with a certain awkwardness. But still Shere Ali did not notice.

"And what was the exception?" he asked eagerly. "What was the other brave deed you have seen fit to rank with this?"

"That, too, happened over there," said the Doctor, seizing upon the question with relief. "During the early days of the siege we were able to send in to the tower water and food. But when the first of August came we could help them no more. The enemy thronged too closely round us, we were attacked by night and by day, and stone sangars, in which the Swatis lay after dark, were built between us and the tower. We sent up water to the tower for the last time at half-past nine on a Saturday morning, and it was not until half-past four on the Monday afternoon that the relieving force marched across the bridge down there and set us free."

"They were without water for all that time—and in August?" cried Shere Ali.

"No," the Doctor answered. "But they would have been had the Sepoy not found his equal. A bheestie"—and he nodded his head to emphasise the word—"not a soldier at all, but a mere water-carrier, a mere camp-follower, volunteered to go down to the river. He crept out of the tower after nightfall with his water-skins, crawled down between the sangars— and I can tell you the hill-side was thick with them—to the brink of the Swat river below there, filled his skins, and returned with them."

"That man, too, earned the Victoria Cross," said Shere Ali.

"Yes," said the Doctor, "no doubt, no doubt."

Something of flurry was again audible in his voice, and this time Shere Ali noticed it.

"Earned—but did not get it?" he went on slowly; and turning to the Doctor he waited quietly for an answer. The answer was given reluctantly, after a pause.

"Well! That is so."

"Why?"

The question was uttered sharply, close upon the words which had preceded it. The Doctor looked upon the ground, shifted his feet, and looked up again. He was a young man, and inexperienced. The question was repeated.

"Why?"

The Doctor's confusion increased. He recognised that his delay in answering only made the answer more difficult to give. It could not be evaded. He blurted out the truth apologetically.

"Well, you see, we don't give the Victoria Cross to natives."

Shere Ali was silent for a while. He stood with his eyes fixed upon the tower, his face quite inscrutable.

"Yes, I guessed that would be the reason," he said quietly.

"Well," said his companion uncomfortably, "I expect some day that will be altered."

Shere Ali shrugged his shoulders, and turned to go down. At the gateway of the Fort, by the wire bridge, his escort, mounted upon their horses, waited for him. He climbed into the saddle without a word. He had been labouring for these last days under a sense of injury, and his thoughts had narrowed in upon himself. He was thinking. "I, too, then, could never win that prize." His conviction that he was really one of the White People, bolstered up as it had been by so many vain arguments, was put to the test of fact. The truth shone in upon his mind. For here was a coveted privilege of the White People from which he was debarred, he and the bheestie and the Sepoy. They were all one, he thought bitterly, to the White People. The invidious bar of his colour was not to be broken.

"Good-bye," he said, leaning down from his saddle and holding out his hand. "Thank you very much."

He shook hands with the Doctor and cantered down the road, with a smile upon his face. But the consciousness of the invidious bar was rankling cruelly at his heart, and it continued to rankle long after he had swung round the bend of the road and had lost sight of Chakdara and the English flag.

He passed through Jandol and climbed the Lowari Pass among the fir trees and the pines, and on the very summit he met three men clothed in brown homespun with their hair clubbed at the sides of their heads. Each man carried a rifle on his back and two of them carried swords besides, and they wore sandals of grass upon their feet. They were talking as they went, and they were talking in the Chilti tongue. Shere Ali hailed them and bade them stop.

"On what journey are you going?" he asked, and one of the three bowed low and answered him.

"Sir, we are going to Mecca."

"To Mecca!" exclaimed Shere Ali. "How will you ever get to

Mecca? Have you money?"

"Sir, we have each six rupees, and with six rupees a man may reach Mecca from Kurrachee. Till we reach Kurrachee, there is no fear that we shall starve. Dwellers in the villages will befriend us."

"Why, that is true," said Shere Ali, "but since you are countrymen of my own and my father's subjects, you shall not tax too heavily your friends upon the road."

He added to their scanty store of rupees, and one after another they thanked him and so went cheerily down the Pass. Shere Ali watched them as they went, wondering that men should take such a journey and endure so much discomfort for their faith. He watched their dwindling figures and understood how far he was set apart from them. He was of their faith himself, nominally at all events, but Mecca—? He shrugged his shoulders at the name. It meant no more to him than it did to the White People who had cast him out. But that chance meeting lingered in his memory, and as he travelled northwards, he would wonder at times by night at what village his three countrymen slept and by day whether their faith still cheered them on their road.

He came at last to the borders of Chiltistan, and travelled thenceforward through a country rich with orchards and green rice and golden amaranth. The terraced slopes of the mountains, ablaze with wild indigo, closed in upon him and widened out. Above the terraces great dark forests of pines and deodars, maples and horse chestnuts clung to the hill sides; and above the forests grass slopes stretched up to bare rock and the snowfields. From the villages the people came out to meet him, and here and there from some castle of a greater importance a chieftain would ride out with his bodyguard, gay in velvets, and silks from Bokhara and chogas of gold kinkob, and offer to him gold dust twisted up in the petal of a flower, which he touched and remitted. He was escorted to polo-grounds and sat for hours witnessing sports and trials of skill, and at night to the music of kettledrums and pipes men and boys danced interminably before him. There was one evening which he particularly remembered. He had set up his camp outside a large village and was sitting alone by his fire in the open air. The night was very still, the sky dark but studded with stars extraordinarily bright—so bright, indeed, that Shere Ali could see upon the water of the river below the low cliff on which his camp fire was lit a trembling golden path made by the rays of a planet. And as he sat, unexpectedly in the hush a boy with a clear, sweet voice began to sing from the darkness behind him. The melody was plaintive and sweet; a few notes of a pipe accompanied him; and as Shere Ali listened in this high valley of the Himalayas on a summer's night, the music took hold upon him and wrung his heart. The yearning for all that he had left behind became a pain almost beyond endurance. The days of his boyhood and his youth went by before his eyes in a glittering procession. His school life, his first summer term at Oxford, the Cherwell with the shadows of the branches overhead dappling the water, the strenuous week of the Eights, his climbs with Linforth, and, above all, London in June, a London bright with lilac and sunshine and the fair faces of women, crowded in upon his memory. He had been steadily of late refusing to remember, but the sweet voice and the plaintive melody had caught him unawares. The ghosts of his dead pleasures trooped out and took life and substance. Particular hours were lived through again—a motor ride alone with Violet Oliver to Pangbourne, a dinner on the lawn outside the inn, the drive back to London in the cool of the evening. It all seemed very far away to-night. Shere Ali sat late beside his fire, nor when he went into his tent did he close his eyes.

The next morning he rode among orchards bright with apricots and mulberries, peaches and white grapes, and in another day he looked down from a high cliff, across which the road was carried on a scaffolding, upon the town of Kohara and the castle of his father rising in terraces upon a hill behind. The nobles and their followers came out to meet him with courteous words and protestations of good will. But they looked him over with curious and not too friendly eyes. News had gone before Shere Ali that the young Prince of Chiltistan was coming to Kohara wearing the dress of the White People. They saw that the news was true, but no word or comment was uttered in his hearing. Joking and laughing they escorted him to the gates of his father's palace. Thus Shere Ali at the last had come home to Kohara. Of the life which he lived there he was to tell something to Violet Oliver.

CHAPTER XIV

IN THE COURTYARD

The investiture was over, and the guests, thronging from the Hall of Audience, came out beneath arches and saw the whole length of the great marble court spread before them. A vast canopy roofed it in, and a soft dim light pervaded it. To those who came from the glitter of the ceremonies it brought a sense of coolness and of peace. From the arches a broad flight of steps led downwards to the floor, where water gleamed darkly in a marble basin. Lilies floated upon its surface, and marble paths crossed it to the steps at the far end; and here and there, in its depth, the reflection of a lamp burned steadily. At the far end steps rose again to a great platform and to gilded arches through which lights poured in a blaze, and gave to that end almost the appearance of a lighted stage, and made of the courtyard a darkened auditorium. From one flight of steps to the other, in the dim cool light, the guests passed across the floor of the court, soldiers in uniforms, civilians in their dress of state, jewelled princes of the native kingdoms, ladies in their bravest array. But now and again one or two would slip from the throng, and, leaving the procession, take their own way about the Fort. Among those who slipped away was Violet Oliver. She went to the side of the courtyard where a couch stood empty. There she seated herself and waited. In front of her the stream of people passed by talking and laughing, within view, within earshot if only one raised one's voice a trifle above the ordinary note. Yet there was no other couch near. One might talk at will and not be overheard. It was, to Violet Oliver's thinking, a good strategic position, and there she proposed to remain till Shere Ali found her, and after he had found her, until he went away.

She wondered in what guise he would come to her: a picturesque figure with a turban of some delicate shade upon his head and pearls about his throat, or—as she wondered, a young man in the evening dress of an Englishman stepped aside from the press of visitors and came towards her. Before she could, in that dim light, distinguish his face, she recognised him by the lightness of his step and the suppleness of his figure. She raised herself into a position a little more upright, and held out her hand. She made room for him on the couch beside her, and when he had taken his seat, she turned at once to speak.

But Shere Ali raised his hand in a gesture of entreaty.

"Hush!" he said with a smile; and the smile pleaded with her as much as did his words. "Just for a moment! We can argue afterwards. Just for a moment, let us pretend."

Violet Oliver had expected anger, accusations, prayers. Even for some threat, some act of violence, she had come prepared. But the quiet wistfulness of his manner, as of a man too tired greatly to long for anything, took her at a disadvantage. But the one thing which she surely understood was the danger of pretence. There had been too much of pretence already.

"No," she said.

"Just for a moment," he insisted. He sat beside her, watching the clear profile of her face, the slender throat, the heavy masses of hair so daintily coiled upon her head. "The last eight months have not been—could not be. Yesterday we were at Richmond, just you and I. It was Sunday—you remember. I called on you in the afternoon, and for a wonder you were alone. We drove down together to Richmond, and dined together in the little room at the end of the passage— the room with the big windows, and the name of the woman who was murdered in France scratched upon the glass. That was yesterday."

"It was last year," said Violet.

"Yesterday," Shere Ali persisted. "I dreamt last night that I had gone back to Chiltistan; but it was only a dream."

"It was the truth," and the quiet assurance of her voice dispelled Shere Ali's own effort at pretence. He leaned forward suddenly, clasping his hands upon his knees in an attitude familiar to her as characteristic of the man. There was a tenseness which gave to him even in repose a look of activity.

"Well, it's the truth, then," he said, and his voice took on an accent of bitterness. "And here's more truth. I never thought to see you here to-night."

"Did you think that I should be afraid?" asked Violet Oliver in a low, steady voice.

"Afraid!" Shere Ali turned towards her in surprise and met her gaze. "No."

"Why, then, should I break my word? Have I done it so often?"

Shere Ali did not answer her directly.

"You promised to write to me," he said, and Violet Oliver replied at once:

"Yes. And I did write."

"You wrote twice," he cried bitterly. "Oh, yes, you kept your word. There's a post every day, winter and summer, into Chiltistan. Sometimes an avalanche or a snowstorm delays it; but on most days it comes. If you could only have guessed how eagerly I looked forward to your letters, you would have written, I think, more often. There's a path over a high ridge by which the courier must come. I could see it from the casement of the tower. I used to watch it through a pair of field-glasses, that I might catch the first glimpse of the man as he rose against the sky. Each day I thought 'Perhaps there's a letter in your handwriting.' And you wrote twice, and in neither letter was there a hint that you were coming out to India."

He was speaking in a low, passionate voice. In spite of herself, Violet Oliver was moved. The picture of him watching from his window in the tower for the black speck against the skyline was clear before her mind, and troubled her. Her voice grew gentle.

"I did not write more often on purpose," she said.

"It was on purpose, too, that you left out all mention of your visit to India?"

Violet nodded her head.

"Yes," she said.

"You did not want to see me again."

Violet turned her face towards him, and leaned forward a little.

"I don't say that," she said softly. "But I thought it would be better that we two should not meet again, if meeting could be avoided. I saw that you cared—I may say that, mayn't I?" and for a second she laid her hand gently upon his sleeve. "I saw that you cared too much. It seemed to me best that it should end altogether."

Shere Ali lifted his head, and turned quickly towards her.

"Why should it end at all?" he cried. His eyes kindled and sought hers. "Violet, why should it end at all?"

Violet Oliver drew back. She cast a glance to the courtyard. Only a few paces away the stream of people passed up and down.

"It must end," she answered. "You know that as well as I."

"I don't know it. I won't know it," he replied. He reached out his hand towards hers, but she was too quick for him. He bent nearer to her.

"Violet," he whispered, "marry me!"

Violet Oliver glanced again to the courtyard. But it was no longer to assure herself that friends of her own race were comfortably near at hand. Now she was anxious that they should not be near enough to listen and overhear.

"That's impossible!" she answered in a startled voice.

"It's not impossible! It's not!" And the desperation in his voice betrayed him. In the depths of his heart he knew that, for this woman, at all events, it was impossible. But he would not listen to that knowledge.

"Other women, here in India, have had the courage."

"And what have their lives been afterwards?" she asked. She had not herself any very strong feeling on the subject of colour. She was not repelled, as men are repelled. But she was aware, nevertheless, how strong the feeling was in others. She had not lived in India for nothing. Marriage with Shere Ali was impossible, even had she wished for it. It meant ostracism and social suicide.

"Where should I live?" she went on. "In Chiltistan? What life would there be there for me?"

"No," he replied. "I would not ask it. I never thought of it. In England. We could live there!" and, ceasing to insist, he began wistfully to plead. "Oh, if you knew how I have hated these past months. I used to sit at night, alone, alone, alone, eating my heart for want of you; for want of everything I care for. I could not sleep. I used to see the morning break. Perhaps here and there a drum would begin to beat, the cries of children would rise up from the streets, and I would lie in my bed with my hands clenched, thinking of the jingle of a hansom cab along the streets of London, and the gas lamps paling as the grey light spread. Violet!"

Violet twisted her hands one within the other. This was just what she had thought to avoid, to shut out from her mind— the knowledge that he had suffered. But the evidence of his pain was too indisputable. There was no shutting it out. It sounded loud in his voice, it showed in his looks. His face had grown white and haggard, the face of a tortured man; his hands trembled, his eyes were fierce with longing.

"Oh, don't," she cried, and so great was her trouble that for once she did not choose her words. "You know that it's impossible. We can't alter these things."

She meant by "these things" the natural law that white shall mate with white, and brown with brown; and so Shere Ali understood her. He ceased to plead. There came a dreadful look upon his face.

"Oh, I know," he exclaimed brutally. "You would be marrying a nigger."

"I never said that," Violet interrupted hastily.

"But you meant it," and he began to laugh bitterly and very quietly. To Violet that laughter was horrible. It frightened her. "Oh, yes, yes," he said. "When we come over to England we are very fine people. Women welcome us and are kind, men make us their friends. But out here! We quickly learn out here that we are the inferior people. Suppose that I wanted to be a soldier, not an officer of my levies, but a soldier in your army with a soldier's chances of promotion and high rank! Do you know what would happen? I might serve for twenty years, and at the end of it the youngest subaltern out of Sandhurst, with a moustache he can't feel upon his lip, would in case of war step over my head and command me. Why, I couldn't win the Victoria Cross, even though I had earned it ten times over. We are the subject races," and he turned to her abruptly. "I am in disfavour to-night. Do you know why? Because I am not dressed in a silk jacket; because I am not wearing jewels like a woman, as those Princes are," and he waved his hand contemptuously towards a group of them. "They are content," he cried. "But I was brought up in England, and I am not."

He buried his face in his hands and was silent; and as he sat thus, Violet Oliver said to him with a gentle reproach:

"When we parted in London last year you spoke in a different way—a better way. I remember very well what you said. For I was glad to hear it. You said: 'I have not forgotten really that there is much to do in my own country. I have not forgotten that I can thank all of you here who have shown me so much kindness by more than mere words. For I can help in Chiltistan—I can really help.'"

Shere All raised his face from his hands with the air of a man listening to strange and curious words.

"I said that?"

"Yes," and in her turn Violet Oliver began to plead. "I wish that to-night you could recapture that fine spirit. I should be very glad of it. For I am troubled by your unhappiness."

But Shere Ali shook his head.

"I have been in Chiltistan since I spoke those words. And they will not let me help."

"There's the road."

"It must not be continued."

"There is, at all events, your father," Violet suggested. "You can help him."

And again Shere Ali laughed. But this time the bitterness had gone from his voice. He laughed with a sense of humour, almost, it seemed to Violet, with enjoyment.

A. E. W. Mason

"My father!" he said. "I'll tell you about my father," and his face cleared for a moment of its distress as he turned towards her. "He received me in the audience chamber of his palace at Kohara. I had not seen him for ten years. How do you think he received me? He was sitting on a chair of brocade with silver legs in great magnificence, and across his knees he held a loaded rifle at full cock. It was a Snider, so that I could be quite sure it was cocked."

Violet stared at him, not understanding.

"But why?" she asked.

"Well, he knew quite well that I was brought back to Kohara in order to replace him, if he didn't mend his ways and spend less money. And he didn't mean to be replaced." The smile broke out again on Shere Ali's face as he remembered the scene. "He sat there with his great beard, dyed red, spreading across his chest, a long velvet coat covering his knees, and the loaded rifle laid over the coat. His eyes watched me, while his fingers played about the trigger."

Violet Oliver was horrified.

"You mean—that he meant to kill you!" she cried incredulously.

"Yes," said Shere Ali calmly. "I think he meant to do that. It's not so very unusual in our family. He probably thought that I might try to kill him. However, he didn't do it. You see, my father's very fond of the English, so I at once began to talk to him about England. It was evening when I went into the reception chamber; but it was broad daylight when I came out. I talked for my life that night—and won. He became so interested that he forgot to shoot me; and at the end I was wise enough to assure him that there was a great deal more to tell."

The ways of the Princes in the States beyond the Frontier were unknown to Violet Oliver. The ruling family of Chiltistan was no exception to the general rule. In its annals there was hardly a page which was not stained with blood. When the son succeeded to the throne, it was, as often as not, after murdering his brothers, and if he omitted that precaution, as often as not he paid the penalty. Shere Ali was fortunate in that he had no brothers. But, on the other hand, he had a father, and there was no great security. Violet was startled, and almost as much bewildered as she was startled. She could not understand Shere Ali's composure. He spoke in so matter-of-fact a tone.

"However," she said, grasping at the fact, "he has not killed you. He has not since tried to kill you."

"No. I don't think he has," said Shere Ali slowly. But he spoke like one in doubt. "You see he realised very soon that I was not after all acceptable to the English. I wouldn't quite do what they wanted," and the humour died out of his face.

"What did they want?"

Shere Ali looked at her in hesitation.

"Shall I tell you? I will. They wanted me to marry—one of my own people. They wanted me to forget," and he broke out in a passionate scorn. "As if I could do either—after I had known you."

"Hush!" said she.

But he was not to be checked.

A. E. W. Mason

"You said it was impossible that you should marry me. It's no less impossible that I should marry now one of my own race. You know that. You can't deny it."

Violet did not try to. He was speaking truth then, she was well aware. A great pity swelled up in her heart for him. She turned to him with a smile, in which there was much tenderness. His life was all awry; and both were quite helpless to set it right.

"I am very sorry," she said in a whisper of remorse. "I did not think. I have done you grave harm."

"Not you," he said quietly. "You may be quite sure of that. Those who have done me harm are those who sent me, ten years ago, to England."

CHAPTER XV

A QUESTION ANSWERED

Thereafter both sat silent for a little while. The stream of people across the courtyard had diminished. High up on the great platform by the lighted arches the throng still pressed and shifted. But here there was quietude. The clatter of voices had died down. A band playing somewhere near at hand could be heard. Violet Oliver for the first time in her life had been brought face to face with a real tragedy. She was conscious of it as something irremediable and terribly sad. And for her own share in bringing it about she was full of remorse. She looked at Shere Ali as he sat beside her, his eyes gazing into the courtyard, his face tired and hopeless. There was nothing to be done. Her thoughts told her so no less clearly than his face. Here was a life spoilt at the beginning. But that was all that she saw. That the spoilt life might become an instrument of evil—she was blind to that possibility: she thought merely of the youth who suffered and still must suffer; who was crippled by the very means which were meant to strengthen him: and pity inclined her towards him with an ever-increasing strength.

"I couldn't do it," she repeated silently to herself. "I couldn't do it. It would be madness."

A. E. W. Mason

Shere Ali raised his head and said with a smile, "I am glad they are not playing the tune which I once heard on the Lake of Geneva, and again in London when I said good-bye to you."

And then Violet sought to comfort him, her mind still working on what he had told her of his life in Chiltistan.

"But it will become easier," she said, beginning in that general way. "In time you will rule in Chiltistan. That is certain." But he checked her with a shake of the head.

"Certain? There is the son of Abdulla Mohammed, who fought against my father when Linforth's father was killed. It is likely enough that those old days will be revived. And I should have the priests against me."

"The Mullahs!" she exclaimed, remembering in what terms he was wont to speak of them to her.

"Yes," he answered, "I have set them against me already. They laid their traps for me while I was on the sea, and I would not fall into them. They would have liked to raise the country against my father and the English, just as they raised it twenty-five years ago. And they would have liked me to join in with them."

He related to Violet the story of his meeting with Safdar Khan at the Gate of Lahore, and he repeated the words which he had used in Safdar Khan's hearing.

"It did not take long for my threats to be repeated in the bazaar of Kohara, and from the bazaar they were quickly carried to the ears of the Mullahs. I had proof of it," he said with a laugh.

Violet asked him anxiously for the proof.

"I can tell to a day when the words were repeated in Kohara. For a fortnight after my coming the Mullahs still had hopes. They had heard nothing, and they met me always with salutations and greetings. Then came the day when I rode up the valley and a Mullah who had smiled the day before passed me as though he had not noticed me at all. The news had come. I was sure of it at the time. I reined in my horse and called sharply to one of the servants riding behind me, 'Who is that?' The Mullah heard the question, and he turned and up went the palm of his hand to his forehead in a flash. But I was not inclined to let him off so easily."

"What did you do?" Violet asked uneasily.

"I said to him, 'My friend, I will take care that you know me the next time we meet upon the road. Show me your hands!' He held them out, and they were soft as a woman's. I was close to a bridge which some workmen were repairing. So I had my friend brought along to the bridge. Then I said to one of the workmen, 'Would you like to earn your day's wage and yet do no work?' He laughed, thinking that I was joking. But I was not. I said to him, 'Very well, then, see that this soft-handed creature does your day's work. You will bring him to me at the Palace this evening, and if I find that he has not done the work, or that you have helped him, you will forfeit your wages and I will whip you both into the bargain.' The Mullah was brought to me in the evening," said Shere Ali, smiling grimly. "He was so stiff he could hardly walk. I made him show me his hands again, and this time they were blistered. So I told him to remember his manners in the future, and I let him go. But he was a man of prominence in the country, and when the story got known he became rather ridiculous." He turned with a smile to Violet Oliver.

A. E. W. Mason

"My people don't like being made ridiculous—least of all Mullahs."

But there was no answering smile on Violet's face. Rather she was troubled and alarmed.

"But surely that was unwise?"

Shere Ali shrugged his shoulders.

"What does it matter?" he said. He did not tell her all of that story. There was an episode which had occurred two days later when Shere Ali was stalking an ibex on the hillside. A bullet had whistled close by his ear, and it had been fired from behind him. He was never quite sure whether his father or the Mullah was responsible for that bullet, but he inclined to attribute it to the Mullah.

"Yes, I have the priests against me," he said. "They call me the Englishman." Then he laughed. "A curious piece of irony, isn't it?"

He stood up suddenly and said: "When I left England I was in doubt. I could not be sure whether my home, my true home, was there or in Chiltistan."

"Yes, I remember," said Violet.

"I am no longer in doubt. It is neither in England nor in Chiltistan. I am a citizen of no country. I have no place anywhere at all."

Violet Oliver stood up and faced him.

"I must be going. I must find my friends," she said, and as he took her hand, she added, "I am so very sorry."

The words, she felt, were utterly inadequate, but no others would come to her lips, and so with a trembling smile she repeated them. She drew her hand from his clasp and moved a step or two away. But he followed her, and she stopped and shook her head.

"This is really good-bye," she said simply and very gravely.

"I want to ask you a question," he explained. "Will you answer it?"

"How can I tell you until you ask it?"

He looked at her for a moment as though in doubt whether he should speak or not. Then he said, "Are you going to marry—Linforth?"

The blood slowly mounted into her face and flushed her forehead and cheeks.

"He has not even asked me to marry him," she said, and moved down into the courtyard.

Shere Ali watched her as she went. That was the last time he should see her, he told himself. The last time in all his life. His eyes followed her, noting the grace of her movements, the whiteness of her skin, all her daintiness of dress and person. A madness kindled in his blood. He had a wild thought of springing down, of capturing her. She mounted the steps and disappeared among the throng.

And they wanted him to marry—to marry one of his own people. Shere Ali suddenly saw the face of the Deputy Commissioner at Lahore calmly suggesting the arrangement, almost ordering it. He sat down again upon the couch and

A. E. W. Mason

once more began to laugh. But the laughter ceased very quickly, and folding his arms upon the high end of the couch, he bowed his head upon them and was still.

CHAPTER XVI

SHERE ALI MEETS AN OLD FRIEND

The carriage which was to take Violet Oliver and her friends
back to their camp had been parked amongst those farthest
from the door. Violet stood for a long while under the
awning, waiting while the interminable procession went by.
The generals in their scarlet coats, the ladies in their satin
gowns, the great officers of state attended by their escorts,
the native princes, mounted into their carriages and were
driven away. The ceremony and the reception which
followed it had been markedly successful even in that land of
ceremonies and magnificence. The voices about her told her
so as they spoke of this or that splendour and recalled the
picturesque figures which had given colour to the scene. But
the laughter, the praise, the very tones of enjoyment had to
her a heartless ring. She watched the pageantry of the great
Indian Administration dissolve, and was blind to its glitter
and conscious only of its ruthlessness. For ruthless she found
it to-night. She had been face to face with a victim of the
system—a youth broken by it, needlessly broken, and as
helpless to recover from his hurt as a wounded animal. The
harm had been done no doubt with the very best intention,
but the harm had been done. She was conscious of her own
share in the blame and she drove miserably home, with the
picture of Shere Ali's face as she had last seen it to bear her

A. E. W. Mason

company, and with his cry, that he had no place anywhere at all, sounding in her ears.

When she reached the privacy of her own tent, and had dismissed her maid, she unlocked one of her trunks and took out from it her jewel case. She had been careful not to wear her necklace of pearls that night, and she took it out of the case now and laid it upon her knees. She was very sorry to part with it. She touched and caressed the pearls with loving fingers, and once she lifted it as though she would place it about her neck. But she checked her hands, fearing that if she put it on she would never bring herself to let it go. Already as she watched and fingered it and bent her head now and again to scrutinise a stone, small insidious voices began to whisper at her heart.

"He asked for nothing when he gave it you."

"You made no promise when you took it."

"It was a gift without conditions hinted or implied."

Violet Oliver took the world lightly on the whole. Only this one passion for jewels and precious stones had touched her deeply as yet. Of love she knew little beyond the name and its aspect in others. She was familiar enough with that, so familiar that she gave little heed to what lay behind the aspect—or had given little heed until to-night. Her husband she had accepted rather than actively welcomed. She had lived with him in a mood of placid and unquestioning good-humour, and she had greatly missed him when he died. But it was the presence in the house that she missed, rather than the lover. To-night, almost for the first time, she had really looked under the surface. Insight had been vouchsafed to her; and in remorse she was minded to put the thing she greatly valued away from her.

She rose suddenly, and, lest the temptation to keep the necklace should prove too strong, laid it away in its case.

A post went every day over the passes into Chiltistan. She wrapped up the case in brown paper, tied it, sealed it, and addressed it. There was need to send it off, she well knew, before the picture of Shere Ali, now so vivid in her mind, lost its aspect of poignant suffering and faded out of her thoughts.

But she slept ill and in the middle of the night she rose from her bed. The tent was pitch dark. She lit her candle; and it was the light of the candle which awoke her maid. The tent was a double one; the maid slept in the smaller portion of it and a canvas doorway gave entrance into her mistress' room. Over this doorway hung the usual screen of green matting. Now these screens act as screens, are as impenetrable to the eye as a door—so long as there is no light behind them. But place a light behind them and they become transparent. This was what Violet Oliver had done. She had lit her candle and at once a part of the interior of her tent was visible to her maid as she lay in bed.

The maid saw the table and the sealed parcel upon it. Then she saw Mrs. Oliver come to the table, break the seals, open the parcel, take out a jewel case—a jewel case which the maid knew well—and carry it and the parcel out of sight. Mrs. Oliver crossed to a corner of the room where her trunks lay; and the next moment the maid heard a key grate in a lock. For a little while the candle still burned, and every now and then a distorted shadow was flung upon the wall of the tent within the maid's vision. It seemed to her that Mrs. Oliver was sitting at a little writing table which stood close by the trunk. Then the light went out again. The maid would have thought no more of this incident, but on entering the room next morning with a cup of tea, she was surprised to

A. E. W. Mason

see the packet once more sealed and fastened on the centre table.

"Adela," said Mrs. Oliver, "I want you to take that parcel to the Post Office yourself and send it off."

The maid took the parcel away.

Violet Oliver, with a sigh of relief, drank her tea. At last, she thought, the end was reached. Now, indeed, her life and Shere Ali's life would touch no more. But she was to see him again. For two days later, as the train which was carrying her northwards to Lahore moved out of the station, she saw from the window of her carriage the young Prince of Chiltistan standing upon the platform. She drew back quickly, fearing that he would see her. But he was watching the train with indifferent eyes; and the spectacle of his indifference struck her as something incongruous and strange. She had been thinking of him with remorse as a man twisting like Hamlet in the coils of tragedy, and wearing like Hamlet the tragic mien. Yet here he was on the platform of a railway station, waiting, like any commonplace traveller, with an uninterested patience for his train. The aspect of Shere Ali diminished Violet Oliver's remorse. She wondered for a moment why he was not travelling upon the same train as herself, for his destination must be northwards too. And then she lost sight of him. She was glad that after all the last vision of him which she was to carry away was not the vision of a youth helpless and despairing with a trouble-tortured face.

Shere Ali was following out the destiny to which his character bound him. He had been made and moulded and fashioned, and though he knew he had been fashioned awry, he could no more change and rebuild himself than the hunchback can will away his hump. He was driven down the ways of circumstance. At present he saw and knew that he was so driven. He knew, too, that he could not resist. This half-year in Chiltistan had taught him that.

So he went southwards to Calcutta. The mere thought of Chiltistan was unendurable. He had to forget. There was no possibility of forgetfulness amongst his own hills and the foreign race that once had been his own people. Southwards he went to Calcutta, and in that city for a time was lost to sight. He emerged one afternoon upon the racecourse, and while standing on the grass in front of the Club stand, before the horses cantered down to the starting post, he saw an elderly man, heavy of build but still erect, approach him with a smile.

Shere Ali would have avoided that man if he could. He hesitated, unwilling to recognise and unable quite to ignore. And while he hesitated, the elderly man held out his hand.

"We know each other, surely. I used to see you at Eton, didn't I? I used to run down to see a young friend of mine and a friend of yours, Dick Linforth. I am Colonel Dewes."

"Yes, I remember," said Shere Ali with some embarrassment; and he took the Colonel's outstretched hand. "I thought that you had left India for good."

"So did I," said Dewes. "But I was wrong." He turned and walked along by the side of Shere Ali. "I don't know why exactly, but I did not find life in London so very interesting."

Shere Ali looked quickly at the Colonel.

"Yet you had looked forward to retiring and going home?" he asked with a keen interest. Colonel Dewes gave himself up to reflection. He sounded the obscurities of his mind. It was a practice to which he was not accustomed. He drew himself erect, his eyes became fixed, and with a puckered forehead he thought.

"I suppose so," he said. "Yes, certainly. I remember. One used to buck at mess of the good time one would have, the comfort of one's club and one's rooms, and the rest of it. It isn't comfortable in India, is it? Not compared with England. Your furniture, your house, and all that sort of thing. You live as if you were a lodger, don't you know, and it didn't matter for a little while whether you were comfortable or not. The little while slips on and on, and suddenly you find you have been in the country twenty or thirty years, and you have never taken the trouble to be comfortable. It's like living in a dak-bungalow."

The Colonel halted and pulled at his moustache. He had made a discovery. He had reflected not without result. "By George!" he said, "that's right. Let me put it properly now, as a fellow would put it in a book, if he hit upon anything as good." He framed his aphorism in different phrases before he was satisfied with it. Then he delivered himself of it with pride.

"At the bottom of the Englishman's conception of life in India, there is always the idea of a dak-bungalow," and he repeated the sentence to commit it surely to memory. "But don't you use it," he said, turning to Shere Ali suddenly. "I thought of that—not you. It's mine."

"I won't use it," said Shere Ali.

"Life in India is based upon the dak-bungalow," said Dewes. "Yes, yes"; and so great was his pride that he relented towards Shere Ali. "You may use it if you like," he conceded. "Only you would naturally add that it was I who thought of it."

Shere Ali smiled and replied:

"I won't fail to do that, Colonel Dewes."

"No? Then use it as much as you like, for it's true. Out here one remembers the comfort of England and looks forward to it. But back there, one forgets the discomfort of India. By George! that's pretty good, too. Shall we look at the horses?"

Shere Ali did not answer that question. With a quiet persistence he kept Colonel Dewes to the conversation. Colonel Dewes for his part was not reluctant to continue it, in spite of the mental wear and tear which it involved. He felt that he was clearly in the vein. There was no knowing what brilliant thing he might not say next. He wished that some of those clever fellows on the India Council were listening to him.

"Why?" asked Shere Ali. "Why back there does one forget the discomfort of India?"

He asked the question less in search of information than to discover whether the feelings of which he was conscious were shared too by his companion.

"Why?" answered Dewes wrinkling his forehead again. "Because one misses more than one thought to miss and one doesn't find half what one thought to find. Come along here!"

He led Shere Ali up to the top of the stand.

"We can see the race quite well from here," he said, "although that is not the reason why I brought you up. This is

A. E. W. Mason

what I wanted to show you."

He waved his hand over towards the great space which the racecourse enclosed. It was thronged with natives robed in saffron and pink, in blue and white, in scarlet and delicate shades of mauve and violet. The whole enclosure was ablaze with colour, and the colours perpetually moved and grouped themselves afresh as the throng shifted. A great noise of cries rose up into the clear air.

"I suppose that is what I missed," said Dewes, "not the noise, not the mere crowd—you can get both on an English racecourse—but the colour."

And suddenly before Shere Ali's eyes there rose a vision of the Paddock at Newmarket during a July meeting. The sleek horses paced within the cool grove of trees; the bright sunlight, piercing the screen of leaves overhead, dappled their backs with flecks of gold. Nothing of the sunburnt grass before his eyes was visible to him. He saw the green turf of the Jockey Club enclosure, the seats, the luncheon room behind with its open doors and windows.

"Yes, I understand," he said. "But you have come back," and a note of envy sounded in his voice. Here was one point in which the parallel between his case and that of Colonel Dewes was not complete. Dewes had missed India as he had missed England. But Dewes was a free man. He could go whither he would. "Yes, you were able to come back. How long do you stay?"

And the answer to that question startled Shere Ali.

"I have come back for good."

"You are going to live here?" cried Shere Ali.

"Not here, exactly. In Cashmere. I go up to Cashmere in a week's time. I shall live there and die there."

Colonel Dewes spoke without any note of anticipation, and without any regret. It was difficult for Shere Ali to understand how deeply he felt. Yet the feeling must be deep. He had cut himself off from his own people, from his own country. Shere Ali was stirred to yet more questions. He was anxious to understand thoroughly all that had moved this commonplace matter-of-fact man at his side.

"You found life in England so dull?" he asked.

"Well, one felt a stranger," said Dewes. "One had lost one's associations. I know there are men who throw themselves into public life and the rest of it. But I couldn't. I hadn't the heart for it even if I had the ability. There was Lawrence, of course. He governed India and then he went on the School Board," and Dewes thumped his fist upon the rail in front of him. "How he was able to do it beats me altogether. I read his life with amazement. He was just as keen about the School Board as he had been about India when he was Viceroy here. He threw himself into it with just as much vigour. That beats me. He was a big man, of course, and I am not. I suppose that's the explanation. Anyway, the School Board was not for me. I put in my winters for some years at Corfu shooting woodcock. And in the summer I met a man or two back on leave at my club. But on the whole it was pretty dull. Yes," and he nodded his head, and for the first time a note of despondency sounded in his voice. "Yes, on the whole it was pretty dull. It will be better in Cashmere."

"It would have been still better if you had never seen India at all," said Shere Ali.

"No; I don't say that. I had my good time in India—twenty-five years of it, the prime of my life. No; I have nothing to complain of," said Dewes.

Here was another difference brought to Shere Ali's eyes. He himself was still young; the prime years were before him, not behind. He looked down, even as Dewes had done, over that wide space gay with colours as a garden of flowers; but in the one man's eyes there was a light of satisfaction, in the other's a gleam almost of hatred.

"You are not sorry you came out to India," he said. "Well, for my part," and his voice suddenly shook with passion, "I wish to heaven I had never seen England."

Dewes turned about, a vacant stare of perplexity upon his face.

"Oh, come, I say!" he protested.

"I mean it!" cried Shere Ali. "It was the worst thing that could have happened. I shall know no peace of mind again, no contentment, no happiness, not until I am dead. I wish I were dead!"

And though he spoke in a low voice, he spoke with so much violence that Colonel Dewes was quite astounded. He was aware of no similiarity between his own case and that of Shere Ali. He had long since forgotten the exhortations of Luffe.

"Oh, come now," he repeated. "Isn't that a little ungrateful—what?"

He could hardly have chosen a word less likely to soothe the exasperated nerves of his companion. Shere Ali laughed harshly.

"I ought to be grateful?" said he.

"Well," said Dewes, "you have been to Eton and Oxford, you have seen London. All that is bound to have broadened your mind. Don't you feel that your mind has broadened?"

"Tell me the use of a broad mind in Chiltistan," said Shere Ali. And Colonel Dewes, who had last seen the valleys of that remote country more than twenty years before, was baffled by the challenge.

"To tell the truth, I am a little out of touch with Indian problems," he said. "But it's surely good in every way that there should be a man up there who knows we have something in the way of an army. When I was there, there was trouble which would have been quite prevented by knowledge of that kind."

"Are you sure?" said Shere Ali quietly; and the two men turned and went down from the roof of the stand.

The words which Dewes had just used rankled in Shere Ali's mind, quietly though he had received them. Here was the one definite advantage of his education in England on which Dewes could lay his finger. He knew enough of the strength of the British army to know also the wisdom of keeping his people quiet. For that he had been sacrificed. It was an advantage—yes. But an advantage to whom? he asked. Why, to those governing people here who had to find the money and the troops to suppress a rising, and to confront at the same time an outcry at home from the opponents of the forward movement. It was to their advantage certainly that he should have been sent to England. And then he was told to be grateful!

As they came out again from the winding staircase and

turned towards the paddock Colonel Dewes took Shere Ali by the arm, and said in a voice of kindliness:

"And what has become of all the fine ambitions you and Dick Linforth used to have in common?"

"Linforth's still at Chatham," replied Shere Ali shortly.

"Yes, but you are here. You might make a beginning by yourself."

"They won't let me."

"There's the road," suggested Dewes.

"They won't let me add an inch to it. They will let me do nothing, and they won't let Linforth come out. I wish they would," he added in a softer voice. "If Linforth were to come out to Chiltistan it might make a difference."

They had walked round to the rails in front of the stand, and Shere Ali looked up the steps to the Viceroy's box. The Viceroy was present that afternoon. Shere Ali saw his tall figure, with the stoop of the shoulders characteristic of him, as he stood dressed in a grey frock-coat, with the ladies of his family and one or two of his *aides-de-camp* about him. Shere Ali suddenly stopped and nodded towards the box.

"Have you any influence there?" he asked of Colonel Dewes; and he spoke with a great longing, a great eagerness, and he waited for the answer in a great suspense.

Dewes shook his head.

"None," he replied; "I am nobody at all."

The hope died out of Shere Ali's face.

"I am sorry," he said; and the eagerness had changed into despair. There was just a chance, he thought, of salvation for himself if only Linforth could be fetched out to India. He might resume with Linforth his old companionship, and so recapture something of his old faith and of his bright ideals. There was sore need that he should recapture them. Shere Ali was well aware of it. More and more frequently sure warnings came to him. Now it was some dim recollection of beliefs once strongly clung to, which came back to him with a shock. He would awaken through some chance word to the glory of the English rule in India, the lessening poverty of the Indian nations, the incorruptibility of the English officials and their justice.

"Yes, yes," he would say with astonishment, "I was sure of these things; I knew them as familiar truths," even as a man gradually going blind might one day see clearly and become aware of his narrowing vision. Or perhaps it would be some sudden unsuspected revulsion of feeling in his heart. Such a revulsion had come to him this afternoon as he had gazed up to the Viceroy's box. A wild and unreasoning wrath had flashed up within him, not against the system, but against that tall stooping man, worn with work, who was at once its representative and its flower. Up there the great man stood— so his thoughts ran—complacent, self-satisfied, careless of the harm which his system wrought. Down here upon the grass walked a man warped and perverted out of his natural course. He had been sent to Eton and to Oxford, and had been filled with longings and desires which could have no fruition; he had been trained to delicate thoughts and habits which must daily be offended and daily be a cause of offence to his countrymen. But what did the tall stooping man care? Shere Ali now knew that the English had something in the way of an army. What did it matter whether he lived in

A. E. W. Mason

unhappiness so long as that knowledge was the price of his unhappiness? A cruel, careless, warping business, this English rule.

Thus Shere Ali felt rather than thought, and realised the while the danger of his bitter heart. Once more he appealed to Colonel Dewes, standing before him with burning eyes.

"Bring Linforth out to India! If you have any influence, use it; if you have none, obtain it. Only bring Linforth out to India, and bring him very quickly!"

Once before a passionate appeal had been made to Colonel Dewes by a man in straits, and Colonel Dewes had not understood and had not obeyed. Now, a quarter of a century later another appeal was made by a man sinking, as surely as Luffe had been sinking before, and once again Dewes did not understand.

He took Shere Ali by the arm, and said in a kindly voice:

"I tell you what it is, my lad. You have been going the pace a bit, eh? Calcutta's no good. You'll only collect debts and a lot of things you are better without. Better get out of it."

Shere Ali's face closed as his lips had done. All expression died from it in a moment. There was no help for him in Colonel Dewes. He said good-bye with a smile, and walked out past the stand. His syce was waiting for him outside the railings.

Shere Ali had come to the races wearing a sun-helmet, and, as the fashion is amongst the Europeans in Calcutta, his syce carried a silk hat for Shere Ali to take in exchange for his helmet when the sun went down. Shere Ali, like most of the Europeanised Indians, was more scrupulous than any

Englishman in adhering to the European custom. But to-day, with an angry gesture, he repelled his syce.

"I am going," he said. "You can take that thing away."

His sense of humour failed him altogether. He would have liked furiously to kick and trample upon that glossy emblem of the civilised world; he had much ado to refrain. The syce carried back the silk hat to Shere Ali's smart trap, and Shere Ali drove home in his helmet. Thus he began publicly to renounce the cherished illusion that he was of the white people, and must do as the white people did.

But Colonel Dewes pointed unwittingly the significance of that trivial matter on the same night. He dined at the house of an old friend, and after the ladies had gone he moved up into the next chair, and so sat beside a weary-looking official from the Punjab named Ralston, who had come down to Calcutta on leave. Colonel Dewes began to talk of his meeting with Shere Ali that afternoon. At the mention of Shere Ali's name the official sat up and asked for more.

"He looked pretty bad," said Colonel Dewes. "Jumpy and feverish, and with the air of a man who has been sitting up all night for a week or two. But this is what interested me most," and Dewes told how the lad had implored him to bring Linforth out to India.

"Who's Linforth?" asked the official quickly. "Not the son of that Linforth who—"

"Yes, that's the man," said the Colonel testily. "But you interrupt me. What interested me was this—when I refused to help, Shere Ali's face changed in a most extraordinary way. All the fire went from his eyes, all the agitation from his face. It was like looking at an open box full of interesting

A. E. W. Mason

things, and then—bang! someone slaps down the lid, and you are staring at a flat piece of wood. It was as if—as if—well, I can't find a better comparison."

"It was as if a European suddenly changed before your eyes into an Oriental."

Dewes was not pleased with Ralston's success in supplying the simile he could not hit upon himself.

"That's a little fanciful," he said grudgingly; and then recognised frankly the justness of its application. "Yet it's true—a European changing into an Oriental! Yes, it just looked like that."

"It may actually have been that," said the official quietly. And he added: "I met Shere Ali last year at Lahore on his way north to Chiltistan. I was interested then; I am all the more interested now, for I have just been appointed to Peshawur."

He spoke in a voice which was grave—so grave that Colonel Dewes looked quickly towards him.

"Do you think there will be trouble up there in Chiltistan?" he asked.

The Deputy-Commissioner, who was now Chief Commissioner, smiled wearily.

"There is always trouble up there in Chiltistan," he said. "That I know. What I think is this—Shere Ali should have gone to the Mayo College at Ajmere. That would have been a compromise which would have satisfied his father and done him no harm. But since he didn't—since he went to Eton, and to Oxford, and ran loose in London for a year or two—why, I think he is right."

"How do you mean—right?" asked the Colonel.

"I mean that the sooner Linforth is fetched out to India and sent up to Chiltistan, the better it will be," said the Commissioner.

CHAPTER XVII

NEWS FROM MECCA

Mr. Charles Ralston, being a bachelor and of an economical mind even when on leave in Calcutta, had taken up his quarters in a grass hut in the garden of his Club. He awoke the next morning with an uncomfortable feeling that there was work to be done. The feeling changed into sure knowledge as he reflected upon the conversation which he had had with Colonel Dewes, and he accordingly arose and went about it. For ten days he went to and fro between the Club and Government House, where he held long and vigorous interviews with officials who did not wish to see him. Moreover, other people came to see him privately—people of no social importance for the most part, although there were one or two officers of the police service amongst them. With these he again held long interviews, asking many inquisitive questions. Then he would go out by himself into those parts of the city where the men of broken fortunes, the jockeys run to seed, and the prize-fighters chiefly preferred to congregate. In the low quarters he sought his information of the waifs and strays who are cast up into the drinking-bars of any Oriental port, and he did not come back empty-handed.

For ten days he thus toiled for the good of the Indian Government, and, above all, of that part of it which had its headquarters at Lahore. And on the morning of the eleventh day, as he was just preparing to leave for Government House, where his persistence had prevailed, a tall, black-bearded and very sunburnt man noiselessly opened the door of the hut and as noiselessly stepped inside. Ralston, indeed, did not at once notice him, nor did the stranger call attention to his presence. He waited, motionless and patient, until Ralston happened to turn and see him.

"Hatch!" cried Ralston with a smile of welcome stealing over his startled face, and making it very pleasant to look upon. "You?"

"Yes," answered the tall man; "I reached Calcutta last night. I went into the Club for breakfast. They told me you were here."

Robert Hatch was of the same age as Ralston. But there was little else which they had in common. The two men had met some fifteen years ago for the first time, in Peshawur, and on that first meeting some subtle chord of sympathy had drawn them together; and so securely that even though they met but seldom nowadays, their friendship had easily survived the long intervals. The story of Hatch's life was a simple one. He had married in his twenty-second year a wife a year younger than himself, and together the couple had settled down upon an estate which Hatch owned in Devonshire. Only a year after the marriage, however, Hatch's wife died, and he, disliking his home, had gone restlessly abroad. The restlessness had grown, a certain taste for Oriental literature and thought had been fostered by his travels. He had become a wanderer upon the face of the earth—a man of many clubs in different quarters of the world, and of many friends, who had come to look upon his unexpected appearance and no less sudden departure as part of the ordinary tenour of their lives. Thus it was not the appearance of Hatch which had

A. E. W. Mason

startled Ralston, but rather the silence of it.

"Why didn't you speak?" he asked. "Why did you stand waiting there for me to look your way?"

Hatch laughed as he sat down in a chair.

"I have got into the habit of waiting, I suppose," he said. "For the last five months I have been a servant in the train of the Sultan of the Maldive Islands."

Ralston was not as a rule to be surprised by any strange thing which Hatch might have chosen to do. He merely glanced at his companion and asked:

"What in the world were you doing in the Maldive Islands?"

"Nothing at all," replied Hatch. "I did not go to them. I joined the Sultan at Suez."

This time Ralston, who had been moving about the room in search of some papers which he had mislaid, came to a stop. His attention was arrested. He sat down in a chair and prepared to listen.

"Go on," he said.

"I wanted to go to Mecca," said Hatch, and Ralston nodded his head as though he had expected just those words.

"I did not see how I was going to get there by myself," Hatch continued, "however carefully I managed my disguise."

"Yet you speak Arabic," said Ralston.

"Yes, the language wasn't the difficulty. Indeed, a great

many of the pilgrims—the people from Central Asia, for instance—don't speak Arabic at all. But I felt sure that if I went down the Red Sea alone on a pilgrim steamer, landed alone at Jeddah, and went up with a crowd of others to Mecca, living with them, sleeping with them, day after day, sooner or later I should make some fatal slip and never reach Mecca at all. If Burton made one mistake, how many should I? So I put the journey off year after year. But this autumn I heard that the Sultan of the Maldive Islands intended to make the pilgrimage. He was a friend of mine. I waited for him at Suez, and he reluctantly consented to take me."

"So you went to Mecca," exclaimed Ralston.

"Yes; I have just come from Mecca. As I told you, I only landed at Calcutta last night."

Ralston was silent for a few moments.

"I think you may be able to help me," he said at length. "There's a man here in Calcutta," and Ralston related what he knew of the history of Shere Ali, dwelling less upon the unhappiness and isolation of the Prince than upon the political consequences of his isolation.

"He has come to grief in Chiltistan," he continued. "He won't marry—there may be a reason for that. I don't know. English women are not always wise in their attitude towards these boys. But it seems to me quite a natural result of his education and his life. He is suspected by his people. When he goes back, he will probably be murdered. At present he is consorting with the lowest Europeans here, drinking with them, playing cards with them, and going to ruin as fast as he can. I am not sure that there's a chance for him at all. A few minutes ago I would certainly have said that there was none. Now, however, I am wondering. You see, I don't know the

A. E. W. Mason

lad well enough. I don't know how many of the old instincts and traditions of his race and his faith are still alive in him, underneath all the Western ideas and the Western feelings to which he has been trained. But if they are dead, there is no chance for him. If they are alive—well, couldn't they be evoked? That's the problem."

Hatch nodded his head.

"He might be turned again into a genuine Mohammedan," he said. "I wonder too."

"At all events, it's worth trying," said Ralston. "For it's the only chance left to try. If we could sweep away the effects of the last few years, if we could obliterate his years in England—oh, I know it's improbable. But help me and let us see."

"How?" asked Hatch.

"Come and dine with me to-morrow night. I'll make Shere Ali come. I *can* make him. For I can threaten to send him back to Chiltistan. Then talk to him of Mecca, talk to him of the city, and the shrine, and the pilgrims. Perhaps something of their devotion may strike a spark in him, perhaps he may have some remnant of faith still dormant in him. Make Mecca a symbol to him, make it live for him as a place of pilgrimage. You could, perhaps, because you have seen with your own eyes, and you know."

"I can try, of course," said Hatch with a shrug of his shoulders. "But isn't there a danger—if I succeed? I might try to kindle faith, I might only succeed in kindling fanaticism. Are the Mohammedans beyond the frontier such a very quiet people that you are anxious to add another to their number?"

Ralston was prepared for the objection. Already, indeed, Shere Ali might be seething with hatred against the English rule. It would be no more than natural if he were. Ralston had pondered the question with an uncomfortable vision before his eyes, evoked by certain words of Colonel Dewes—a youth appealing for help, for the only help which could be of service to him, and then, as the appeal was rejected, composing his face to a complete and stolid inexpressiveness, no longer showing either his pain or his desire—reverting, as it were, from the European to the Oriental.

"Yes, there is that danger," he admitted. "Seeking to restore a friend, we might kindle an enemy." And then he rose up and suddenly burst out: "But upon my word, were that to come to pass, we should deserve it. For we are to blame—we who took him from Chiltistan and sent him to be petted by the fine people in England." And once more it was evident from his words that he was thinking not of Shere Ali—not of the human being who had just his one life to live, just his few years with their opportunities of happiness, and their certain irrevocable periods of distress—but of the Prince of Chiltistan who might or might not be a cause of great trouble to the Government of the Punjab.

"We must take the risk," he cried as one arguing almost against himself. "It's the only chance. So we must take the risk. Besides, I have been at some pains already to minimise it. Shere Ali has a friend in England. We are asking for that friend. A telegram goes to-day. So come to-morrow night and do your best."

"Very well, I will," said Hatch, and, taking up his hat, he went away. He had no great hopes that any good would come of the dinner. But at the worst, he thought, it would leave matters where they were.

In that, however, he was wrong. For there were important moments in the history of the young Prince of Chiltistan of which both Hatch and Ralston were quite unaware. And because they were unaware the dinner which was to help in straightening out the tangle of Shere Ali's life became a veritable catastrophe. Shere Ali was brought reluctantly to the table in the corner of the great balcony upon the first floor. He had little to say, and it was as evident to the two men who entertained him as it had been to Colonel Dewes that the last few weeks had taken their toll of him. There were dark, heavy pouches beneath his eyes, his manner was feverish, and when he talked at all it was with a boisterous and a somewhat braggart voice.

Ralston turned the conversation on to the journey which Hatch had taken, and for a little while the dinner promised well. At the mere mention of Mecca, Shere Ali looked up with a swift interest. "Mecca!" he cried, "you have been there! Tell me of Mecca. On my way up to Chiltistan I met three of my own countrymen on the summit of the Lowari Pass. They had a few rupees apiece—just enough, they told me, to carry them to Mecca. I remember watching them as they went laughing and talking down the snow on their long journey. And I wondered—" He broke off abruptly and sat looking out from the balcony. The night was coming on. In front stretched the great grass plain of the Maidan with its big trees and the wide carriage-road bisecting it. The carriages had driven home; the road and the plain were empty. Beyond them the high chimney-stacks of the steamers on the river could still be seen, some with a wisp of smoke curling upwards into the still air; and at times the long, melancholy hoot of a steam-syren broke the stillness of the evening.

Shere Ali turned to Hatch again and said in a quiet voice which had some note of rather pathetic appeal: "Will you tell me what you thought of Mecca? I should like to know."

The vision of the three men descending the Lowari Pass was present to him as he listened. And he listened, wondering what strange, real power that sacred place possessed to draw men cheerfully on so long and hazardous a pilgrimage. But the secret was not yet to be revealed to him. Hatch talked well. He told Shere Ali of the journey down the Red Sea, and the crowded deck at the last sunset before Jeddah was reached, when every one of the pilgrims robed himself in spotless white and stood facing the east and uttering his prayers in his own tongue. He described the journey across the desert, the great shrine of the Prophet in Mecca, the great gathering for prayer upon the plain two miles away. Something of the fervour of the pilgrims he managed to make real by his words, but Shere Ali listened with the picture of the three men in his thoughts, and with a deep envy of their contentment.

Then Hatch made his mistake. He turned suddenly towards Ralston and said:

"But something curious happened—something very strange and curious—which I think you ought to know, for the matter can hardly be left where it is."

Ralston leaned forward.

"Wait a moment," he said, and he called to the waiter. "Light a cigar before you begin, Hatch," he continued.

The cigars were brought, and Hatch lighted one.

"In what way am I concerned?" asked Ralston.

"My story has to do with India," Hatch replied, and in his turn he looked out across the Maidan. Darkness had come and lights gleamed upon the carriage-way; the funnels of the

A. E. W. Mason

ships had disappeared, and above, in a clear, dark sky, glittered a great host of stars.

"With India, but not with the India of to-day," Hatch continued. "Listen"; and over his coffee he told his story. "I was walking down a narrow street of Mecca towards the big tank, when to my amazement I saw written up on a signboard above a door the single word 'Lodgings.' It was the English word, written, too, in the English character. I could hardly believe my eyes when I saw it. I stood amazed. What was an English announcement, that lodgings were to be had within, doing in a town where no Englishman, were he known to be such, would live for a single hour? I had half a mind to knock at the door and ask. But I noticed opposite to the door a little shop in which a man sat with an array of heavy country-made bolts and locks hung upon the walls and spread about him as he squatted on the floor. I crossed over to the booth, and sitting down upon the edge of the floor, which was raised a couple of feet or so from the ground, I made some small purchase. Then, looking across to the sign, I asked him what the writing on it meant. I suppose that I did not put my question carelessly enough, for the shopkeeper leaned forward and peered closely into my face.

"'Why do you ask?' he said, sharply."

"'Because I do not understand,' I replied."

"The man looked me over again. There was no mistake in my dress, and with my black beard and eyes I could well pass for an Arab. It seemed that he was content, for he continued: 'How should I know what the word means? I have heard a story, but whether it is true or not, who shall say?'"

Hatch paused for a moment and lighted his cigar again.

"Well, the account which he gave me was this. Among the pilgrims who come up to Mecca, there are at times Hottentots from South Africa who speak no language intelligible to anyone in Mecca; but they speak English, and it is for their benefit that the sign was hung up."

"What a strange thing!" said Shere Ali.

"The explanation," continued Hatch, "is not very important to my story, but what followed upon it is; for the very next day, as I was walking alone, I heard a voice in my ear, whispering: 'The Englishwoman would like to see you this evening at five.' I turned round in amazement, and there stood the shopkeeper of whom I had made the inquiries. I thought, of course, that he was laying a trap for me. But he repeated his statement, and, telling me that he would wait for me on this spot at ten minutes to five, he walked away.

"I did not know what to do. One moment I feared treachery and proposed to stay away, the next I was curious and proposed to go. How in the world could there be an Englishwoman in Mecca—above all, an Englishwoman who was in a position to ask me to tea? Curiosity conquered in the end. I tucked a loaded revolver into my waist underneath my jellaba and kept the appointment."

"Go on," said Shere Ali, who was leaning forward with a great perplexity upon his face.

"The shopkeeper was already there. 'Follow me,' he said, 'but not too closely.' We passed in that way through two or three streets, and then my guide turned into a dead alley closed in at the end by a house. In the wall of the house there was a door. My guide looked cautiously round, but there was no one to oversee us. He rapped gently with his knuckles on the door, and immediately the door was opened. He beckoned to me,

A. E. W. Mason

and went quickly in. I followed him no less quickly. At once the door was shut behind me, and I found myself in darkness. For a moment I was sure that I had fallen into a trap, but my guide laid a hand upon my arm and led me forward. I was brought into a small, bare room, where a woman sat upon cushions. She was dressed in white like a Mohammedan woman of the East, and over her face she wore a veil. But a sort of shrivelled aspect which she had told me that she was very old. She dismissed the guide who had brought me to her, and as soon as we were alone she said:

"'You are English.'"

"And she spoke in English, though with a certain rustiness of speech, as though that language had been long unfamiliar to her tongue."

"'No,' I replied, and I expressed my contempt of that infidel race in suitable words."

"The old woman only laughed and removed her veil. She showed me an old wizened face in which there was not a remnant of good looks—a face worn and wrinkled with hard living and great sorrows."

"'You are English,' she said, 'and since I am English too, I thought that I would like to speak once more with one of my own countrymen.'"

"I no longer doubted. I took the hand she held out to me and—"

"'But what are you doing here in Mecca?' I asked."

"'I live in Mecca,' she replied quietly. 'I have lived here for twenty years.'

"I looked round that bare and sordid little room with horror. What strange fate had cast her up there? I asked her, and she told me her story. Guess what it was!"

Ralston shook his head.

"I can't imagine."

Hatch turned to Shere Ali.

"Can you?" he asked, and even as he asked he saw that a change had come over the young Prince's mood. He was no longer oppressed with envy and discontent. He was leaning forward with parted lips and a look in his eyes which Hatch had not seen that evening—a look as if hope had somehow dared to lift its head within him. And there was more than a look of hope; there was savagery too.

"No. I want to hear," replied Shere Ali. "Go on, please! How did the Englishwoman come to Mecca?"

"She was a governess in the family of an officer at Cawnpore when the Mutiny broke out, more than forty years ago," said Hatch.

Ralston leaned back in his chair with an exclamation of horror. Shere Ali said nothing. His eyes rested intently and brightly upon Hatch's face. Under the table, and out of sight, his fingers worked convulsively.

"She was in that room," continued Hatch, "in that dark room with the other Englishwomen and children who were murdered. But she was spared. She was very pretty, she told me, in her youth, and she was only eighteen when the massacre took place. She was carried up to the hills and forced to become a Mohammedan. The man who had spared

A. E. W. Mason

her married her. He died, and a small chieftain in the hills took her and married her, and finally brought her out with him when he made the pilgrimage to Mecca. While he was at Mecca, however, he fell ill, and in his turn he died. She was left alone. She had a little money, and she stayed. Indeed, she could not get away. A strange story, eh?"

And Hatch leaned back in his chair, and once more lighted his cigar which for a second time had gone out.

"You didn't bring her back?" exclaimed Ralston.

"She wouldn't come," replied Hatch. "I offered to smuggle her out of Mecca, but she refused. She felt that she wouldn't and couldn't face her own people again. She should have died at Cawnpore, and she did not die. Besides, she was old; she had long since grown accustomed to her life, and in England she had long since been given up for dead. She would not even tell me her real name. Perhaps she ought to be fetched away. I don't know."

Ralston and Hatch fell to debating that point with great earnestness. Neither of them paid heed to Shere Ali, and when he rose they easily let him go. Nor did their thoughts follow him upon his way. But he was thinking deeply as he went, and a queer and not very pleasant smile played about his lips.

CHAPTER XVIII

SYBIL LINFORTH'S LOYALTY

A fortnight after Shere Ali had dined with Ralston in Calcutta, a telegram was handed to Linforth at Chatham. It was Friday, and a guest-night. The mess-room was full, and here and there amongst the scarlet and gold lace the sombre black of a civilian caught the eye. Dinner was just over, and at the ends of the long tables the mess-waiters stood ready to draw, with a single jerk, the strips of white tablecloth from the shining mahogany. The silver and the glasses had been removed, the word was given, and the strips of tablecloth vanished as though by some swift legerdemain. The port was passed round, and while the glasses were being filled the telegram was handed to Linforth by his servant.

He opened it carelessly, but as he read the words his heart jumped within him. His importunities had succeeded, he thought. At all events, his opportunity had come; for the telegram informed him of his appointment to the Punjab Commission. He sat for a moment with his thoughts in a whirl. He could hardly believe the good news. He had longed so desperately for this one chance that it had seemed to him of late impossible that he should ever obtain it. Yet here it had come to him, and upon that his neighbour jogged him in the ribs and said:

A. E. W. Mason

"Wake up!"

He waked to see the Colonel at the centre of the top table standing on his feet with his glass in his hand.

"Gentlemen, the Queen. God bless her!" and all that company arose and drank to the toast. The prayer, thus simply pronounced amongst the men who had pledged their lives in service to the Queen, had always been to Linforth a very moving thing. Some of those who drank to it had already run their risks and borne their sufferings in proof of their sincerity; the others all burned to do the like. It had always seemed to him, too, to link him up closely and inseparably with the soldiers of the regiment who had fallen years ago or had died quietly in their beds, their service ended. It gave continuity to the regiment of Sappers, so that what each man did increased or tarnished its fair fame. For years back that toast had been drunk, that prayer uttered in just those simple words, and Linforth was wont to gaze round the walls on the portraits of the famous generals who had looked to these barracks and to this mess-room as their home. They, too, had heard that prayer, and, carrying it in their hearts, without parade or needless speech had gone forth, each in his turn, and laboured unsparingly.

But never had Linforth been so moved as he was tonight. He choked in his throat as he drank. For his turn to go forth had at the last come to him. And in all humility of spirit he sent up a prayer on his own account, that he might not fail—and again that he might not fail.

He sat down and told his companions the good news, and rejoiced at their congratulations. But he slipped away to his own quarters very quietly as soon as the Colonel rose, and sat late by himself.

There was one, he knew very well, to whom the glad tidings would be a heavy blow—but he could not—no, not even for her sake—stand aside. For this opportunity he had lived, training alike his body and mind against its coming. He could not relinquish it. There was too strong a constraint upon him.

"Over the passes to the foot of the Hindu Kush," he murmured; and in his mind's eye he saw the road—a broad, white, graded road—snake across the valleys and climb the cliffs.

Was Russia at work? he wondered. Was he to be sent to Chiltistan? What was Shere Ali doing? He turned the questions over in his mind without being at much pains to answer them. In such a very short time now he would know. He was to embark before a month had passed.

He travelled down the very next day into Sussex, and came to the house under the Downs at twelve o'clock. It was early spring, and as yet there were no buds upon the trees, no daffodils upon the lawns. The house, standing apart in its bare garden of brown earth, black trees, and dull green turf, had a desolate aspect which somehow filled him with remorse. He might have done more, perhaps, to fill this house with happiness. He feared that, now that it was too late to do the things left undone. He had been so absorbed in his great plans, which for a moment lost in his eyes their magnitude.

Dick Linforth found his mother in the study, through the window of which she had once looked from the garden in the company of Colonel Dewes. She was writing her letters, and when she saw him enter, she sprang up with a cry of joy.

"Dick!" she cried, coming towards him with outstretched

A. E. W. Mason

hands. But she stopped half-way. The happiness died out of her. She raised a hand to her heart, and her voice once more repeated his name; but her voice faltered as she spoke, and the hand was clasped tight upon her breast.

"Dick," she said, and in his face she read the tidings he had brought. The blow so long dreaded had at last fallen.

"Yes, mother, it's true," he said very gently; and leading her to a chair, he sat beside her, stroking her hand, almost as a lover might do. "It's true. The telegram came last night. I start within the month."

"For Chiltistan?"

Dick looked at her for a moment.

"For the Punjab," he said, and added: "But it will mean Chiltistan. Else why should I be sent for? It has been always for Chiltistan that I have importuned them."

Sybil Linforth bowed her head. The horror which had been present with her night and day for so long a while twenty-five years ago rushed upon her afresh, so that she could not speak. She sat living over again the bitter days when Luffe was shut up with his handful of men in the fort by Kohara. She remembered the morning when the postman came up the garden path with the official letter that her husband had been slain. And at last in a whisper she said:

"The Road?"

Dick, even in the presence of her pain, could not deny the implication of her words.

"We Linforths belong to the Road," he answered gravely.

The words struck upon a chord of memory. Sybil Linforth sat upright, turned to her sort and greatly surprised him. He had expected an appeal, a prayer. What he heard was something which raised her higher in his thoughts than ever she had been, high though he had always placed her.

"Dick," she said, "I have never said a word to dissuade you, have I? Never a word? Never a single word?" and her tone besought him to assure her.

"Never a word, mother," he replied.

But still she was not content.

"When you were a boy, when the Road began to take hold on you—when we were much together, playing cricket out there in the garden," and her voice broke upon the memory of those golden days, "when I might have been able, perhaps, to turn you to other thoughts, I never tried to, Dick? Own to that! I never tried to. When I came upon you up on the top of the Down behind the house, lying on the grass, looking out—always—always towards the sea—oh, I knew very well what it was that was drawing you; but I said nothing, Dick. Not a word—not a word!"

Dick nodded his head.

"That's true, mother. You never questioned me. You never tried to dissuade me."

Sybil's face shone with a wan smile. She unlocked a drawer in her writing-table, and took out an envelope. From the envelope she drew a sheet of paper covered with a faded and yellow handwriting.

"This is the last letter your father ever wrote to me," she said.

"Harry wrote on the night that he—that he died. Oh, Dick, my boy, I have known for a long time that I would have one day to show it to you, and I wanted you to feel when that time came that I had not been disloyal."

She had kept her face steady, even her voice calm, by a great effort. But now the tears filled her eyes and brimmed over, and her voice suddenly shook between a laugh and a sob. "But oh, Dick," she cried, "I have so often wanted to be disloyal. I was so often near to it—oh, very, very near."

She handed him the faded letter, and, turning towards the window, stood with her back to him while he read. It was that letter, with its constant refrain of "I am very tired," which Linforth had written in his tent whilst his murderers crouched outside waiting for sleep to overcome him.

"I am sitting writing this by the light of a candle," Dick read. "The tent door is open. In front of me I can see the great snow-mountains. All the ugliness of the shale-slopes is hidden. By such a moonlight, my dear, may you always look back upon my memory. For it is all over, Sybil."

Then followed the advice about himself and his school; and after that advice the message which was now for the first time delivered:

"Whether he will come out here, it is too early to think about. But the Road will not be finished—and I wonder. If he wants to, let him! We Linforths belong to the Road."

Dick folded the letter reverently, and crossing to his mother's side, put his arm about her waist.

"Yes," he said. "My father knew it as I know it. He used the words which I in my turn have used. We Linforths belong to the Road."

His mother took the letter from his hand and locked it away.

"Yes," she said bravely, and called a smile to her face. "So you must go."

Dick nodded his head.

"Yes. You see, the Road has not advanced since my father died. It almost seems, mother, that it waits for me."

He stayed that day and that night with Sybil, and in the morning both brought haggard faces to the breakfast table. Sybil, indeed, had slept, but, with her memories crowding hard upon her, she had dreamed again one of those almost forgotten dreams which, in the time of her suspense, had so tortured her. The old vague terror had seized upon her again. She dreamed once more of a young Englishman who pursued a young Indian along the wooden galleries of the road above the torrents into the far mists. She could tell as of old the very dress of the native who fled. A thick sheepskin coat swung aside as he ran and gave her a glimpse of gay silk; soft high leather boots protected his feet; and upon his face there was a look of fury and wild fear. But this night there was a difference in the dream. Her present distress added a detail. The young Englishman who pursued turned his face to her as he disappeared amongst the mists, and she saw that it was the face of Dick.

But of this she said nothing at all at the breakfast table, nor when she bade Dick good-bye at the stile on the further side of the field beyond the garden.

"You will come down again, and I shall go to Marseilles to see you off," she said, and so let him go.

A. E. W. Mason

There was something, too, stirring in Dick's mind of which he said no word. In the letter of his father, certain sentences had caught his eye, and on his way up to London they recurred to his thoughts, as, indeed, they had more than once during the evening before.

"May he meet," Harry Linforth had written to Sybil of his son Dick—"may he meet a woman like you, my dear, when his time comes, and love her as I love you."

Dick Linforth fell to thinking of Violet Oliver. She was in India at this moment. She might still be there when he landed. Would he meet her, he wondered, somewhere on the way to Chiltistan?

CHAPTER XIX

A GIFT MISUNDERSTOOD

The month was over before Linforth at last steamed out of the harbour at Marseilles. He was as impatient to reach Bombay as a year before Shere Ali had been reluctant. To Shere Ali the boat had flown with wings of swiftness, to Linforth she was a laggard. The steamer passed Stromboli on a wild night of storm and moonlight. The wrack of clouds scurrying overhead, now obscured, now let the moonlight through, and the great cone rising sheer from a tempestuous sea glowed angrily. Linforth, in the shelter of a canvas screen, watched the glow suddenly expand, and a stream of bright sparkling red flow swiftly along the shoulder of the mountain, turn at a right angle, and plunge down towards the sea. The bright red would become dull, the dull red grow black, the glare of light above the cone contract for a little while and then burst out again. Yet men lived upon the slope of Stromboli, even as Englishmen—the thought flashed into his mind—lived in India, recognising the peril and going quietly about their work. There was always that glare of menacing light over the hill-districts of India as above the crater of Stromboli, now contracting, now expanding and casting its molten stream down towards the plains.

At the moment when Linforth watched the crown of light

A. E. W. Mason

above Stromboli, the glare was widening over the hill country of Chiltistan. Ralston so far away as Peshawur saw it reddening the sky and was the more troubled in that he could not discover why just at this moment the menace should glow red. The son of Abdulla Mohammed was apparently quiet and Shere Ali had not left Calcutta. The Resident at Kohara admitted the danger. Every despatch he sent to Peshawur pointed to the likelihood of trouble. But he too was at fault. Unrest was evident, the cause of it quite obscure. But what was hidden from Government House in Peshawur and the Old Mission House at Kohara was already whispered in the bazaars. There among the thatched booths which have their backs upon the brink of the water-channel in the great square, men knew very well that Shere Ali was the cause, though Shere Ali knew nothing of it himself. One of those queer little accidents possible in the East had happened within the last few weeks. A trifling gift had been magnified into a symbol and a message, and the message had run through Chiltistan like fire through a dry field of stubble. And then two events occurred in Peshawur which gave to Ralston the key of the mystery.

The first was the arrival in that city of a Hindu lady from Gujerat who had lately come to the conclusion that she was a reincarnation of the Goddess Devi. She arrived in great pomp, and there was some trouble in the streets as the procession passed through to the temple which she had chosen as her residence. For the Hindus, on the one hand, firmly believed in her divinity. The lady came of a class which, held in dishonour in the West, had its social position and prestige in India. There was no reason in the eyes of the faithful why she should say she was the Goddess Devi if she were not. Therefore they lined the streets to acclaim her coming. The Mohammedans, on the other hand, Afghans from the far side of the Khyber, men of the Hassan and the Aka and the Adam Khel tribes, Afridis from Kohat and Tirah and the Araksai country, any who happened to be in that wild and crowded town, turned out, too—to keep order, as they pleasantly termed it, when their leaders were subsequently asked for explanations. In the end a good many heads were broken before the lady was safely lodged in her temple. Nor did the trouble end there. The presence of a reincarnated Devi at once kindled the Hindus to fervour and stimulated to hostility against them the fanatical Mohammedans. Futteh Ali Shah, a merchant, a municipal councillor and a landowner of some importance, headed a deputation of elderly gentlemen who begged Ralston to remove the danger from the city.

Danger there was, as Ralston on his morning rides through the streets could not but understand. The temple was built in the corner of an open space, and upon that open space a noisy and excited crowd surged all day; while from the countryside around pilgrims in a mood of frenzied piety and Pathans spoiling for a fight trooped daily in through the gates of Peshawur. Ralston understood that the time had come for definite steps to be taken; and he took them with that unconcerned half-weary air which was at once natural to him and impressive to these particular people with whom he had to deal.

He summoned two of his native levies and mounted his horse.

"But you will take a guard," said Colonel Ward, of the Oxfordshires, who had been lunching with Ralston. "I'll send a company down with you."

"No, thank you," said Ralston listlessly, "I think my two men will do."

The Colonel stared and expostulated.

A. E. W. Mason

"You know, Ralston, you are very rash. Your predecessor never rode into the City without an escort."

"I do every morning."

"I know," returned the Colonel, "and that's where you are wrong. Some day something will happen. To go down with two of your levies to-day is madness. I speak seriously. The place is in a ferment."

"Oh, I think I'll be all right," said Ralston, and he rode at a trot down from Government House into the road which leads past the gaol and the Fort to the gate of Peshawur. At the gate he reduced the trot to a walk, and so, with his two levies behind him, passed up along the streets like a man utterly undisturbed. It was not bravado which had made him refuse an escort. On the contrary, it was policy. To assume that no one questioned his authority was in Ralston's view the best way and the quickest to establish it. He pushed forward through the crowd right up to the walls of the temple, seemingly indifferent to every cry or threat which was uttered as he passed. The throng closed in behind him, and he came to a halt in front of a low door set in the whitewashed wall which enclosed the temple and its precincts. Upon this door he beat with the butt of his crop and a little wicket in the door was opened. At the bars of the wicket an old man's face showed for a moment and then drew back in fear.

"Open!" cried Ralston peremptorily.

The face appeared again.

"Your Excellency, the goddess is meditating. Besides, this is holy ground. Your Excellency would not wish to set foot on it. Moreover, the courtyard is full of worshippers. It would not be safe."

Ralston broke in upon the old man's fluttering protestations. "Open the door, or my men will break it in."

A murmur of indignation arose from the crowd which thronged about him. Ralston paid no heed to it. He called to his two levies:

"Quick! Break that door in!"

As they advanced the door was opened. Ralston dismounted, and bade one of his men do likewise and follow him. To the second man he said,

"Hold the horses!"

He strode into the courtyard and stood still.

"It will be touch and go," he said to himself, as he looked about him.

The courtyard was as thronged as the open space without, and four strong walls enclosed it. The worshippers were strangely silent. It seemed to Ralston that suspense had struck them dumb. They looked at the intruder with set faces and impassive eyes. At the far end of the courtyard there was a raised stone platform, and this part was roofed. At the back in the gloom he could see a great idol of the goddess, and in front, facing the courtyard, stood the lady from Gujerat. She was what Ralston expected to see—a dancing girl of Northern India, a girl with a good figure, small hands and feet, and a complexion of an olive tint. Her eyes were large and lustrous, with a line of black pencilled upon the edges of the eyelids, her eyebrows arched and regular, her face oval, her forehead high. The dress was richly embroidered with

A. E. W. Mason

gold, and she had anklets with silver bells upon her feet.

Ralston pushed his way through the courtyard until he reached the wall of the platform.

"Come down and speak to me," he cried peremptorily to the lady, but she took no notice of his presence. She did not move so much as an eyelid. She gazed over his head as one lost in meditation. From the side an old priest advanced to the edge of the platform.

"Go away," he cried insolently. "You have no place here. The goddess does not speak to any but her priests," and through the throng there ran a murmur of approval. There, was a movement, too—a movement towards Ralston. It was as yet a hesitating movement—those behind pushed, those in front and within Ralston's vision held back. But at any moment the movement might become a rush.

Ralston spoke to the priest.

"Come down, you dog!" he said quite quietly.

The priest was silent. He hesitated. He looked for help to the crowd below, which in turn looked for leadership to him. "Come down," once more cried Ralston, and he moved towards the steps as though he would mount on to the platform and tear the fellow down.

"I come, I come," said the priest, and he went down and stood before Ralston.

Ralston turned to the Pathan who accompanied him. "Turn the fellow into the street."

Protests rose from the crowd; the protests became cries of

anger; the throng swayed and jostled. But the Pathan led the priest to the door and thrust him out.

Again Ralston turned to the platform.

"Listen to me," he called out to the lady from Gujerat. "You must leave Peshawur. You are a trouble to the town. I will not let you stay."

But the lady paid no heed. Her mind floated above the earth, and with every moment the danger grew. Closer and closer the throng pressed in upon Ralston and his attendant. The clamour rose shrill and menacing. Ralston cried out to his Pathan in a voice which rang clear and audible even above the clamour:

"Bring handcuffs!"

The words were heard and silence fell upon all that crowd, the sudden silence of stupefaction. That such an outrage, such a defilement of a holy place, could be contemplated came upon the worshippers with a shock. But the Pathan levy was seen to be moving towards the door to obey the order, and as he went the cries and threats rose with redoubled ardour. For a moment it seemed to Ralston that the day would go against him, so fierce were the faces which shouted in his ears, so turbulent the movement of the crowd. It needed just one hand to be laid upon the Pathan's shoulder as he forced his way towards the door, just one blow to be struck, and the ugly rush would come. But the hand was not stretched out, nor the blow struck; and the Pathan was seen actually at the threshold of the door. Then the Goddess Devi came down to earth and spoke to another of her priests quickly and urgently. The priest went swiftly down the steps.

"The goddess will leave Peshawur, since your Excellency so

A. E. W. Mason

wills it," he said to Ralston. "She will shake the dust of this city from her feet. She will not bring trouble upon its people." So far he had got when the goddess became violently agitated. She beckoned to the priest and when he came to her side she spoke quickly to him in an undertone. For the last second or two the goddess had grown quite human and even feminine. She was rating the priest well and she did it spitefully. It was a crestfallen priest who returned to Ralston.

"The goddess, however, makes a condition," said he. "If she goes there must be a procession."

The goddess nodded her head emphatically. She was clearly adamant upon that point.

Ralston smiled.

"By all means. The lady shall have a show, since she wants one," said he, and turning towards the door, he signalled to the Pathan to stop.

"But it must be this afternoon," said he. "For she must go this afternoon."

And he made his way out of the courtyard into the street. The lady from Gujerat left Peshawur three hours later. The streets were lined with levies, although the Mohammedans assured his Excellency that there was no need for troops.

"We ourselves will keep order," they urged. Ralston smiled, and ordered up a company of Regulars. He himself rode out from Government House, and at the bend of the road he met the procession, with the lady from Gujerat at its head in a litter with drawn curtains of tawdry gold.

As the procession came abreast of him a little brown hand was thrust out from the curtains, and the bearers and the rabble behind came to a halt. A man in a rough brown homespun cloak, with a beggar's bowl attached to his girdle, came to the side of the litter, and thence went across to Ralston.

"Your Highness, the Goddess Devi has a word for your ear alone." Ralston, with a shrug of his shoulders, walked his horse up to the side of the litter and bent down his head. The lady spoke through the curtains in a whisper.

"Your Excellency has been very kind to me, and allowed me to leave Peshawur with a procession, guarding the streets so that I might pass in safety and with great honour. Therefore I make a return. There is a matter which troubles your Excellency. You ask yourself the why and the wherefore, and there is no answer. But the danger grows."

Ralston's thoughts flew out towards Chiltistan. Was it of that country she was speaking?

"Well?" he asked. "Why does the danger grow?"

"Because bags of grain and melons were sent," she replied, "and the message was understood."

She waved her hand again, and the bearers of the litter stepped forward on their march through the cantonment. Ralston rode up the hill to his home, wondering what in the world was the meaning of her oracular words. It might be that she had no meaning—that was certainly a possibility. She might merely be keeping up her pose as a divinity. On the other hand, she had been so careful to speak in a low whisper, lest any should overhear.

"Some melons and bags of grain," he said to himself. "What

A. E. W. Mason

message could they convey? And who sent them? And to whom?"

He wrote that night to the Resident at Kohara, on the chance that he might be able to throw some light upon the problem.

"Have you heard anything of a melon and a bag of grain?" he wrote. "It seems an absurd question, but please make inquiries. Find out what it all means."

The messenger carried the letter over the Malakand Pass and up the road by Dir, and in due time an answer was returned. Ralston received the answer late one afternoon, when the light was failing, and, taking it over to the window, read it through. Its contents fairly startled him.

"I have made inquiries," wrote Captain Phillips, the Resident, "as you wished, and I have found out that some melons and bags of grain were sent by Shere Ali's orders a few weeks ago as a present to one of the chief Mullahs in the town."

Ralston was brought to a stop. So it was Shere Ali, after all, who was at the bottom of the trouble. It was Shere Ali who had sent the present, and had sent it to one of the Mullahs. Ralston looked back upon the little dinner party, whereby he had brought Hatch and Shere Ali together. Had that party been too successful, he wondered? Had it achieved more than he had wished to bring about? He turned in doubt to the letter which he held.

"It seems," he read, "that there had been some trouble between this man and Shere Ali. There is a story that Shere Ali set him to work for a day upon a bridge just below Kohara. But I do not know whether there is any truth in the story. Nor can I find that any particular meaning is attached to the present. I imagine that Shere Ali realised that it would be wise—as undoubtedly it was—for him to make his peace with the Mullah, and sent him accordingly the melons and the bags of grain as an earnest of his good-will."

There the letter ended, and Ralston stood by the window as the light failed more and more from off the earth, pondering with a heavy heart upon its contents. He had to make his choice between the Resident at Kohara and the lady of Gujerat. Captain Phillips held that the present was not interpreted in any symbolic sense. But the lady of Gujerat had known of the present. It was matter of talk, then, in the bazaars, and it would hardly have been that had it meant no more than an earnest of good-will. She had heard of the present; she knew what it was held to convey. It was a message. There was that glare broadening over Chiltistan. Surely the lady of Gujerat was right.

So far his thoughts had carried him when across the window there fell a shadow, and a young officer of the Khyber Rifles passed by to the door. Captain Singleton was announced, and a boy—or so he looked—dark-haired and sunburnt, entered the office. For eighteen months he had been stationed in the fort at Landi Kotal, whence the road dips down between the bare brown cliffs towards the plains and mountains of Afghanistan. With two other English officers he had taken his share in the difficult task of ruling that regiment of wild tribesmen which, twice a week, perched in threes on some rocky promontory, or looking down from a machicolated tower, keeps open the Khyber Pass from dawn to dusk and protects the caravans. The eighteen months had written their history upon his face; he stood before Ralston, for all his youthful looks, a quiet, self-reliant man.

"I have come down on leave, sir," he said. "On the way I fetched Rahat Mian out of his house and brought him in to Peshawur."

Ralston looked up with interest.

"Any trouble?" he asked.

"I took care there should be none."

Ralston nodded.

"He had better be safely lodged. Where is he?"

"I have him outside."

Ralston rang for lights, and then said to Singleton: "Then, I'll see him now."

And in a few minutes an elderly white-bearded man, dressed from head to foot in his best white robes, was shown into the room.

"This is his Excellency," said Captain Singleton, and Rahat Mian bowed with dignity and stood waiting. But while he stood his eyes roamed inquisitively about the room.

"All this is strange to you, Rahat Mian," said Ralston. "How long is it since you left your house in the Khyber Pass?"

"Five years, your Highness," said Rahat Mian, quietly, as though there were nothing very strange in so long a confinement within his doors.

"Have you never crossed your threshold for five years?" asked Ralston.

"No, your Highness. I should not have stepped back over it again, had I been so foolish. Before, yes. There was a deep trench dug between my house and the road, and I used to crawl along the trench when no-one was about. But after a little my enemies saw me walking in the road, and watched the trench."

Rahat Mian lived in one of the square mud windowless houses, each with a tower at a corner which dot the green wheat fields in the Khyber Pass wherever the hills fall back and leave a level space. His house was fifty yards from the road, and the trench stretched to it from his very door. But not two hundred yards away there were other houses, and one of these held Rahat Mian's enemies. The feud went back many years to the date when Rahat Mian, without asking anyone's leave or paying a single farthing of money, secretly married the widowed mother of Futteh Ali Shah. Now Futteh Ali Shah was a boy of fourteen who had the right to dispose of his mother in second marriage as he saw fit, and for the best price he could obtain. And this deprivation of his rights kindled in him a great anger against Rahat Mian. He nursed it until he became a man and was able to buy for a couple of hundred rupees a good pedigree rifle—a rifle which had belonged to a soldier killed in a hill-campaign and for which inquiries would not be made. Armed with his pedigree rifle, Futteh Ali Shah lay in wait vainly for Rahat Mian, until an unexpected bequest caused a revolution in his fortunes. He went down to Bombay, added to his bequest by becoming a money-lender, and finally returned to Peshawur, in the neighbourhood of which city he had become a landowner of some importance. Meanwhile, however, he had not been forgetful of Rahat Mian. He left relations behind to carry on the feud, and in addition he set a price on Rahat Mian's head. It was this feud which Ralston had it in his mind to settle.

He turned to Rahat Mian.

"You are willing to make peace?"

A. E. W. Mason

"Yes," said the old man.

"You will take your most solemn oath that the feud shall end. You will swear to divorce your wife, if you break your word?"

For a moment Rahat Mian hesitated. There was no oath more binding, more sacred, than that which he was called upon to take. In the end he consented.

"Then come here at eight to-morrow morning," said Ralston, and, dismissing the man, he gave instructions that he should be safely lodged. He sent word at the same time to Futteh Ali Shah, with whom, not for the first time, he had had trouble.

Futteh Ali Shah arrived late the next morning in order to show his independence. But he was not so late as Ralston, who replied by keeping him waiting for an hour. When Ralston entered the room he saw that Futteh Ali Shah had dressed himself for the occasion. His tall high-shouldered frame was buttoned up in a grey frock coat, grey trousers clothed his legs, and he wore patent-leather shoes upon his feet.

"I hope you have not been waiting very long. They should have told me you were here," said Ralston, and though he spoke politely, there was just a suggestion that it was not really of importance whether Futteh Ali Shah was kept waiting or not.

"I have brought you here that together we may put an end to your dispute with Rahat Mian," said Ralston, and, taking no notice of the exclamation of surprise which broke from the Pathan's lips, he rang the bell and ordered Rahat Mian to be shown in.

"Now let us see if we cannot come to an understanding," said

Ralston, and he seated himself between the two antagonists.

But though they talked for an hour, they came no nearer to a settlement. Futteh Ali Shah was obdurate; Rahat Mian's temper and pride rose in their turn. At the sight of each other the old grievance became fresh as a thing of yesterday in both their minds. Their dark faces, with the high cheek-bones and the beaked noses of the Afridi, became passionate and fierce. Finally Futteh Ali Shah forgot all his Bombay manners; he leaned across Ralston, and cried to Rahat Mian:

"Do you know what I would like to do with you? I would like to string my bedstead with your skin and lie on it."

And upon that Ralston arrived at the conclusion that the meeting might as well come to an end.

He dismissed Rahat Mian, promising him a safe conveyance to his home. But he had not yet done with Futteh Ali Shah.

"I am going out," he said suavely. "Shall we walk a little way together?"

Futteh Ali Shah smiled. Landowner of importance that he was, the opportunity to ride side by side through Peshawur with the Chief Commissioner did not come every day. The two men went out into the porch. Ralston's horse was waiting, with a scarlet-clad syce at its head. Ralston walked on down the steps and took a step or two along the drive. Futteh Ali Shah lagged behind.

"Your Excellency is forgetting your horse."

"No," said Ralston. "The horse can follow. Let us walk a little. It is a good thing to walk."

It was nine o'clock in the morning, and the weather was getting hot. And it is said that the heat of Peshawur is beyond the heat of any other city from the hills to Cape Comorin. Futteh Ali Shah, however, could not refuse. Regretfully he signalled to his own groom who stood apart in charge of a fine dark bay stallion from the Kirghiz Steppes. The two men walked out from the garden and down the road towards Peshawur city, with their horses following behind them.

"We will go this way," said Ralston, and he turned to the left and walked along a mud-walled lane between rich orchards heavy with fruit. For a mile they thus walked, and then Futteh Ali Shah stopped and said:

"I am very anxious to have your Excellency's opinion of my horse. I am very proud of it."

"Later on," said Ralston, carelessly. "I want to walk for a little"; and, conversing upon indifferent topics, they skirted the city and came out upon the broad open road which runs to Jamrud and the Khyber Pass.

It was here that Futteh Ali Shah once more pressingly invited Ralston to try the paces of his stallion. But Ralston again refused.

"I will with pleasure later on," he said. "But a little exercise will be good for both of us; and they continued to walk along the road. The heat was overpowering; Futteh Ali Shah was soft from too much good living; his thin patent-leather shoes began to draw his feet and gall his heels; his frock coat was tight; the perspiration poured down his face. Ralston was hot, too. But he strode on with apparent unconcern, and talked with the utmost friendliness on the municipal affairs of Peshawur."

"It is very hot," said Futteh Ali Shah, "and I am afraid for your Excellency's health. For myself, of course, I am not troubled, but so much walking will be dangerous to you"; and he halted and looked longingly back to his horse.

"Thank you," said Ralston. "But my horse is fresh, and I should not be able to talk to you so well. I do not feel that I am in danger."

Futteh Ali Shah mopped his face and walked on. His feet blistered; he began to limp, and he had nothing but a riding-switch in his hand. Now across the plain he saw in the distance the round fort of Jamrud, and he suddenly halted:

"I must sit down," he said. "I cannot help it, your Excellency, I must stop and sit down."

Ralston turned to him with a look of cold surprise.

"Before me, Futteh Ali Shah? You will sit down in my presence before I sit down? I think you will not."

Futteh Ali Shah gazed up the road and down the road, and saw no help anywhere. Only this devilish Chief Commissioner stood threateningly before him. With a gesture of despair he wiped his face and walked on. For a mile more he limped on by Ralston's side, the while Ralston discoursed upon the great question of Agricultural Banks. Then he stopped again and blurted out:

"I will give you no more trouble. If your Excellency will let me go, never again will I give you trouble. I swear it."

Ralston smiled. He had had enough of the walk himself.

"And Rahat Mian?" he asked.

There was a momentary struggle in the zemindar's mind. But his fatigue and exhaustion were too heavy upon him.

"He, too, shall go his own way. Neither I nor mine shall molest him."

Ralston turned at once and mounted his horse. With a sigh of relief Futteh Ali Shah followed his example.

"Shall we ride back together?" said Ralston, pleasantly. And as on the way out he had made no mention of any trouble between the landowner and himself, so he did not refer to it by a single word on his way back.

But close to the city their ways parted and Futteh Ali Shah, as he took his leave, said hesitatingly,

"If this story goes abroad, your Excellency—this story of how we walked together towards Jamrud—there will be much laughter and ridicule."

The fear of ridicule—there was the weak point of the Afridi, as Ralston very well knew. To be laughed at—Futteh Ali Shah, who was wont to lord it among his friends, writhed under the mere possibility. And how they would laugh in and round about Peshawur! A fine figure he would cut as he rode through the streets with every ragged bystander jeering at the man who was walked into docility and submission by his Excellency the Chief Commissioner.

"My life would be intolerable," he said, "were the story to get about."

Ralston shrugged his shoulders.

"But why should it get about?"

"I do not know, but it surely will. It may be that the trees have ears and eyes and a mouth to speak." He edged a little nearer to the Commissioner. "It may be, too," he said cunningly, "that your Excellency loves to tell a good story after dinner. Now there is one way to stop that story."

Ralston laughed. "If I could hold my tongue, you mean," he replied.

Futteh Ali Shah came nearer still. He rode up close and leaned a little over towards Ralston.

"Your Excellency would lose the story," he said, "but on the other hand there would be a gain—a gain of many hours of sleep passed otherwise in guessing."

He spoke in an insinuating fashion, which made Ralston disinclined to strike a bargain—and he nodded his head like one who wishes to convey that he could tell much if only he would. But Ralston paused before he answered, and when he answered it was only to put a question.

"What do you mean?" he asked.

And the reply came in a low quick voice.

"There was a message sent through Chiltistan."

Ralston started. Was it in this strange way the truth was to come to him? He sat his horse carelessly. "I know," he said. "Some melons and some bags of grain."

Futteh Ali Shah was disappointed. This devilish Chief Commissioner knew everything. Yet the story of the walk must not get abroad in Peshawur, and surely it would unless the Chief Commissioner were pledged to silence. He drew a

A. E. W. Mason

bow at a venture.

"Can your Excellency interpret the message? As they interpret it in Chiltistan?" and it seemed to him that he had this time struck true. "It is a little thing I ask of your Excellency."

"It is not a great thing, to be sure," Ralston admitted. He looked at the zemindar and laughed. "But I could tell the story rather well," he said doubtfully. "It would be an amusing story as I should tell it. Yet—well, we will see," and he changed his tone suddenly. "Interpret to me that present as it is interpreted in the villages of Chiltistan."

Futteh Ali Shah looked about him fearfully, making sure that there was no one within earshot. Then in a whisper he said: "The grain is the army which will rise up from the hills and descend from the heavens to destroy the power of the Government. The melons are the forces of the Government; for as easily as melons they will be cut into pieces."

He rode off quickly when he had ended, like a man who understands that he has said too much, and then halted and returned.

"You will not tell that story?" he said.

"No," answered Ralston abstractedly. "I shall never tell that story."

He understood the truth at last. So that was the message which Shere Ali had sent. No wonder, he thought, that the glare broadened over Chiltistan.

CHAPTER XX

THE SOLDIER AND THE JEW

These two events took place at Peshawur, while Linforth was still upon the waters of the Red Sea. To be quite exact, on that morning when Ralston was taking his long walk towards Jamrud with the zemindar Futteh Ali Shah, Linforth was watching impatiently from his deck-chair the high mosque towers, the white domes and great houses of Mocha, as they shimmered in the heat at the water's edge against a wide background of yellow sand. It seemed to him that the long narrow city so small and clear across the great level of calm sea would never slide past the taffrail. But it disappeared, and in due course the ship moved slowly through the narrows into Aden harbour. This was on a Thursday evening, and the steamer stopped in Aden for three hours to coal. The night came on hot, windless and dark. Linforth leaned over the side, looking out upon the short curve of lights and the black mass of hill rising dimly above them. Three and a half more days and he would be standing on Indian soil. A bright light flashed towards the ship across the water and a launch came alongside, bearing the agent of the company.

He had the latest telegrams in his hand.

"Any trouble on the Frontier?" Linforth asked.

A. E. W. Mason

"None," the agent replied, and Linforth's fever of impatience was assuaged. If trouble were threatening he would surely be in time—since there were only three and a half more days.

But he did not know why he had been brought out from England, and the three and a half days made him by just three and a half days too late. For on this very night when the steamer stopped to coal in Aden harbour Shere Ali made his choice.

He was present that evening at a prize-fight which took place in a music-hall at Calcutta. The lightweight champion of Singapore and the East, a Jew, was pitted against a young soldier who had secured his discharge and had just taken to boxing as a profession. The soldier brought a great reputation as an amateur. This was his first appearance as a professional, and his friends had gathered in numbers to encourage him. The hall was crowded with soldiers from the barracks, sailors from the fleet, and patrons of the fancy in Calcutta. The heat was overpowering, the audience noisy, and overhead the electric fans, which hung downwards from the ceiling, whirled above the spectators with so swift a rotation that those looking up saw only a vague blur in the air. The ring had been roped off upon the stage, and about three sides of the ring chairs for the privileged had been placed. The fourth side was open to the spectators in the hall, and behind the ropes at the back there sat in the centre of the row of chairs a fat red-faced man in evening-dress who was greeted on all sides as Colonel Joe. "Colonel Joe" was the referee, and a person on these occasions of great importance.

There were several preliminary contests and before each one Colonel Joe came to the front and introduced the combatants with a short history of their achievements. A Hindu boy was matched against a white one, a couple of wrestlers came next, and then two English sailors, with more spirit than skill, had a set-to which warmed the audience into enthusiasm and ended amid shouts, whistles, shrill cat-calls, and thunders of applause. Meanwhile the heat grew more and more intense, the faces shinier, the air more and more smoke-laden and heavy.

Shere Ali came on to the stage while the sailors were at work. He exchanged a nod with "Colonel Joe," and took his seat in the front row of chairs behind the ropes.

It was a rough gathering on the whole, though there were some men in evening-dress besides Colonel Joe, and of these two sat beside Shere Ali. They were talking together, and Shere Ali at the first paid no heed to them. The trainers, the backers, the pugilists themselves were the men who had become his associates in Calcutta. There were many of them present upon the stage, and in turn they approached Shere Ali and spoke to him with familiarity upon the chances of the fight. Yet in their familiarity there was a kind of deference. They were speaking to a patron. Moreover, there was some flattery in the attention with which they waited to catch his eye and the eagerness with which they came at once to his side.

"We are all glad to see you, sir," said a small man who had been a jockey until he was warned off the turf.

"Yes," said Shere Ali with a smile, "I am among friends."

"Now who would you say was going to win this fight?" continued the jockey, cocking his head with an air of shrewdness, which said as plainly as words, "You are the one to tell if you will only say."

Shere Ali expanded. Deference and flattery, however gross, so long as they came from white people were balm to his wounded vanity. The weeks in Calcutta had worked more

A. E. W. Mason

harm than Ralston had suspected. Shy of meeting those who had once treated him as an equal, imagining when he did meet them that now they only admitted him to their company on sufferance and held him in their thoughts of no account, he had become avid for recognition among the riff-raff of the town.

"I have backed the man from Singapore," he replied, "I know him. The soldier is a stranger to me"; and gradually as he talked the voices of his two neighbours forced themselves upon his consciousness. It was not what they said which caught his attention. But their accents and the pitch of their voices arrested him, and swept him back to his days at Eton and at Oxford. He turned his head and looked carelessly towards them. They were both young; both a year ago might have been his intimates and friends. As it was, he imagined bitterly, they probably resented his sitting even in the next chair to them.

The stage was now clear; the two sailors had departed, the audience sat waiting for the heroes of the evening and calling for them with impatient outbursts of applause. Shere Ali waited too. But there was no impatience on his part, as there was no enthusiasm. He was just getting through the evening; and this hot and crowded den, with its glitter of lights, promised a thrill of excitement which would for a moment lift him from the torture of his thoughts.

But the antagonists still lingered in their dressing-rooms while their trainers put the final touch to their preparations. And while the antagonists lingered, the two young men next to him began again to talk, and this time the words fell on Shere Ali's ears.

"I think it ought to be stopped," said one. "It can't be good for us. Of course the fellow who runs the circus doesn't care, although he is an Englishman, and although he must have understood what was being shouted."

"He is out for money, of course," replied the other.

"Yes. But not half a mile away, just across the Maidan there, is Government House. Surely it ought to be stopped."

The speaker was evidently serious. He spoke, indeed, with some heat. Shere Ali wondered indifferently what it was that went on in the circus in the Maidan half a mile from the Government House. Something which ought to be stopped, something which could not be "good for us." Shere Ali clenched his hands in a gust of passion. How well he knew the phrase! Good for us, good for the magic of British prestige! How often he had used the words himself in the days when he had been fool enough to believe that he belonged to the white people. He had used it in the company of just such youths as those who sat next to him now, and he writhed in his seat as he imagined how they must have laughed at him in their hearts. What was it that was not "good for us" in the circus on the Maidan?

As he wondered there was a burst of applause, and on the opposite side of the ring the soldier, stripped to the waist, entered with his two assistants. Shere Ali was sitting close to the lower corner of the ring on the right-hand side of the stage; the soldier took his seat in the upper corner on the other side. He was a big, heavily-built man, but young, active, and upon his open face he had a look of confidence. It seemed to Shere Ali that he had been trained to the very perfection of his strength, and when he moved the muscles upon his shoulders and back worked under his skin as though they lived. Shouts greeted him, shouts in which his surname and his Christian name and his nicknames were mingled, and he smiled pleasantly back at his friends. Shere Ali looked at him. From his cheery, honest face to the firm set of his feet upon the floor, he was typical of his class and race.

"Oh, I hope he'll be beaten!"

Shere Ali found himself repeating the words in a whisper. The wish had suddenly sprung up within him, but it grew in intensity; it became a great longing. He looked anxiously for the appearance of the Jew from Singapore. He was glad that, knowing little of either man, he had laid his money against the soldier.

Meanwhile the two youths beside him resumed their talk, and Shere Ali learned what it was that was not "good for us"!

"There were four girls," said the youth who had been most indignant. "Four English girls dancing a *pas de quatre* on the sand of the circus. The dance was all right, the dresses were all right. In an English theatre no one would have had a word to say. It was the audience that was wrong. The cheaper parts at the back of the tent were crowded with natives, tier above tier—and I tell you—I don't know much Hindustani, but the things they shouted made my blood boil. After all, if you are going to be the governing race it's not a good thing to let your women be insulted, eh?"

Shere Ali laughed quietly. He could picture to himself the whole scene, the floor of the circus, the tiers of grinning faces rising up against the back walls of the tent.

"Did the girls themselves mind?" asked the other of the youths.

"They didn't understand." And again the angry utterance followed. "It ought to be stopped! It ought to be stopped!"

Shere Ali turned suddenly upon the speaker.

"Why?" he asked fiercely, and he thrust a savage face towards him.

The young man was taken by surprise; for a second it warmed Shere Ali to think that he was afraid. And, indeed, there was very little of the civilised man in Shere Ali's look at this moment. His own people were claiming him. It was one of the keen grim tribesmen of the hills who challenged the young Englishman. The Englishman, however, was not afraid. He was merely disconcerted by the unexpected attack. He recovered his composure the next moment.

"I don't think that I was speaking to you," he said quietly, and then turned away.

Shere Ali half rose in his seat. But he was not yet quite emancipated from the traditions of his upbringing. To create a disturbance in a public place, to draw all eyes upon himself, to look a fool, eventually to be turned ignominiously into the street—all this he was within an ace of doing and suffering, but he refrained. He sat down again quickly, feeling hot and cold with shame, just as he remembered he had been wont to feel when he had committed some gaucherie in his early days in England.

At that moment the light-weight champion from Singapore came out from his dressing-room and entered the ring. He was of a slighter build than his opponent, but very quick upon his feet. He was shorter, too. Colonel Joe introduced the antagonists to the audience, standing before the footlights as he did so. And it was at once evident who was the favourite. The shouts were nearly all for the soldier.

The Jew took his seat in a chair down in the corner where

Shere Ali was sitting, and Shere Ali leaned over the ropes and whispered to him fiercely,

"Win! Win! I'll double the stake if you do!"

The Jew turned and smiled at the young Prince.

"I'll do my best."

Shere Ali leaned back in his chair and the fight began. He followed it with an excitement and a suspense which were astonishing even to him. When the soldier brought his fist home upon the prominent nose of the Singapore champion and plaudits resounded through the house, his heart sank with bitter disappointment. When the Jew replied with a dull body-blow, his hopes rebounded. He soon began to understand that in the arts of prize-fighting the soldier was a child compared with the man from Singapore. The Champion of the East knew his trade. He was as hard as iron. The sounding blows upon his forehead and nose did no more than flush his face for a few moments. Meanwhile he struck for the body. Moreover, he had certain tricks which lured his antagonist to an imprudent confidence. For instance, he breathed heavily from the beginning of the second round, as though he were clean out of condition. But each round found him strong and quick to press an advantage. After one blow, which toppled his opponent through the ropes, Shere Ali clapped his hands.

"Bravo!" he cried; and one of the youths at his side said to his companion:

"This fellow's a Jew, too. Look at his face."

For twelve rounds the combatants seemed still to be upon equal terms, though those in the audience who had knowledge began to shake their heads over the chances of the soldier. Shere Ali, however, was still racked by suspense. The fight had become a symbol, almost a message to him, even as his gift to the Mullah had become a message to the people of Chiltistan. All that he had once loved, and now furiously raged against, was represented by the soldier, the confident, big, heavily built soldier, while, on the other hand, by the victory of the Jew all the subject peoples would be vindicated. More and more as the fight fluctuated from round to round the people and the country of Chiltistan claimed its own. The soldier represented even those youths at his side, whose women must on no account be insulted.

"Why should they be respected?" he cried to himself.

For at the bottom of his heart lay the thought that he had been set aside as impossible by Violet Oliver. There was the real cause of his bitterness against the white people. He still longed for Violet Oliver, still greatly coveted her. But his own people and his own country were claiming him; and he longed for her in a different way. Chivalry—the chivalry of the young man who wants to guard and cherish—respect, the desire that the loved one should share ambitions, life work, all—what follies and illusions these things were!

"I know," said Shere Ali to himself. "I know. I am myself the victim of them," and he lowered his head and clasped his hands tightly together between his knees. He forgot the prize-fight, the very sound of the pugilists' feet upon the bare boards of the stage ceased to be audible to his ears. He ached like a man bruised and beaten; he was possessed with a sense of loneliness, poignant as pain. "If I had only taken the easier way, bought and never cared!" he cried despairingly. "But at all events there's no need for respect. Why should one respect those who take and do not give?"

As he asked himself the question, there came a roar from the audience. He looked up. The soldier was standing, but he was stooping and the fingers of one hand touched the boards. Over against the soldier the man from Singapore stood waiting with steady eyes, and behind the ropes Colonel Joe was counting in a loud voice:

"One, two, three, four."

Shere Ali's eyes lit up. Would the soldier rise? Would he take the tips of those fingers from the floor, stand up again and face his man? Or was he beaten?

"Five, six, seven, eight"—the referee counted, his voice rising above the clamour of voices. The audience had risen, men stood upon their benches, cries of expostulation were shouted to the soldier.

"Nine, ten," counted the referee, and the fight was over. The soldier had been counted out.

Shere Ali was upon his feet like the rest of the enthusiasts.

"Well done!" he cried. "Well done!" and as the Jew came back to his corner Shere Ali shook him excitedly by the hand. The sign had been given; the subject race had beaten the soldier. Shere Ali was livid with excitement. Perhaps, indeed, the young Englishmen had been right, and some dim racial sympathy stirred Shere Ali to his great enthusiasm.

CHAPTER XXI

SHERE ALI IS CLAIMED BY CHILTISTAN

While these thoughts were seething in his mind, while the excitement was still at its height, the cries still at their loudest, Shere All heard a quiet penetrating voice speak in his ear. And the voice spoke in Pushtu.

The mere sound of the language struck upon Shere Ali's senses at that moment of exultation with a strange effect. He thrilled to it from head to foot. He heard it with a feeling of joy. And then he took note of the spoken words.

"The man who wrote to your Highness from Calcutta waits outside the doors. As you stand under the gas lamps, take your handkerchief from your pocket if you wish to speak with him."

Shere Ali turned back from the ropes. But the spectators were already moving from their chairs to the steps which led from the stage to the auditorium. There was a crowd about those steps, and Shere Ali could not distinguish among it the man who was likely to have whispered in his ear. All seemed bent upon their own business, and that business was to escape from the close heat-laden air of the building as quickly as might be.

A. E. W. Mason

Shere Ali stood alone and pondered upon the words.

The man who had written to him from Calcutta! That was the man who had sent the anonymous letter which had caused him one day to pass through the Delhi Gate of Lahore. A money-lender at Calcutta, but a countryman from Chiltistan. So he had gathered from Safdar Khan, while heaping scorn upon the message.

But now, and on this night of all nights, Shere Ali was in a mood to listen. There were intrigues on foot—there were always intrigues on foot. But to-night he would weigh those intrigues. He went out from the music-hall, and under the white glare of the electric lamps above the door he stood for a moment in full view. Then he deliberately took his handkerchief from his pocket. From the opposite side of the road, a man in native dress, wearing a thick dark cloak over his white shirt and pyjamas, stepped forward. Shere Ali advanced to meet him.

"Huzoor, huzoor," said the man, bending low, and he raised Shere Ali's hand and pressed his forehead upon it, in sign of loyalty.

"You wish to speak to me?" said Shere Ali.

"If your Highness will deign to follow. I am Ahmed Ismail. Your Highness has heard of me, no doubt."

Shere Ali did not so much as smile, nor did he deny the statement. He nodded gravely. After all, vanity was not the prerogative of his people alone in all the world.

"Yes," he said, "I will follow."

Ahmed Ismail crossed the road once more out of the lights

into the shadows, and walked on, keeping close to the lines of houses. Shere Ali followed upon his heels. But these two were not alone to take that road. A third man, a Bengali, bespectacled, and in appearance most respectable, came down the steps of the musichall, a second after Shere Ali had crossed the road. He, too, had been a witness of the prize-fight. He hurried after Shere Ali and caught him up.

"Very good fight, sir," he said. "Would Prince of Chiltistan like to utter some few welcome words to great Indian public on extraordinary skill of respective pugilists? I am full-fledged reporter of *Bande Mataram*, great Nationalist paper."

He drew out a note-book and a pencil as he spoke. Ahmed Ismail stopped and turned back towards the two men. The Babu looked once, and only once, at the money-lender. Then he stood waiting for Shere Ali's answer.

"No, I have nothing to say," said Shere Ali civilly. "Good-night," and he walked on.

"Great disappointment for Indian public," said the Bengali. "Prince of Chiltistan will say nothing. I make first-class leading article on reticence of Indian Prince in presence of high-class spectacular events. Good-night, sir," and the Babu shut up his book and fell back.

Shere Ali followed upon the heels of Ahmed Ismail. The money-lender walked down the street to the Maidan, and then turned to the left. The Babu, on the other hand, hailed a third-class gharry and, ascending into it gave the driver some whispered instructions.

The gharry drove on past the Bengal Club, and came, at length, to the native town. At the corner of a street the Babu descended, paid the driver, and dismissed him.

"I will walk the rest of the way," he said. "My home is quite near and a little exercise is good. I have large varicose veins in the legs, or I should have tramped hand and foot all the way."

He walked slowly until the driver had turned his gharry and was driving back. Then, for a man afflicted with varicose veins the Babu displayed amazing agility. He ran through the silent and deserted street until he came to a turning. The lane which ran into the main road was a blind alley. Mean hovels and shuttered booths flanked it, but at the end a tall house stood. The Babu looked about him and perceived a cart standing in the lane. He advanced to it and looked in.

"This is obvious place for satisfactory concealment," he said, as with some difficulty he clambered in. Over the edge of the cart he kept watch. In a while he heard the sound of a man walking. The man was certainly at some distance from the turning, but the Babu's head went down at once. The man whose footsteps he heard was wearing boots, but there would be one walking in front of that man who was wearing slippers—Ahmed Ismail.

Ahmed Ismail, indeed, turned an instant afterwards into the lane, passed the cart and walked up to the door of the big house. There he halted, and Shere Ali joined him.

"The gift was understood, your Highness," he said. "The message was sent from end to end of Chiltistan."

"What gift?" asked Shere Ali, in genuine surprise.

"Your Highness has forgotten? The melons and the bags of grain."

Shere Ali was silent for a few moments. Then he said:

"And how was the gift interpreted?"

Ahmed Ismail smiled in the darkness.

"There are wise men in Chiltistan, and they found the riddle easy to read. The melons were the infidels which would be cut to pieces, even as a knife cuts a melon. The grain was the army of the faithful."

Again Shere Ali was silent. He stood with his eyes upon his companion.

"Thus they understand my gift to the Mullah?" he said at length.

"Thus they understood it," said Ahmed Ismail. "Were they wrong?" and since Shere Ali paused before he answered, Ahmed repeated the question, holding the while the key of his door between his fingers.

"Were they wrong, your Highness?"

"No," said Shere Ali firmly. "They were right."

Ahmed Ismail put the key into the lock. The bolt shot back with a grating sound, the door opened upon blackness.

"Will your Highness deign to enter?" he said, standing aside.

"Yes," said Shere Ali, and he passed in. His own people, his own country, had claimed and obtained him.

A. E. W. Mason

CHAPTER XXII

THE CASTING OF THE DIE

Ahmed Ismail crossed the threshold behind Shere Ali. He closed the door quietly, bolted and locked it. Then for a space of time the two men stood silent in the darkness, and both listened intently—Ahmed Ismail for the sound of someone stirring in the house, Shere Ali for a quiet secret movement at his elbow. The blackness of the passage gaping as the door opened had roused him to suspicion even while he had been standing in the street. But he had not thought of drawing back. He had entered without fear, just as now he stood, without fear, drawn up against the wall. There was, indeed, a smile upon his face. Then he reached out his hand. Ahmed Ismail, who still stood afraid lest any of his family should have been disturbed, suddenly felt a light touch, like a caress, upon his face, and then before he could so much as turn his head, five strong lean fingers gripped him by the throat and tightened.

"Ahmed, I have enemies in Chiltistan," said Shere Ali, between a whisper and a laugh. "The son of Abdulla Mohammed, for instance," and he loosened his grip a little upon Ahmed's throat, but held him still with a straight arm. Ahmed did not struggle. He whispered in reply:

"I am not of your Highness's enemies. Long ago I gave your Highness a sign of friendship when I prayed you to pass by the Delhi Gate of Lahore."

Shere Ali turned Ahmed Ismail towards the inner part of the house and loosed his neck.

"Go forward, then. Light a lamp," he said, and Ahmed moved noiselessly along the passage. Shere Ali heard the sound of a door opening upstairs, and then a pale light gleamed from above. Shere Ali walked to the end of the passage, and mounting the stairs found Ahmed Ismail in the doorway of a little room with a lighted lamp in his hand.

"I was this moment coming down," said Ahmed Ismail as he stood aside from the door. Shere Ali walked in. He crossed to the window, which was unglazed but had little wooden shutters. These shutters were closed. Shere Ali opened one and looked out. The room was on the first floor, and the window opened on to a small square courtyard. A movement of Ahmed Ismail's brought him swiftly round. He saw the money-lender on his knees with his forehead to the ground, grovelling before his Prince's feet.

"The time has come, oh, my Lord," he cried in a low, eager voice, and again, "the time has come."

Shere Ali looked down and pleasure glowed unwontedly within him. He did not answer, he did not give Ahmed Ismail leave to rise from the ground. He sated his eyes and his vanity with the spectacle of the man's abasement. Even his troubled heart ached with a duller pain.

"I have been a fool," he murmured, "I have wasted my years. I have tortured myself for nothing. Yes, I have been a fool."

A. E. W. Mason

A wave of anger swept over him, drowning his pride—anger against himself. He thought of the white people with whom he had lived.

"I sought for a recognition of my equality with them," he went on. "I sought it from their men and from their women. I hungered for it like a dog for a bone. They would not give it—neither their men, nor their women. And all the while here were my own people willing at a sign to offer me their homage."

He spoke in Pushtu, and Ahmed Ismail drank in every word.

"They wanted a leader, Huzoor," he said.

"I turned away from them like a fool," replied Shere Ali, "while I sought favours from the white women like a slave."

"Your Highness shall take as a right what you sought for as a favour."

"As a right?" cried Shere Ali, his heart leaping to the incense of Ahmed Ismail's flattery. "What right?" he asked, suddenly bending his eyes upon his companion.

"The right of a conqueror," cried Ahmed Ismail, and he bowed himself again at his Prince's feet. He had spoken Shere Ali's wild and secret thought. But whereas Shere Ali had only whispered it to himself, Ahmed Ismail spoke it aloud, boldly and with a challenge in his voice, like one ready to make good his words. An interval of silence followed, a fateful interval as both men knew. Not a sound from without penetrated into that little shuttered room, but to Shere Ali it seemed that the air throbbed and was heavy with unknown things to come. Memories and fancies whirled in his disordered brain without relation to each other or consequence in his thoughts. Now it was the two Englishmen seated side by side behind the ropes and quietly talking of what was "not good for us," as though they had the whole of India, and the hill-districts, besides, in their pockets. He saw their faces, and, quietly though he stood and impassive as he looked, he was possessed with a longing to behold them within reach, so that he might strike them and disfigure them for ever. Now it was Violet Oliver as she descended the steps into the great courtyard of the Fort, dainty and provoking from the arched slipper upon her foot to the soft perfection of her hair. He saw her caught into the twilight swirl of pale white faces and so pass from his sight, thinking that at the same moment she passed from his life. Then it was the Viceroy in his box at the racecourse and all Calcutta upon the lawn which swept past his eyes. He saw the Eurasian girls prinked out in their best frocks to lure into marriage some unwary Englishman. And again it was Colonel Dewes, the man who had lost his place amongst his own people, even as he, Shere Ali, had himself. A half-contemptuous smile of pity for a moment softened the hard lines of his mouth as he thought upon that forlorn and elderly man taking his loneliness with him into Cashmere.

"That shall not be my way," he said aloud, and the lines of his mouth hardened again. And once more before his eyes rose the vision of Violet Oliver.

Ahmed Ismail had risen to his feet and stood watching his Prince with eager, anxious eyes. Shere Ali crossed to the table and turned down the lamp, which was smoking. Then he went to the window and thrust the shutters open. He turned round suddenly upon Ahmed.

"Were you ever in Mecca?"

"Yes, Huzoor," and Ahmed's eyes flashed at the question.

"I met three men from Chiltistan on the Lowari Pass. They were going down to Kurachi. I, too, must make the pilgrimage to Mecca."

He stood watching the flame of the lamp as he spoke, and spoke in a monotonous dull voice, as though what he said were of little importance. But Ahmed Ismail listened to the words, not the voice, and his joy was great. It was as though he heard a renegade acknowledge once more the true faith.

"Afterwards, Huzoor," he said, significantly. "Afterwards." Shere Ali nodded his head.

"Yes, afterwards. When we have driven the white people down from the hills into the plains."

"And from the plains into the sea," cried Ahmed Ismail. "The angels will fight by our side—so the Mullahs have said—and no man who fights with faith will be hurt. All will be invulnerable. It is written, and the Mullahs have read the writing and translated it through Chiltistan."

"Is that so?" said Shere Ali, and as he put the question there was an irony in his voice which Ahmed Ismail was quick to notice. But Shere Ali put it yet a second time, after a pause, and this time there was no trace of irony.

"But I will not go alone," he said, suddenly raising his eyes from the flame of the lamp and looking towards Ahmed Ismail.

Ahmed did not understand. But also he did not interrupt, and Shere Ali spoke again, with a smile slowly creeping over his face.

"I will not go alone to Mecca. I will follow the example of

Sirdar Khan."

The saying was still a riddle to Ahmed Ismail.

"Sirdar Khan, your Highness?" he said. "I do not know him."

Shere Ali turned his eyes again upon the flame of the lamp, and the smile broadened upon his face, a thing not pleasant to see. He wetted his lips with the tip of his tongue and told his story.

"Sirdar Khan is dead long since," he said, "but he was one of the five men of the bodyguard of Nana, who went into the Bibigarh at Cawnpore on July 12 of the year 1857. Have you heard of that year, Ahmed Ismail, and of the month and of the day? Do you know what was done that day in the Bibigarh at Cawnpore?"

Ahmed Ismail watched the light grow in Shere Ali's eyes, and a smile crept into his face, too.

"Huzoor, Huzoor," he said, in a whisper of delight. He knew very well what had happened in Cawnpore, though he knew nothing of the month or the day, and cared little in what year it had happened.

"There were 206 women and children, English women, English children, shut up in the Bibigarh. At five o'clock— and it is well to remember the hour, Ahmed Ismail—at five o'clock in the evening the five men of the Nana's bodyguard went into the Bibigarh and the doors were closed upon them. It was dark when they came out again and shut the doors behind them, saying that all were dead. But it was not true. There was an Englishwoman alive in the Bibigarh, and Sirdar Khan came back in the night and took her away."

A. E. W. Mason

"And she is in Mecca now?" cried Ahmed Ismail.

"Yes. An old, old woman," said Shere Ali, dwelling upon the words with a quiet, cruel pleasure. He had the picture clear before his eyes, he saw it in the flame of the lamp at which he gazed so steadily—an old, wizened, shrunken woman, living in a bare room, friendless and solitary, so old that she had even ceased to be aware of her unhappiness, and so coarsened out of all likeness to the young, bright English girl who had once dwelt in Cawnpore, that even her own countryman had hardly believed she was of his race. He set another picture side by side with that—the picture of Violet Oliver as she turned to him on the steps and said, "This is really good-bye." And in his imagination, he saw the one picture merge and coarsen into the other, the dainty trappings of lace and ribbons change to a shapeless cloak, the young face wither from its beauty into a wrinkled and yellow mask. It would be a just punishment, he said to himself. Anger against her was as a lust at his heart. He had lost sight of her kindness, and her pity; he desired her and hated her in the same breath.

"Are you married, Ahmed Ismail?" he asked.

Ahmed Ismail smiled.

"Truly, Huzoor."

"Do you carry your troubles to your wife? Is she your companion as well as your wife? Your friend as well as your mistress?"

Ahmed Ismail laughed.

"Yet that is what the Englishwomen are," said Shere Ali.

"Perhaps, Huzoor," replied Ahmed, cunningly, "it is for that reason that there are some who take and do not give."

He came a little nearer to his Prince.

"Where is she, Huzoor?"

Shere Ali was startled by the question out of his dreams. For it had been a dream, this thought of capturing Violet Oliver and plucking her out of her life into his. He had played with it, knowing it to be a fancy. There had been no settled plan, no settled intention in his mind. But to-night he was carried away. It appeared to him there was a possibility his dream might come true. It seemed so not alone to him but to Ahmed Ismail too. He turned and gazed at the man, wondering whether Ahmed Ismail played with him or not. But Ahmed bore the scrutiny without a shadow of embarrassment.

"Is she in India, Huzoor?"

Shere Ali hesitated. Some memory of the lessons learned in England was still alive within him, bidding him guard his secret. But the memory was no longer strong enough. He bowed his head in assent.

"In Calcutta?"

"Yes."

"Your Highness shall point her out to me one evening as she drives in the Maidan," said Ahmed Ismail, and again Shere Ali answered—

"Yes."

But he caught himself back the next moment. He flung away

A. E. W. Mason

from Ahmed Ismail with a harsh outburst of laughter.

"But this is all folly," he cried. "We are not in the days of the uprising," for thus he termed now what a month ago he would have called "The Mutiny." "Cawnpore is not Calcutta," and he turned in a gust of fury upon Ahmed Ismail. "Do you play with me, Ahmed Ismail?"

"Upon my head, no! Light of my life, hope of my race, who would dare?" and he was on the ground at Shere Ali's feet. "Do I indeed speak follies? I pray your Highness to bethink you that the summer sets its foot upon the plains. She will go to the hills, Huzoor. She will go to the hills. And your people are not fools. They have cunning to direct their strength. See, your Highness, is there a regiment in Peshawur whose rifles are safe, guard them howsoever carefully they will? Every week they are brought over the hills into Chiltistan that we may be ready for the Great Day," and Ahmed Ismail chuckled to himself. "A month ago, Huzoor, so many rifles had been stolen that a regiment in camp locked their rifles to their tent poles, and so thought to sleep in peace. But on the first night the cords of the tents were cut, and while the men waked and struggled under the folds of canvas, the tent poles with the rifles chained to them were carried away. All those rifles are now in Kohara. Surely, Huzoor, if they can steal the rifles from the middle of a camp, they can steal a weak girl among the hills."

Ahmed Ismail waited in suspense, with his forehead bowed to the ground, and when the answer came he smiled. He had made good use of this unexpected inducement which had been given to him. He knew very well that nothing but an unlikely chance would enable him to fulfil his promise. But that did not matter. The young Prince would point out the Englishwoman in the Maidan and, at a later time when all was ready in Chiltistan, a fine and obvious attempt should be made to carry her off. The pretence might, if occasion served, become a reality, to be sure, but the attempt must be as public as possible. There must be no doubt as to its author. Shere Ali, in a word, must be committed beyond any possibility of withdrawal. Ahmed Ismail himself would see to that.

"Very well. I will point her out to you," said Shere Ali, and Ahmed Ismail rose to his feet. He waited before his master, silent and respectful. Shere Ali had no suspicion that he was being jockeyed by that respectful man into a hopeless rebellion. He had, indeed, lost sight of the fact that the rebellion must be hopeless.

"When," he asked, "will Chiltistan be ready?"

"As soon as the harvest is got in," replied Ahmed Ismail.

Shere Ali nodded his head.

"You and I will go northwards to-morrow," he said.

"To Kohara?" asked Ahmed Ismail.

"Yes."

For a little while Ahmed Ismail was silent. Then he said: "If your Highness will allow his servant to offer a contemptible word of advice—"

"Speak," said Shere Ali.

"Then it might be wise, perhaps, to go slowly to Kohara. Your Highness has enemies in Chiltistan. The news of the melons and the bags of grain is spread abroad, and jealousy is aroused. For there are some who wish to lead when they should serve."

"The son of Abdulla Mohammed," said Shere Ali.

Ahmed Ismail shrugged his shoulders as though the son of Abdulla Mohammed were of little account. There was clearly another in his mind, and Shere Ali was quick to understand him.

"My father," he said quietly. He remembered how his father had received him with his Snider rifle cocked and laid across his knees. This time the Snider would be fired if ever Shere Ali came within range of its bullet. But it was unlikely that he would get so far, unless he went quickly and secretly at an appointed time.

"I had a poor foolish thought," said Ahmed Ismail, "not worthy a moment's consideration by my Prince."

Shere Ali broke in impatiently upon his words.

"Speak it."

"If we travelled slowly to Ajmere, we should come to that town at the time of pilgrimage. There in secret the final arrangements can be made, so that the blow may fall upon an uncovered head."

"The advice is good," said Shere Ali. But he spoke reluctantly. He wanted not to wait at all. He wanted to strike now while his anger was at its hottest. But undoubtedly the advice was good.

Ahmed Ismail, carrying the light in his hand, went down the stairs before Shere Ali and along the passage to the door. There he extinguished the lamp and cautiously drew back the bolts. He looked out and saw that the street was empty.

"There is no one," he said, and Shere Ali passed out to the mouth of the blind alley and turned to the left towards the Maidan. He walked thoughtfully and did not notice a head rise cautiously above the side of a cart in the mouth of the alley. It was the head of the reporter of Bande Mataram, whose copy would be assuredly too late for the press.

Shere Ali walked on through the streets. It was late, and he met no one. There had come upon him during the last hours a great yearning for his own country. He ran over in his mind, with a sense of anger against himself, the miserable wasted weeks in Calcutta—the nights in the glaring bars and halls, the friends he had made, the depths in which he had wallowed. He came to the Maidan, and, standing upon that empty plain, gazed round on the great silent city. He hated it, with its statues of Viceroys and soldiers, its houses of rich merchants, its insolence. He would lead his own people against all that it symbolised. Perhaps, some day, when all the frontier was in flame, and the British power rolled back, he and his people might pour down from the hills and knock even against the gates of Calcutta. Men from the hills had come down to Tonk, and Bhopal, and Rohilcund, and Rampur, and founded kingdoms for themselves. Why should he and his not push on to Calcutta?

He bared his head to the night wind. He was uplifted, and fired with mad, impossible dreams. All that he had learned was of little account to him now. It might be that the English, as Colonel Dewes had said, had something of an army. Let them come to Chiltistan and prove their boast.

"I will go north to the hills," he cried, and with a shock he understood that, after all, he had recovered his own place. The longing at his heart was for his own country—for his

A. E. W. Mason

own people. It might have been bred of disappointment and despair. Envy of the white people might have cradled it, desire for the white woman might have nursed it into strength. But it was alive now. That was all of which Shere Ali was conscious. The knowledge filled all his thoughts. He had his place in the world. Greatly he rejoiced.

CHAPTER XXIII

SHERE ALI'S PILGRIMAGE

There were times when Ralston held aloft his hands and cursed the Indian administration by all his gods. But he never did so with a more whole-hearted conviction than on the day when he received word that Linforth had been diverted to Rawal Pindi, in order that he might take up purely military duties. It took Ralston just seven months to secure his release, and it was not until the early days of autumn had arrived that Linforth at last reached Peshawur. A landau, with a coachman and groom in scarlet liveries, was waiting for him at the station, and he drove along the broad road through the cantonment to Government House. As the carriage swung in at the gates, a tall, thin man came from the croquet-ground on the left. He joined Dick in the porch.

"You are Mr. Linforth?" he said.

"Yes."

For a moment a pair of grey, tired eyes ran Dick over from head to foot in a careless scrutiny. Apparently, however, the scrutiny was favourable.

"I am the Chief Commissioner. I am glad that you have

A. E. W. Mason

come. My sister will give you some tea, and afterwards, if you are not tired, we might go for a ride together. You would like to see your room first."

Ralston spoke with his usual indifference. There was no intonation in his voice which gave to any one sentence a particular meaning; and for a particular meaning Dick Linforth was listening with keen ears. He followed Ralston across the hall to his room, and disappointment gained upon him with every step. He had grown familiar with disappointment of late years, but he was still young enough in years and spirit to expect the end of disappointment with each change in his fortunes. He had expected it when the news of his appointment had reached him in Calcutta, and disappointment had awaited him in Bombay. He had expected it again when, at last, he was sent from Rawal Pindi to Peshawur. All the way up the line he had been watching the far hills of Cashmere, and repeating to himself, "At last! At last!"

The words had been a song at his heart, tuned to the jolt and rhythm of the wheels. Ralston of Peshawur had asked for him. So much he had been told. His longing had explained to him why Ralston of Peshawur had asked for him, and easily he had believed the explanation. He was a Linforth, one of the Linforths of the Road. Great was his pride. He would not have bartered his position to be a General in command of a division. Ralston had sent for him because of his hereditary title to work upon the Road, the broad, permanent, graded Road which was to make India safe.

And now he walked behind a tired and indifferent Commissioner, whose very voice officialdom had made phlegmatic, and on whose aspect was writ large the habit of routine. In this mood he sat, while Miss Ralston prattled to him about the social doings of Peshawur, the hunt, the golf; and in this mood he rode out with Ralston to the Gate of the City.

They passed through the main street, and, turning to the right, ascended to an archway, above which rose a tower. At the archway they dismounted and climbed to the roof of the tower. Peshawur, with its crowded streets, its open bazaars, its balconied houses of mud bricks built into wooden frames, lay mapped beneath them. But Linforth's eyes travelled over the trees and the gardens northwards and eastwards, to where the foothills of the Himalayas were coloured with the violet light of evening.

"Linforth," Ralston cried. He was leaning on the parapet at the opposite side of the tower, and Dick crossed and leaned at his side.

"It was I who had you sent for," said Ralston in his dull voice. "When you were at Chatham, I mean. I worried them in Calcutta until they sent for you."

Dick took his elbows from the parapet and stood up. His face took life and fire, there came a brightness as of joy into his eyes. After all, then, this time he was not to be disappointed.

"I wanted you to come to Peshawur straight from Bombay six months ago," Ralston went on. "But I counted without the Indian Government. They brought you out to India, at my special request, for a special purpose, and then, when they had got you, they turned you over to work which anyone else could have done. So six months have been wasted. But that's their little way."

"You have special work for me?" said Linforth quietly enough, though his heart was beating quickly in his breast. An answer came which still quickened its beatings.

"Work that you alone can do," Ralston replied gravely. But he was a man who had learned to hope for little, and to

A. E. W. Mason

expect discouragements as his daily bread, and he added:

"That is, if you can do it."

Linforth did not answer at once. He was leaning with his elbows on the parapet, and he raised a hand to the side of his face, that side on which Ralston stood. And so he remained, shutting himself in with his thoughts, and trying to think soberly. But his head whirled. Below him lay the city of Peshawur. Behind him the plains came to an end, and straight up from them, like cliffs out of the sea, rose the dark hills, brown and grey and veined with white. Here on this tower of Northern India, the long dreams, dreamed for the first time on the Sussex Downs, and nursed since in every moment of leisure—in Alpine huts in days of storm, in his own quarters at Chatham—had come to their fulfilment.

"I have lived for this work," he said in a low voice which shook ever so little, try as he might to quiet it. "Ever since I was a boy I have lived for it, and trained myself for it. It is the Road."

Linforth's evident emotion came upon Ralston as an unexpected thing. He was carried back suddenly to his own youth, and was surprised to recollect that he, too, had once cherished great plans. He saw himself as he was to-day, and, side by side with that disillusioned figure, he saw himself as he had been in his youth. A smile of friendliness came over his face.

"If I had shut my eyes," he said, "I should have thought it was your father who was speaking."

Linforth turned quickly to Ralston.

"My father. You knew him?"

"Yes."

"I never did," said Dick regretfully.

Ralston nodded his head and continued:

"Twenty-six years ago we were here in Peshawur together. We came up on to the top of this tower, as everyone does who comes to Peshawur. He was like you. He was dreaming night and day of the Great Road through Chiltistan to the foot of the Hindu Kush. Look!" and Ralston pointed down to the roof-tops of the city, whereon the women and children worked and played. For the most part they were enclosed within brick walls, and the two men looked down into them as you might look in the rooms of a doll's house by taking off the lid. Ralston pointed to one such open chamber just beneath their eyes. An awning supported on wooden pillars sheltered one end of it, and between two of these pillars a child swooped backwards and forwards in a swing. In the open, a woman, seated upon a string charpoy, rocked a cradle with her foot, while her hands were busy with a needle, and an old woman, with a black shawl upon her shoulders and head, sat near by, inactive. But she was talking. For at times the younger woman would raise her head, and, though at that distance no voice could be heard, it was evident that she was answering. "I remember noticing that roof when your father and I were talking up here all those years ago. There was just the same family group as you see now. I remember it quite clearly, for your father went away to Chiltistan the next day, and never came back. It was the last time I saw him, and we were both young and full of all the great changes we were to bring about." He smiled, half it seemed in amusement, half in regret. "We talked of the Road, of course. Well, there's just one change. The old woman, sitting there with the shawl upon her shoulders now, was in those days the young woman rocking the cradle and

A. E. W. Mason

working with her needle. That's all. Troubles there have been, disturbances, an expedition or two—but there's no real change. Here are you talking of the Road just as your father did, not ambitious for yourself," he explained with a kindly smile which illumined his whole face, "but ambitious for the Road, and the Road still stops at Kohara."

"But it will go on—now," cried Linforth.

"Perhaps," said Ralston slowly. Then he stood up and confronted Linforth.

"It was not that you might carry on the Road that I brought you out from England," he skid. "On the contrary."

Once more disappointment seized upon Dick Linforth, and he found it all the more bitter in that he had believed a minute since that his dreams were to be fulfilled. He looked down upon Peshawur, and the words which Ralston had lately spoken, half in amusement, half with regret, suddenly took for him their full meaning. Was it true that there was no change but the change from the young woman to the old one, from enthusiasm to acquiescence? He was young, and the possibility chilled him and even inspired him with a kind of terror. Was he to carry the Road no further than his father had done? Would another Linforth in another generation come to the tower in Peshawur with hopes as high as his and with the like futility?

"On the contrary?" he asked. "Then why?"

"That you might stop the Road from going on," said Ralston quietly.

In the very midst of his disappointment Linforth realised that he had misjudged his companion. Here was no official, here was a man. The attitude of indifference had gone, the air of lassitude with it. Here was a man quietly exacting the hardest service which it was in his power to exact, claiming it as a right, and yet making it clear by some subtle sympathy that he understood very well all that the service would cost to the man who served.

"I am to hinder the making of that Road?" cried Linforth.

"You are to do more. You are to prevent it."

"I have lived so that it should be made."

"So you have told me," said Ralston quietly, and Dick was silent. With each quiet sentence Ralston had become more and more the dominating figure. He was so certain, so assured. Linforth recognised him no longer as the man to argue with; but as the representative of Government which overrides predilections, sympathies, ambitions, and bends its servants to their duty.

"I will tell you more," Ralston continued. "You alone can prevent the extension of the Road. I believe it—I know it. I sent to England for you, knowing it. Do your duty, and it may be that the Road will stop at Kohara—an unfinished, broken thing. Flinch, and the Road runs straight to the Hindu Kush. You will have your desire; but you will have failed."

There was something implacable and relentless in the tone and the words. There was more, too. There was an intimation, subtly yet most clearly conveyed, that Ralston who spoke had in his day trampled his ambitions and desires beneath his feet in service to the Government, and asked no more now from Linforth than he himself had in his turn performed. "I, too, have lived in Arcady," he added. It twas this last intimation which subdued the protests in Linforth's

A. E. W. Mason

mind. He looked at the worn face of the Commissioner, then he lifted his eyes and swept the horizon with his gaze. The violet light upon the hills had lost its brightness and its glamour. In the far distance the hills themselves were withdrawn. Somewhere in that great barrier to the east was the gap of the Malakand Pass, where the Road now began. Linforth turned away from the hills towards Peshawur.

"What must I do?" he asked simply.

Ralston nodded his head. His attitude relaxed, his voice lost its dominating note.

"What you have to understand is this," he explained. "To drive the Road through Chiltistan means war. It would be the cause of war if we insisted upon it now, just as it was the cause of war when your father went up from Peshawur twenty-six years ago. Or it might be the consequence of war. If the Chiltis rose in arms, undoubtedly we should carry it on to secure control of the country in the future. Well, it is the last alternative that we are face to face with now."

"The Chiltis might rise!" cried Linforth.

"There is that possibility," Ralston returned. "We don't mean on our own account to carry on the Road; but the Chiltis might rise."

"And how should I prevent them?" asked Dick Linforth in perplexity.

"You know Shere Ali?" said Ralston

"Yes."

"You are a friend of his?"

"Yes."

"A great friend. His chief friend?"

"Yes."

"You have some control over him?"

"I think so," said Linforth.

"Very well," said Ralston. "You must use that control."

Linforth's perplexity increased. That danger should come from Shere Ali—here was something quite incredible. He remembered their long talks, their joint ambition. A day passed in the hut in the Promontoire of the Meije stood out vividly in his memories. He saw the snow rising in a swirl of white over the Breche de la Meije, that gap in the rock-wall between the Meije and the Rateau, and driving down the glacier towards the hut. He remembered the eagerness, the enthusiasm of Shere Ali.

"But he's loyal," Linforth cried. "There is no one in India more loyal."

"He was loyal, no doubt," said Ralston, with a shrug of his shoulders, and, beginning with his first meeting with Shere Ali in Lahore, he told Linforth all that he knew of the history of the young Prince.

"There can be no doubt," he said, "of his disloyalty," and he recounted the story of the melons and the bags of grain. "Since then he has been intriguing in Calcutta."

"Is he in Calcutta now?" Linforth asked.

"No," said Ralston. "He left Calcutta just about the time when you landed in Bombay. And there is something rather strange—something, I think, very disquieting in his movements since he left Calcutta. I have had him watched, of course. He came north with one of his own countrymen, and the pair of them have been seen at Cawnpore, at Lucknow, at Delhi."

Ralston paused. His face had grown very grave, very troubled.

"I am not sure," he said slowly. "It is difficult, however long you stay in India, to get behind these fellows' minds, to understand the thoughts and the motives which move them. And the longer you stay, the more difficult you realise it to be. But it looks to me as if Shere Ali had been taken by his companion on a sort of pilgrimage."

Linforth started.

"A pilgrimage!" and he added slowly, "I think I understand. A pilgrimage to all the places which could most inflame the passions of a native against the English race," and then he broke out in protest. "But it's impossible. I know Shere Ali. It's not reasonable—"

Ralston interrupted him upon the utterance of the word.

"Reasonable!" he cried. "You are in India. Do ever white men act reasonably in India?" and he turned with a smile. "There was a great-uncle of yours in the days of the John Company, wasn't there? Your father told me about him here on this tower. When his time was up, he sent his money home and took his passage, and then came back—came back to the mountains and disappeared. Very likely he may be sitting somewhere beyond that barrier of hills by a little shrine to this hour, an old, old man, reverenced as a saint, with a strip of cloth about his loins, and forgetful of the days when he ruled a district in the Plains. I should not wonder. It's not a reasonable country."

Ralston, indeed, was not far out in his judgment. Ahmed Ismail had carried Shere Ali off from Calcutta. He had taken him first of all to Cawnpore, and had led him up to the gate of the enclosure, wherein are the Bibigarh, where the women and children were massacred, and the well into which their bodies were flung. An English soldier turned them back from that enclosure, refusing them admittance. Ahmed Ismail, knowing well that it would be so, smiled quietly under his moustache; but Shere Ali angrily pointed to some English tourists who were within the enclosure.

"Why should we remain outside?" he asked.

"They are Bilati," said Ahmed Ismail in a smooth voice as they moved away. "They are foreigners. The place is sacred to the foreigners. It is Indian soil; but the Indian may not walk on it; no, not though he were born next door. Yet why should we grumble or complain? We are the dirt beneath their feet. We are dogs and sons of dogs, and a hireling will turn our Princes from the gate lest the soles of our shoes should defile their sacred places. And are they not right, Huzoor?" he asked cunningly. "Since we submit to it, since we cringe at their indignities and fawn upon them for their insults, are they not right?"

"Why, that's true, Ahmed Ismail," replied Shere Ali bitterly. He was in the mood to make much of any trifle. This reservation of the enclosure at Cawnpore was but one sign of the overbearing arrogance of the foreigners, the Bilati—the men from over the sea. He had fawned upon them himself in the days of his folly.

"But turn a little, Huzoor," Ahmed whispered in his ear, and led him back. "Look! There is the Bibigarh where the women were imprisoned. That is the house. Through that opening Sirdar Khan and his four companions went—and shut the door behind them. In that room the women of Mecca knelt and prayed for mercy. Come away, Huzoor. We have seen. Those were days when there were men upon the plains of India."

And Shere Ali broke out with a fierce oath.

"Amongst the hills, at all events, there are men today. There is no sacred ground for them in Chiltistan."

"Not even the Road?" asked Ahmed Ismail; and Shere Ali stopped dead, and stared at his companion with startled eyes. He walked away in silence after that; and for the rest of that day he said little to Ahmed Ismail, who watched him anxiously. At night, however, Ahmed was justified of his policy. For Shere Ali appeared before him in the white robes of a Mohammedan. Up till then he had retained the English dress. Now he had discarded it. Ahmed Ismail fell at his feet, and bowed himself to the ground.

"My Lord! My Lord!" he cried, and there was no simulation in his outburst of joy. "Would that your people could behold you now! But we have much to see first. To-morrow we go to Lucknow."

Accordingly the two men travelled the next day to Lucknow. Shere Ali was led up under the broken archway by Evans's Battery into the grounds of the Residency. He walked with Ahmed Ismail at his elbow on the green lawns where the golden-crested hoopoes flashed in the sunlight and the ruined buildings stood agape to the air. They looked peaceful enough, as they strolled from one battery to another, but all the while Ahmed Ismail preached his sermon into Shere Ali's ears. There Lawrence had died; here at the top of the narrow lane had stood Johannes's house whence Nebo the Nailer had watched day after day with his rifle in his hand. Hardly a man, be he never so swift, could cross that little lane from one quarter of the Residency to another, so long as daylight lasted and so long as Nebo the Nailer stood behind the shutters of Johannes's house. Shere Ali was fired by the story of that siege. By so little was the garrison saved. Ahmed Ismail led him down to a corner of the grounds and once more a sentry barred the way.

"This is the graveyard," said Ahmed Ismail, and Shere Ali, looking up, stepped back with a look upon his face which Ahmed Ismail did not understand.

"Huzoor!" he said anxiously, and Shere Ali turned upon him with an imperious word.

"Silence, dog!" he cried. "Stand apart. I wish to be alone."

His eyes were on the little church with the trees and the wall girding it in. At the side a green meadow with high trees, had the look of a playing-ground—the playing-ground of some great public school in England. Shere Ali's eyes took in the whole picture, and then saw it but dimly through a mist. For the little church, though he had never seen it before, was familiar and most moving. It was a model of the Royal Chapel at Eton, and, in spite of himself, as he gazed the tears filled his eyes and the memory of his schooldays ached at his heart. He yearned to be back once more in the shadow of that chapel with his comrades and his friends. Not yet had he wholly forgotten; he was softened out of his bitterness; the burden of his jealousy and his anger fell for awhile from his shoulders. When he rejoined Ahmed Ismail, he bade him follow and speak no word. He drove back to the town, and

A. E. W. Mason

then only he spoke to Ahmed Ismail.

"We will go from Lucknow to-day," he said. "I will not sleep in this town."

"As your Highness wills," said Ahmed Ismail humbly, and he went into the station and bought tickets for Delhi. It was on a Thursday morning that the pair reached that town; and that day Ahmed Ismail had an unreceptive listener for his sermons. The monument before the Post Office, the tablets on the arch of the arsenal, even the barracks in the gardens of the Moghul Palace fired no antagonism in the Prince, who so short a time ago had been a boy at Eton. The memories evoked by the little church at Lucknow had borne him company all night and still clung to him that day. He was homesick for his school. Only twice was he really roused.

The first instance took place when he was driving along the Chandni Chauk, the straight broad tree-fringed street which runs from the Lahore Gate to the Fort. Ahmed Ismail sat opposite to him, and, leaning forward, he pointed to a tree and to a tall house in front of the tree.

"My Lord," said he, "could that tree speak, what groans would one hear!"

"Why?" said Shere Ali listlessly.

"Listen, your Highness," said Ahmed Ismail. Like the rest of his countrymen, he had a keen love for a story. And the love was the keener when he himself had the telling of it. He sat up alertly. "In that house lived an Englishman of high authority. He escaped when Delhi was seized by the faithful. He came back when Delhi was recaptured by the infidels. And there he sat with an English officer, at his window, every morning from eight to nine. And every morning from eight to nine every native who passed his door was stopped and hanged upon that tree, while he looked on. Huzoor, there was no inquiry. It might be some peaceable merchant, some poor man from the countryside. What did it matter? There was a lesson to be taught to this city. And so whoever walked down the Chandni Chauk during that hour dangled from those branches. Huzoor, for a week this went on—for a whole week."

The story was current in Delhi. Ahmed Ismail found it to his hand, and Shere Ali did not question it. He sat up erect, and something of the fire which this last day had been extinct kindled again in his sombre eyes. Later on he drove along the sinuous road on the top of the ridge, and as he looked over Delhi, hidden amongst its foliage, he saw the great white dome of the Jumma Musjid rising above the tree-tops, like a balloon. "The Mosque," he said, standing up in his carriage. "To-morrow we will worship there."

Before noon the next day he mounted the steep broad flight of steps and passed under the red sandstone arch into the vast enclosure. He performed his ablutions at the fountain, and, kneeling upon the marble tiles, waited for the priest to ascend the ladder on to the wooden platform. He knelt with Ahmed Ismail at his side, in the open, amongst the lowliest. In front of him rows of worshippers knelt and bowed their foreheads to the tiles—rows and rows covering the enclosure up to the arches of the mosque itself. There were others too—rows and rows within the arches, in the dusk of the mosque itself, and from man to man emotion passed like a spark upon the wind. The crowd grew denser, there came a suspense, a tension. It gained upon all, it laid its clutch upon Shere Ali. He ceased to think, even upon his injuries, he was possessed with expectancy. And then a man kneeling beside him interrupted his prayers and began to curse fiercely beneath his breath.

"May they burn, they and their fathers and their children, to the last generation!" And he added epithets of a surprising ingenuity. The while he looked backwards over his shoulder.

Shere Ali followed his example. He saw at the back of the enclosure, in the galleries which surmounted the archway and the wall, English men and English women waiting. Shere Ali's blood boiled at the sight. They were laughing, talking. Some of them had brought sandwiches and were eating their lunch. Others were taking photographs with their cameras. They were waiting for the show to begin.

Shere Ali followed the example of his neighbour and cursed them. All his anger kindled again and quickened into hatred. They were so careful of themselves, so careless of others!

"Not a Mohammedan," he cried to himself, "must set foot in their graveyard at Lucknow, but they come to our mosque as to a show."

Suddenly he saw the priest climb the ladder on to the high wooden platform in front of the central arch of the mosque and bow his forehead to the floor. His voice rang out resonant and clear and confident over that vast assemblage.

"There is only one God."

And a shiver passed across the rows of kneeling men, as though unexpectedly a wind had blown across a ripe field of corn. Shere Ali was moved like the rest, but all the while at the back of his mind there was the thought of those white people in the galleries.

"They are laughing at us, they are making a mock of us, they think we are of no account." And fiercely he called upon his God, the God of the Mohammedans, to root them out from the land and cast them as weeds in the flame.

The priest stood up erect upon the platform, and with a vibrating voice, now plaintive and conveying some strange sense of loneliness, now loud in praise, now humble in submission, he intoned the prayers. His voice rose and sank, reverberating back over the crowded courtyard from the walls of the mosque. Shere Ali prayed too, but he prayed silently, with all the fervour of a fanatic, that it might be his hand which should drive the English to their ships upon the sea.

When he rose and came out from the mosque he turned to Ahmed Ismail.

"There are some of my people in Delhi?"

Ahmed Ismail bowed.

"Let us go to them," said Shere Ali; he sought refuge amongst them from the thought of those people in the galleries. Ahmed Ismail was well content with the results of his pilgrimage. Shere Ali, as he paced the streets of Delhi with a fierce rapt look in his eyes, had the very aspect of a Ghazi fresh from the hills and bent upon murder and immolation.

CHAPTER XXIV

NEWS FROM AJMERE

Something of this pilgrimage Ralston understood; and what he understood he explained to Dick Linforth on the top of the tower at Peshawur. Linforth, however, was still perplexed, still unconvinced.

"I can't believe it," he cried; "I know Shere Ali so well."

Ralston shook his head.

"England overlaid the real man with a pretty varnish," he said. "That's all it ever does. And the varnish peels off easily when the man comes back to an Indian sun. There's not one of these people from the hills but has in him the makings of a fanatic. It's a question of circumstances whether the fanaticism comes to the top or not. Given the circumstances, neither Eton, nor Oxford, nor all the schools and universities rolled into one would hinder the relapse."

"But why?" exclaimed Linforth. "Why should Shere Ali have relapsed?"

"Disappointment here, flattery in England—there are many reasons. Usually there's a particular reason."

"And what is that?" asked Linforth.

"The love of a white woman."

Ralston was aware that Linforth at his side started. He started ever so slightly. But Ralston was on the alert. He made no sign, however, that he had noticed anything.

"I know that reason held good in Shere Ali's case," Ralston went on; and there came a change in Linforth's voice. It grew rather stern, rather abrupt.

"Why? Has he talked?"

"Not that I know of. Nevertheless, I am sure that there was one who played a part in Shere Ali's life," said Ralston. "I have known it ever since I first met him—more than a year ago on his way northwards to Chiltistan. He stopped for a day at Lahore and rode out with me. I told him that the Government expected him to marry as soon as possible, and settle down in his own country. I gave him that advice deliberately. You see I wanted to find out. And I did find out. His consternation, his anger, answered me clearly enough. I have no doubt that there was someone over there in England—a woman, perhaps an innocent woman, who had been merely careless—perhaps—"

But he did not finish the sentence. Linforth interrupted him before he had time to complete it. And he interrupted without flurry or any sign of agitation.

"There was a woman," he said. "But I don't think she was thoughtless. I don't see how she could have known that there was any danger in her friendliness. For she was merely friendly to Shere Ali. I know her myself."

The answer was given frankly and simply. For once Ralston was outwitted. Dick Linforth had Violet Oliver to defend, and the defence was well done. Ralston was left without a suspicion that Linforth had any reason beyond the mere truth of the facts to spur him to defend her.

"Yes, that's the mistake," said Ralston. "The woman's friendly and means no more than she says or looks. But these fellows don't understand such friendship. Shere Ali is here dreaming of a woman he knows he can never marry—because of his race. And so he's ready to run amuck. That's what it comes to."

He turned away from the city as he spoke and took a step or two towards the flight of stone stairs which led down from the tower.

"Where is Shere Ali now?" Linforth asked, and Ralston stopped and came back again.

"I don't know," he said. "But I shall know, and very soon. There may be a letter waiting for me at home. You see, when there's trouble brewing over there behind the hills, and I want to discover to what height it has grown and how high it's likely to grow, I select one of my police, a Pathan, of course, and I send him to find out."

"You send him over the Malakand," said Linforth, with a glance towards the great hill-barrier. He was to be astonished by the answer Ralston gave.

"No. On the contrary, I send him south. I send him to Ajmere, in Rajputana."

"In Ajmere?" cried Linforth.

"Yes. There is a great Mohammedan shrine. Pilgrims go there from all parts, but mostly from beyond the frontier. I get my fingers on the pulse of the frontier in Ajmere more surely than I should if I sent spies up into the hills. I have a man there now. But that's not all. There's a great feast in Ajmere this week. And I think I shall find out from there where Shere Ali is and what he's doing. As soon as I do find out, I want you to go to him."

"I understand," said Linforth. "But if he has changed so much, he will have changed to me."

"Yes," Ralston admitted. He turned again towards the steps, and the two men descended to their horses. "That's likely enough. They ought to have sent you to me six months ago. Anyway, you must do your best." He climbed into the saddle, and Linforth did the same.

"Very well," said Dick, as they rode through the archway. "I will do my best," and he turned towards Ralston with a smile. "I'll do my best to hinder the Road from going on."

It was a queer piece of irony that the first real demand made upon him in his life was that he should stop the very thing on the accomplishment of which his hopes were set. But there was his friend to save. He comforted himself with that thought. There was his friend rushing blindly upon ruin. Linforth could not doubt it. How in the world could Shere Ali, he wondered. He could not yet dissociate the Shere Ali of to-day from the boy and the youth who had been his chum.

They passed out of the further gate of Peshawur and rode along the broad white road towards Government House. It was growing dark, and as they turned in at the gateway of the garden, lights shone in the windows ahead of them. The lights recalled to Ralston's mind a fact which he had forgotten to mention.

"By the way," he said, turning towards Linforth, "we have a lady staying with us who knows you."

Linforth leaned forward in his saddle and stooped as if to adjust a stirrup, and it was thus a second or two before he answered.

"Indeed!" he said. "Who is she?"

"A Mrs. Oliver," replied Ralston, "She was at Srinagar in Cashmere this summer, staying with the Resident. My sister met her there, I think she told Mrs. Oliver you were likely to come to us about this time."

Dick's heart leaped within him suddenly. Had Violet Oliver arranged her visit so that it might coincide with his? It was at all events a pleasant fancy to play with. He looked up at the windows of the house. She was really there! After all these months he would see her. No wonder the windows were bright. As they rode up to the porch and the door was opened, he heard her voice. She was singing in the drawing-room, and the door of the drawing-room stood open. She sang in a low small voice, very pretty to the ear, and she was accompanying herself softly on the piano. Dick stood for a while listening in the lofty hall, while Ralston looked over his letters which were lying upon a small table. He opened one of them and uttered an exclamation.

"This is from my man at Ajmere," he said, but Dick paid no attention. Ralston glanced through the letter.

"He has found him," he cried. "Shere Ali is in Ajmere."

It took a moment or two for the words to penetrate to Linforth's mind. Then he said slowly:

"Oh! Shere Ali's in Ajmere. I must start for Ajmere to-morrow."

Ralston looked up from his letters and glanced at Linforth. Something in the abstracted way in which Linforth had spoken attracted his attention. He smiled:

"Yes, it's a pity," he said. But again it seemed that Linforth did not hear. And then the voice at the piano stopped abruptly as though the singer had just become aware that there were people talking in the hall. Linforth moved forward, and in the doorway of the drawing-room he came face to face with Violet Oliver. Ralston smiled again.

"There's something between those two," he said to himself. But Linforth had kept his secrets better half an hour ago. For it did not occur to Ralston to suspect that there had been something also between Violet Oliver and Shere Ali.

CHAPTER XXV

IN THE ROSE GARDEN

"Let us go out," said Linforth.

It was after dinner on the same evening, and he was standing with Violet Oliver at the window of the drawing-room. Behind them an officer and his wife from the cantonment were playing "Bridge" with Ralston and his sister. Violet Oliver hesitated. The window opened upon the garden. Already Linforth's hand was on the knob.

"Very well," she said. But there was a note of reluctance in her voice.

"You will need a cloak," he said.

"No," said Violet Oliver. She had a scarf of lace in her hand, and she twisted it about her throat. Linforth opened the long window and they stepped out into the garden. It was a clear night of bright stars. The chill of sunset had passed, the air was warm. It was dark in spite of the stars. The path glimmered faintly in front of them.

"I was hoping very much that I should meet you somewhere in India," said Dick. "Lately I had grown afraid that you would be going home before the chance came."

"You left it to chance," said Violet.

The reluctance had gone from her voice; but in its place there was audible a note of resentment. She had spoken abruptly and a little sharply, as though a grievance present in her mind had caught her unawares and forced her to give it utterance.

"No," replied Linforth, turning to her earnestly. "That's not fair. I did not know where you were. I asked all who might be likely to know. No one could tell me. I could not get away from my station. So that I had to leave it to chance."

They walked down the drive, and then turned off past the croquet lawn towards a garden of roses and jasmine and chrysanthemums.

"And chance, after all, has been my friend," he said with a smile.

Violet Oliver stopped suddenly. Linforth turned to her. They were walking along a narrow path between high bushes of rhododendrons. It was very dark, so that Linforth could only see dimly her face and eyes framed in the white scarf which she had draped over her hair. But even so he could see that she was very grave.

"I was wondering whether I should tell you," she said quietly. "It was not chance which brought me here—which brought us together again."

Dick came to her side.

"No?" he asked, looking down into her face. He spoke very

A. E. W. Mason

gently, and with a graver voice than he had used before.

"No," she answered. Her eyes were raised to his frankly and simply. "I heard that you were to be here. I came on that account. I wanted to see you again."

As she finished she walked forward again, and again Linforth walked at her side. Dick, though his settled aim had given to him a manner and an aspect beyond his age, was for the same reason younger than his years in other ways. Very early in his youth he had come by a great and definite ambition, he had been inspired by it, he had welcomed and clung to it with the simplicity and whole-heartedness which are of the essence of youth. It was always new to him, however long he pondered over it; his joy in it was always fresh. He had never doubted either the true gold of the thing he desired, or his capacity ultimately to attain it. But he had ordered his life towards its attainment with the method of a far older man, examining each opportunity which came his way with always the one question in his mind—"Does it help?"—and leaving or using that opportunity according to the answer. Youth, however, was the truth of him. The inspiration, the freshness, the simplicity of outlook—these were the dominating elements in his character, and they were altogether compact of youth. He looked upon the world with expectant eyes and an unfaltering faith. Nor did he go about to detect intrigues in men or deceits in women. Violet's words therefore moved him not merely to tenderness, but to self-reproach.

"It is very kind of you to say that," he said, and he turned to her suddenly. "Because you mean it."

"It is true," said Violet simply; and the next moment she was aware that someone very young was standing before her in that Indian garden beneath the starlit sky and faltering out statements as to his unworthiness. The statements were familiar to her ears, but there was this which was unfamiliar: they stirred her to passion.

She stepped back, throwing out a hand as if to keep him from her.

"Don't," she whispered. "Don't!"

She spoke like one who is hurt. Amongst the feelings which had waked in her, dim and for the most part hardly understood, two at all events were clear. One a vague longing for something different from the banal path she daily trod, the other a poignant regret that she was as she was.

But Linforth caught the hand which she held out to thrust him off, and, clasping it, drew her towards him.

"I love you," he said; and she answered him in desperation:

"But you don't know me."

"I know that I want you. I know that I am not fit for you."

And Violet Oliver laughed harshly.

But Dick Linforth paid no attention to that laugh. His hesitation had gone. He found that for this occasion only he had the gift of tongues. There was nothing new and original in what he said. But, on the other hand, he said it over and over again, and the look upon his face and the tone of his voice were the things which mattered. At the opera it is the singer you listen to, and not the words of the song. So in this rose garden Violet Oliver listened to Dick Linforth rather than to what he said. There was audible in his voice from sentence to sentence, ringing through them, inspiring them, the reverence a young man's heart holds for the woman whom he loves.

"You ought to marry, not me, but someone better," she cried. "There is someone I know—in—England—who—"

But Linforth would not listen. He laughed to scorn the notion that there could be anyone better than Violet Oliver; and with each word he spoke he seemed to grow younger. It was as though a miracle had happened. He remained in her eyes what he really was, a man head and shoulders above her friends, and in fibre altogether different. Yet to her, and for her, he was young, and younger than the youngest. In spite of herself, the longing at her heart cried with a louder voice. She sought to stifle it.

"There is the Road," she cried. "That is first with you. That is what you really care for."

"No," he replied quietly. She had hoped to take him at a disadvantage. But he replied at once:

"No. I have thought that out. I do not separate you from the Road. I put neither first. It is true that there was a time when the Road was everything to me. But that was before I met you—do you remember?—in the inn at La Grave."

Violet Oliver looked curiously at Linforth—curiously, and rather quickly. But it seemed that he at all events did not remember that he had not come alone down to La Grave.

"It isn't that I have come to care less for the Road," he went on. "Not by one jot. Rather, indeed, I care more. But I can't dissociate you from the Road. The Road's my life-work; but it will be the better done if it's done with your help. It will be done best of all if it's done for you."

Violet Oliver turned away quickly, and stood with her head averted. Ardently she longed to take him at his word. A glimpse of a great life was vouchsafed to her, such as she had not dreamt of. That some time she would marry again, she had not doubted. But always she had thought of her husband to be, as a man very rich, with no ambition but to please her, no work to do which would thwart her. And here was another life offered, a life upon a higher, a more difficult plane; but a life much more worth living. That she saw clearly enough. But out of her self-knowledge sprang the insistent question:

"Could I live it?"

There would be sacrifices to be made by her. Could she make them? Would not dissatisfaction with herself follow very quickly upon her marriage? Out of her dissatisfaction would there not grow disappointment in her husband? Would not bitterness spring up between them and both their lives be marred?

Dick was still holding her hand.

"Let me see you," he said, drawing her towards him. "Let me see your face!"

She turned and showed it. There was a great trouble in her eyes, her voice was piteous as she spoke.

"Dick, I can't answer you. When I told you that I came here on purpose to meet you, that I wanted to see you again, it was true, all true. But oh, Dick, did I mean more?"

"How should I know?" said Dick, with a quiet laugh—a laugh of happiness.

A. E. W. Mason

"I suppose that I did. I wanted you to say just what you have said to-night. Yet now that you have said it—" she broke off with a cry. "Dick, I have met no one like you in my life. And I am very proud. Oh, Dick, my boy!" And she gave him her other hand. Tears glistened in her eyes.

"But I am not sure," she went on. "Now that you have spoken, I am not sure. It would be all so different from what my life has been, from what I thought it would be. Dick, you make me ashamed."

"Hush!" he said gently, as one might chide a child for talking nonsense. He put an arm about her, and she hid her face in his coat.

"Yes, that's the truth, Dick. You make me ashamed."

So she remained for a little while, and then she drew herself away.

"I will think and tell you, Dick," she said.

"Tell me now!"

"No, not yet. It's all your life and my life, you know, Dick. Give me a little while."

"I go away to-morrow."

"To-morrow?" she cried.

"Yes, I go to Ajmere. I go to find my friend. I must go."

Violet started. Into her eyes there crept a look of fear, and she was silent.

"The Prince?" she asked with a queer suspense in her voice.

"Yes—Shere Ali," and Dick became perceptibly embarrassed. "He is not as friendly to us as he used to be. There is some trouble," he said lamely.

Violet looked him frankly in the face. It was not her habit to flinch. She read and understood his embarrassment. Yet her eyes met his quite steadily.

"I am afraid that I am the trouble," she said quietly.

Dick did not deny the truth of what she said. On the other hand, he had as yet no thought or word of blame for her. There was more for her to tell. He waited to hear it.

"I tried to avoid him here in India, as I told you I meant to do," she said. "I thought he was safe in Chiltistan. I did not let him know that I was coming out. I did not write to him after I had landed. But he came down to Agra—and we met. There he asked me to marry him."

"He asked *you!*" cried Linforth. "He must have been mad to think that such a thing was possible."

"He was very unhappy," Violet Oliver explained. "I told him that it was impossible. But he would not see. I am afraid that is the cause of his unfriendliness."

"Yes," said Dick. Then he was silent for a little while.

"But you are not to blame," he added at length, in a quiet but decisive voice; and he turned as though the subject were now closed.

But Violet was not content. She stayed him with a gesture.

A. E. W. Mason

She was driven that night to speak out all the truth. Certainly he deserved that she should make no concealment. Moreover, the truth would put him to the test, would show to her how deep his passion ran. It might change his thoughts towards her, and so she would escape by the easiest way the difficult problem she had to solve. And the easiest way was the way which Violet Oliver always chose to take.

"I am to blame," she said. "I took jewels from him in London. Yes." She saw Dick standing in front of her, silent and with a face quite inscrutable, and she lowered her head and spoke with the submission of a penitent to her judge. "He offered me jewels. I love them," and she spread out her hands. "Yes, I cannot help it. I am a foolish lover of beautiful things. I took them. I made no promises, he asked for none. There were no conditions, he stipulated for none. He just offered me the pearls, and I took them. But very likely he thought that my taking them meant more than it did."

"And where are they now?" asked Dick.

She was silent for a perceptible time. Then she said:

"I sent them back." She heard Dick draw a breath of relief, and she went on quickly, as though she had been in doubt what she should say and now was sure. "The same night—after he had asked me to marry him—I packed them up and sent them to him."

"He has them now, then?" asked Linforth.

"I don't know. I sent them to Kohara. I did not know in what camp he was staying. I thought it likely he would go home at once."

"Yes," said Dick.

They turned and walked back towards the house. Dick did not speak. Violet was afraid. She walked by his side, stealing every now and then a look at his set face. It was dark; she could see little but the profile. But she imagined it very stern, and she was afraid. She regretted now that she had spoken. She felt now that she could not lose him.

"Dick," she whispered timidly, laying a hand upon his arm; but he made no answer. The lighted windows of the house blazed upon the night. Would he reach the door, pass in and be gone the next morning without another word to her except a formal goodnight in front of the others?

"Oh, Dick," she said again, entreatingly; and at that reiteration of his name he stopped.

"I am very sorry," he said gently. "But I know quite well—others have taken presents from these princes. It is a pity.... One rather hates it. But you sent yours back," and he turned to her with a smile. "The others have not always done as much. Yes, you sent yours back."

Violet Oliver drew a breath of relief. She raised her face towards his. She spoke with pleading lips.

"I am forgiven then?"

"Hush!"

And in a moment she was in his arms. Passion swept her away. It seemed to her that new worlds were opening before her eyes. There were heights to walk upon for her—even for her who had never dreamed that she would even see them near. Their lips touched.

"Oh, Dick," she murmured. Her hands were clasped about

A. E. W. Mason

his neck. She hid her face against his coat, and when he would raise it she would not suffer him. But in a little while she drew herself apart, and, holding his hands, looked at him with a great pride.

"My Dick," she said, and she laughed—a low sweet laugh of happiness which thrilled to the heart of her lover.

"I'll tell you something," she said. "When I said good-bye to him—to the Prince—he asked me if I was going to marry you."

"And you answered?"

"That you hadn't asked me."

"Now I have. Violet!" he whispered.

But now she held him off, and suddenly her face grew serious.

"Dick, I will tell you something," she said, "now, so that I may never tell you it again. Remember it, Dick! For both our sakes remember it!"

"Well?" he asked. "What is it?"

"Don't forgive so easily," she said very gravely, "when we both know that there is something real to be forgiven." She let go of his hands before he could answer, and ran from him up the steps into the house. Linforth saw no more of her that night.

CHAPTER XXVI

THE BREAKING OF THE PITCHER

It is a far cry from Peshawur to Ajmere, and Linforth travelled in the train for two nights and the greater part of two days before he came to it. A little State carved out of Rajputana and settled under English rule, it is the place of all places where East and West come nearest to meeting. Within the walls of the city the great Dargah Mosque, with its shrine of pilgrimage and its ancient rites, lies close against the foot of the Taragarh Hill. Behind it the mass of the mountain rises steeply to its white crown of fortress walls. In front, its high bright-blue archway, a thing of cupolas and porticoes, faces the narrow street of the grain-sellers and the locksmiths. Here is the East, with its memories of Akbar and Shah Jehan, its fiery superstitions and its crudities of decoration. Gaudy chandeliers of coloured glass hang from the roof of a marble mosque, and though the marble may crack and no one give heed to it, the glass chandeliers will be carefully swathed in holland bags. Here is the East, but outside the city walls the pile of Mayo College rises high above its playing-grounds and gives to the princes and the chiefs of Rajputana a modern public school for the education of their sons.

From the roof top of the college tower Linforth looked to the city huddled under the Taragarh Hill, and dimly made out the

A. E. W. Mason

high archway of the mosque. He turned back to the broad playing-fields at his feet where a cricket match was going on. There was the true solution of the great problem, he thought.

"Here at Ajmere," he said to himself, "Shere Ali could have learned what the West had to teach him. Had he come here he would have been spared the disappointments, and the disillusions. He would not have fallen in with Violet Oliver. He would have married and ruled in his own country."

As it was, he had gone instead to Eton and to Oxford, and Linforth must needs search for him over there in the huddled city under the Taragarh Hill. Ralston's Pathan was even then waiting for Linforth at the bottom of the tower.

"Sir," he said, making a low salaam when Linforth had descended, "His Highness Shere Ali is now in Ajmere. Every morning between ten and eleven he is to be found in a balcony above the well at the back of the Dargah Mosque, and to-morrow I will lead you to him."

"Every morning!" said Linforth. "What does he do upon this balcony?"

"He watches the well below, and the water-carriers descending with their jars," said the Pathan, "and he talks with his friends. That is all."

"Very well," said Linforth. "To-morrow we will go to him."

He passed up the steps under the blue portico a little before the hour on the next morning, and entered a stone-flagged court which was thronged with pilgrims. On each side of the archway a great copper vat was raised upon stone steps, and it was about these two vats that the crowd thronged. Linforth and his guide could hardly force their way through. On the steps of the vats natives, wrapped to the eyes in cloths to save themselves from burns, stood emptying the caldrons of boiling ghee. And on every side Linforth heard the name of Shere Ali spoken in praise.

"What does it mean?" he asked of his guide, and the Pathan replied:

"His Highness the Prince has made an offering. He has filled those caldrons with rice and butter and spices, as pilgrims of great position and honour sometimes do. The rice is cooked in the vats, and so many jars are set aside for the strangers, while the people of Indrakot have hereditary rights to what is left. Sir, it is an act of great piety to make so rich an offering."

Linforth looked at the swathed men scrambling, with cries of pain, for the burning rice. He remembered how lightly Shere Ali had been wont to speak of the superstitions of the Mohammedans and in what contempt he held the Mullahs of his country. Not in those days would he have celebrated his pilgrimage to the shrine of Khwajah Mueeyinudin Chisti by a public offering of ghee.

Linforth looked back upon the Indrakotis struggling and scrambling and burning themselves on the steps about the vast caldrons, and the crowd waiting and clamouring below. It was a scene grotesque enough in all conscience, but Linforth was never further from smiling than at this moment. A strong intuition made him grave.

"Does this mark Shere Ali's return to the ways of his fathers?" he asked himself. "Is this his renunciation of the White People?"

He moved forward slowly towards the inner archway, and

the Pathan at his side gave a new turn to his thoughts.

"Sir, that will be talked of for many months," the Pathan said. "The Prince will gain many friends who up till now distrust him."

"It will be taken as a sign of faith?" asked Linforth.

"And more than that," said the guide significantly. "This one thing done here in Ajmere to-day will be spread abroad through Chiltistan and beyond."

Linforth looked more closely at the crowd. Yes, there were many men there from the hills beyond the Frontier to carry the news of Shere Ali's munificence to their homes.

"It costs a thousand rupees at the least to fill one of those caldrons," said the Pathan. "In truth, his Highness has done a wise thing if—" And he left the sentence unfinished.

But Linforth could fill in the gap.

"If he means to make trouble."

But he did not utter the explanation aloud.

"Let us go in," he said; and they passed through the high inner archway into the great court where the saint's tomb, gilded and decked out with canopies and marble, stands in the middle.

"Follow me closely," said the Pathan. "There may be bad men. Watch any who approach you, and should one spit, I beseech your Excellency to pay no heed."

The huge paved square, indeed, was thronged like a bazaar.

Along the wall on the left hand booths were erected, where food and sweetmeats were being sold. Stone tombs dotted the enclosure; and amongst them men walked up and down, shouting and talking. Here and there big mango and peepul trees threw a welcome shade.

The Pathan led Linforth to the right between the Chisti's tomb and the raised marble court surrounded by its marble balustrade in front of the long mosque of Shah Jehan. Behind the tomb there were more trees, and the shrine of a dancing saint, before which dancers from Chitral were moving in and out with quick and flying steps. The Pathan led Linforth quickly through the groups, and though here and there a man stood in their way and screamed insults, and here and there one walked along beside them with a scowling face and muttered threats, no one molested them.

The Pathan turned to the right, mounted a few steps, and passed under a low stone archway. Linforth found himself upon a balcony overhanging a great ditch between the Dargah and Taragarh Hill. He leaned forward over the balustrade, and from every direction, opposite to him, below him, and at the ends, steps ran down to the bottom of the gulf—twisting and turning at every sort of angle, now in long lines, now narrow as a stair. The place had the look of some ancient amphitheatre. And at the bottom, and a little to the right of the balcony, was the mouth of an open spring.

"The Prince is here, your Excellency."

Linforth looked along the balcony. There were only three men standing there, in white robes, with white turbans upon their heads. The turban of one was hemmed with gold. There was gold, too, upon his robe.

"No," said Linforth. "He has not yet come," and even as he

turned again to look down into that strange gulf of steps the man with the gold-hemmed turban changed his attitude and showed Linforth the profile of his face.

Linforth was startled.

"Is that the Prince?" he exclaimed. He saw a man, young to be sure, but older than Shere Ali, and surely taller too. He looked more closely. That small carefully trimmed black beard might give the look of age, the long robe add to his height. Yes, it was Shere Ali. Linforth walked along the balcony, and as he approached, Shere Ali turned quickly towards him. The blood rushed into his dark face; he stood staring at Linforth like a man transfixed.

Linforth held out his hand with a smile.

"I hardly knew you again," he said.

Shere Ali did not take the hand outstretched to him; he did not move; neither did he speak. He just stood with his eyes fixed upon Linforth. But there was recognition in his eyes, and there was something more. Linforth recalled something that Violet Oliver had told to him in the garden at Peshawur—"Are you going to marry Linforth?" That had been Shere Ali's last question when he had parted from her upon the steps of the courtyard of the Fort. Linforth remembered it now as he looked into Shere Ali's face. "Here is a man who hates me," he said to himself. And thus, for the first time since they had dined together in the mess-room at Chatham, the two friends met.

"Surely you have not forgotten me, Shere Ali?" said Linforth, trying to force his voice in to a note of cheery friendliness. But the attempt was not very successful. The look of hatred upon Shere Ali's face had died away, it is true.

But mere impassivity had replaced it. He had aged greatly during those months. Linforth recognised that clearly now. His face was haggard, his eyes sunken. He was a man, moreover. He had been little more than a boy when he had dined with Linforth in the mess-room at Chatham.

"After all," Linforth continued, and his voice now really had something of genuine friendliness, for he understood that Shere Ali had suffered—had suffered deeply; and he was inclined to forgive his temerity in proposing marriage to Violet Oliver—"after all, it is not so much more than a year ago when we last talked together of our plans."

Shere Ali turned to the younger of the two who stood beside him and spoke a few words in a tongue which Linforth did not yet understand. The youth—he was a youth with a soft pleasant voice, a graceful manner and something of the exquisite in his person—stepped smoothly forward and repeated the words to Linforth's Pathan.

"What does he say?" asked Linforth impatiently. The Pathan translated:

"His Highness the Prince would be glad to know what your Excellency means by interrupting him."

Linforth flushed with anger. But he had his mission to fulfil, if it could be fulfilled.

"What's the use of making this pretence?" he said to Shere Ali. "You and I know one another well enough."

And as he ended, Shere Ali suddenly leaned over the balustrade of the balcony. His two companions followed the direction of his eyes; and both their faces became alert with some expectancy. For a moment Linforth imagined that

A. E. W. Mason

Shere Ali was merely pretending to be absorbed in what he saw. But he, too, looked, and it grew upon him that here was some matter of importance—all three were watching in so eager a suspense.

Yet what they saw was a common enough sight in Ajmere, or in any other town of India. The balcony was built out from a brick wall which fell sheer to the bottom of the foss. But at some little distance from the end of the balcony and at the head of the foss, a road from the town broke the wall, and a flight of steep steps descended to the spring. The steps descended along the wall first of all towards the balcony, and then just below the end of it they turned, so that any man going down to the well would have his face towards the people on the balcony for half the descent and his back towards them during the second half.

A water-carrier with an earthen jar upon his head had appeared at the top of the steps a second before Shere Ali had turned so abruptly away from Linforth. It was this man whom the three were watching. Slowly he descended. The steps were high and worn, smooth and slippery. He went down with his left hand against the wall, and the lizards basking in the sunlight scuttled into their crevices as he approached. On his right hand the ground fell in a precipice to the bottom of the gulf. The three men watched him, and, it seemed to Linforth, with a growing excitement as he neared the turn of the steps. It was almost as though they waited for him to slip just at that turn, where a slip was most likely to occur.

Linforth laughed at the thought, but the thought suddenly gained strength, nay, conviction in his mind. For as the water-carrier reached the bend, turned in safety and went down towards the well, there was a simultaneous movement made by the three—a movement of disappointment. Shere

Ali did more than merely move. He struck his hand upon the balustrade and spoke impatiently. But he did not finish the sentence, for one of his companions looked significantly towards Linforth and his Pathan. Linforth stepped forward again.

"Shere Ali," he said, "I want to speak to you. It is important that I should."

Shere Ali leaned his elbows on the balustrade, and gazing across the foss to the Taragarh Hill, hummed to himself a tune.

"Have you forgotten everything?" Linforth went on. He found it difficult to say what was in his mind. He seemed to be speaking to a stranger—so great a gulf was between them now—a gulf as wide, as impassable, as this one at his feet between the balcony and the Taragarh Hill. "Have you forgotten that night when we sat in the doorway of the hut under the Aiguilles d'Arve? I remember it very clearly. You said to me, of your own accord, 'We will always be friends. No man, no woman, shall come between us. We will work together and we will always be friends.'"

By not so much as the flicker of an eyelid did Shere Ali betray that he heard the words. Linforth sought to revive that night so vividly that he needs must turn, needs must respond to the call, and needs must renew the pledge.

"We sat for a long while that night, smoking our pipes on the step of the door. It was a dark night. We watched a planet throw its light upwards from behind the amphitheatre of hills on the left, and then rise clear to view in a gap. There was a smell of hay, like an English meadow, from the hut behind us. You pledged your friendship that night. It's not so very long ago—two years, that's all."

He came to a stop with a queer feeling of shame. He remembered the night himself, and always had remembered it. But he was not given to sentiment, and here he had been talking sentiment and to no purpose.

Shere Ali spoke again to his courtier, and the courtier stepped forward more bland than ever.

"His Highness would like to know if his Excellency is still talking, and if so, why?" he said to the Pathan, who translated it.

Linforth gave up the attempt to renew his friendship with Shere Ali. He must go back to Peshawur and tell Ralston that he had failed. Ralston would merely shrug his shoulders and express neither disappointment nor surprise. But it was a moment of bitterness to Linforth. He looked at Shere Ali's indifferent face, he listened for a second or two to the tune he still hummed, and he turned away. But he had not taken more than a couple of steps towards the entrance of the balcony when his guide touched him cautiously upon the elbow.

Linforth stopped and looked back. The three men were once more gazing at the steps which led down from the road to the well. And once more a water-carrier descended with his great earthen jar upon his head. He descended very cautiously, but as he came to the turn of the steps his foot slipped suddenly.

Linforth uttered a cry, but the man had not fallen. He had tottered for a moment, then he had recovered himself. But the earthen jar which he carried on his head had fallen and been smashed to atoms.

Again the three made a simultaneous movement, but this

time it was a movement of joy. Again an exclamation burst from Shere Ali's lips, but now it was a cry of triumph.

He stood erect, and at once he turned to go. As he turned he met Linforth's gaze. All expression died out of his face, but he spoke to his young courtier, who fluttered forward sniggering with amusement.

"His Highness would like to know if his Excellency is interested in a Road. His Highness thinks it a damn-fool road. His Highness much regrets that he cannot even let it go beyond Kohara. His Highness wishes his Excellency good-morning."

Linforth made no answer to the gibe. He passed out into the courtyard, and from the courtyard through the archway into the grain-market. Opposite to him at the end of the street, a grass hill, with the chalk showing at one bare spot on the side of it, ridged up against the sky curiously like a fragment of the Sussex Downs. Linforth wondered whether Shere Ali had ever noticed the resemblance, and whether some recollection of the summer which he had spent at Poynings had ever struck poignantly home as he had stood upon these steps. Or were all these memories quite dead within his breast?

In one respect Shere Ali was wrong. The Road would go on—now. Linforth had done his best to hinder it, as Ralston had bidden him to do, but he had failed, and the Road would go on to the foot of the Hindu Kush. Old Andrew Linforth's words came back to his mind:

"Governments will try to stop it; but the power of the Road will be greater than the power of any Government. It will wind through valleys so deep that the day's sunshine is gone within the hour. It will be carried in galleries along the faces of the mountains, and for eight months of the year sections

A. E. W. Mason

of it will be buried deep in snow. Yet it will be finished."

How rightly Andrew Linforth had judged! But Dick for once felt no joy in the accuracy of the old man's forecast. He walked back through the city silent and with a heavy heart. He had counted more than he had thought upon Shere Ali's co-operation. His friendship for Shere Ali had grown into a greater and a deeper force than he had ever imagined it until this moment to be. He stopped with a sense of weariness and disillusionment, and then walked on again. The Road would never again be quite the bright, inspiring thing which it had been. The dream had a shadow upon it. In the Eton and Oxford days he had given and given and given so much of himself to Shere Ali that he could not now lightly and easily lose him altogether out of his life. Yet he must so lose him, and even then that was not all the truth. For they would be enemies, Shere Ali would be ruined and cast out, and his ruin would be the opportunity of the Road.

He turned quickly to his companion.

"What was it that the Prince said," he asked, "when the first of those water-carriers came down the steps and did not slip? He beat his hands upon the balustrade of the balcony and cried out some words. It seemed to me that his companion warned him of your presence, and that he stopped with the sentence half spoken."

"That is the truth," Linforth's guide replied. "The Prince cried out in anger, 'How long must we wait?'"

Linforth nodded his head.

"He looked for the pitcher to fall and it did not fall," he said. "The breaking of the pitcher was to be a sign."

"And the sign was given. Do not forget that, your Excellency. The sign was given."

But what did the sign portend? Linforth puzzled his brains vainly over that problem. He had not the knowledge by which a man might cipher out the intrigues of the hill-folk beyond the Frontier. Did the breaking of the pitcher mean that some definite thing had been done in Chiltistan, some breaking of the British power? They might look upon the *Raj* as a heavy burden on their heads, like an earthen pitcher and as easily broken. Ralston would know.

"You must travel back to Peshawur to-night," said Linforth. "Go straight to his Excellency the Chief Commissioner and tell him all that you saw upon the balcony and all that you heard. If any man can interpret it, it will be he. Meanwhile, show me where the Prince Shere Ali lodges in Ajmere."

The policeman led Linforth to a tall house which closed in at one end a short and narrow street.

"It is here," he said.

"Very well," said Linforth, "I will seek out the Prince again. I will stay in Ajmere and try by some way or another to have talk with him."

But again Linforth was to fail. He stayed for some days in Ajmere, but could never gain admittance to the house. He was put off with the politest of excuses, delivered with every appearance of deep regret. Now his Highness was unwell and could see no one but his physician. At another time he was better—so much better, indeed, that he was giving thanks to Allah for the restoration of his health in the Mosque of Shah Jehan. Linforth could not reach him, nor did he ever see him in the streets of Ajmere.

He stayed for a week, and then coming to the house one morning he found it shuttered. He knocked upon the door, but no one answered his summons; all the reply he got was the melancholy echo of an empty house.

A Babu from the Customs Office, who was passing at the moment, stopped and volunteered information.

"There is no one there, Mister," he said gravely. "All have skedaddled to other places."

"The Prince Shere Ali, too?" asked Linforth.

The Babu laughed contemptuously at the title.

"Oho, the Prince! The Prince went away a week ago."

Linforth turned in surprise.

"Are you sure?" he asked.

The Babu told him the very day on which Shere Ali had gone from Ajmere. It was on the day when the pitcher had fallen on the steps which led down to the well. Linforth had been tricked by the smiling courtier like any schoolboy.

"Whither did the Prince go?"

The Babu shrugged his shoulders.

"How should I know? They are not of my people, these poor ignorant hill-folk."

He went on his way. Linforth was left with the assurance that now, indeed, he had really failed. He took the train that night back to Peshawur.

CHAPTER XXVII

AN ARRESTED CONFESSION

Linforth related the history of his failure to Ralston in the office at Peshawur.

"Shere Ali went away on the day the pitcher was broken," he said. "It was the breaking of the pitcher which gave him the notice to go; I am sure of it. If one only knew what message was conveyed—" and Ralston handed to him a letter.

The letter had been sent by the Resident at Kohara and had only this day reached Peshawur. Linforth took it and read it through. It announced that the son of Abdulla Mahommed had been murdered.

"You see?" said Ralston. "He was shot in the back by one of his attendants when he was out after Markhor. He was the leader of the rival faction, and was bidding for the throne against Shere Ali. His murder clears the way. I have no doubt your friend is over the Lowari Pass by this time. There will be trouble in Chiltistan. I would have stopped Shere Ali on his way up had I known."

"But you don't think Shere Ali had this man murdered!" cried Linforth.

A. E. W. Mason

Ralston shrugged his shoulders.

"Why not? What else was he waiting for from ten to eleven in the balcony above the well, except just for this news?"

He stopped for a moment, and went on again in a voice which was very grave.

"That seems to you horrible. I am very much afraid that another thing, another murder much more horrible, will be announced down to me in the next few days. The son of Abdulla Mahommed stood in Shere Ali's way a week ago and he is gone. But the way is still not clear. There's still another in his path."

Linforth interpreted the words according to the gravity with which they were uttered.

"His father!" he said, and Ralston nodded his head.

"What can we do?" he cried. "We can threaten—but what is the use of threatening without troops? And we mayn't use troops. Chiltistan is an independent kingdom. We can advise, but we can't force them to follow our advice. We accept the status quo. That's the policy. So long as Chiltistan keeps the peace with us we accept Chiltistan as it is and as it may be. We can protect if our protection is asked. But our protection has not been asked. Why has Shere Ali fled so quickly back to his country? Tell me that if you can."

None the less, however, Ralston telegraphed at once to the authorities at Lahore. Linforth, though he had failed to renew his old comradeship with Shere Ali, had not altogether failed. He had brought back news which Ralston counted as of great importance. He had linked up the murder in Chiltistan with the intrigues of Shere Ali. That the glare was rapidly broadening over that country of hills and orchards Ralston was very well aware. But it was evident now that at any moment the eruption might take place, and fire pour down the hills. In these terms he telegraphed to Lahore. Quietly and quickly, once more after twenty-five years, troops were being concentrated at Nowshera for a rush over the passes into Chiltistan. But even so Ralston was urgent that the concentration should be hurried.

He sent a letter in cipher to the Resident at Kohara, bidding him to expect Shere Ali, and with Shere Ali the beginning of the trouble.

He could do no more for the moment. So far as he could see he had taken all the precautions which were possible. But that night an event occurred in his own house which led him to believe that he had not understood the whole extent of the danger.

It was Mrs. Oliver who first aroused his suspicions. The four of them—Ralston and his sister, Linforth and Violet Oliver were sitting quietly at dinner when Violet suddenly said:

"It's a strange thing. Of course there's nothing really in it, and I am not at all frightened, but the last two nights, on going to bed, I have found that one of my windows was no longer bolted."

Linforth looked up in alarm. Ralston's face, however, did not change.

"Are you sure that it was bolted before?"

"Yes, quite sure," said Violet. "The room is on the ground floor, and outside one of the windows a flight of steps leads down from the verandah to the ground. So I have always taken care to bolt them myself."

"When?" asked Ralston.

"After dressing for dinner," she replied. "It is the last thing I do before leaving the room."

Ralston leaned back in his chair, as though a momentary anxiety were quite relieved.

"It is one of the servants, no doubt," he said. "I will speak about it afterwards"; and for the moment the matter dropped.

But Ralston returned to the subject before dinner was finished.

"I don't think you need be uneasy, Mrs. Oliver," he said. "The house is guarded by sentinels, as no doubt you know. They are native levies, of course, but they are quite reliable"; and in this he was quite sincere. So long as they wore the uniform they would be loyal. The time might come when they would ask to be allowed to go home. That permission would be granted, and it was possible that they would be found in arms against the loyal troops immediately afterwards. But they would ask to be allowed to go first.

"Still," he resumed, "if you carry valuable jewellery about with you, it would be as well, I think, if you locked it up."

"I have very little jewellery, and that not valuable," said Violet, and suddenly her face flushed and she looked across the table at Linforth with a smile. The smile was returned, and a minute later the ladies rose.

The two men were left alone to smoke.

"You know Mrs. Oliver better than I do," said Ralston. "I will tell you frankly what I think. It may be a mere nothing. There may be no cause for anxiety at all. In any case anxiety is not the word" he corrected himself, and went on. "There is a perfectly natural explanation. The servants may have opened the window to air the room when they were preparing it for the night, and may easily have forgotten to latch the bolt afterwards."

"Yes, I suppose that is the natural explanation," said Linforth, as he lit a cigar. "It is hard to conceive any other."

"Theft," replied Ralston, "is the other explanation. What I said about the levies is true. I can rely on them. But the servants—that is perhaps a different question. They are Mahommedans all of them, and we hear a good deal about the loyalty of Mahommedans, don't we?" he said, with a smile. "They wear, if not a uniform, a livery. All these things are true. But I tell you this, which is no less true. Not one of those Mahommedan servants would die wearing the livery, acknowledging their service. Every one of them, if he fell ill, if he thought that he was going to die, would leave my service to-morrow. So I don't count on them so much. However, I will make some inquiries, and to-morrow we will move Mrs. Oliver to another room."

He went about the business forthwith, and cross-examined his servants one after another. But he obtained no admission from any one of them. No one had touched the window. Was a single thing missing of all that the honourable lady possessed? On their lives, no!

Meanwhile Linforth sought out Violet Oliver in the drawing-room. He found her alone, and she came eagerly towards him and took his hands.

A. E. W. Mason

"Oh, Dick," she said, "I am glad you have come back. I am nervous."

"There's no need," said Dick with a laugh. "Let us go out."

He opened the window, but Violet drew back.

"No, let us stay here," she said, and passing her arm through his she stared for a few moments with a singular intentness into the darkness of the garden.

"Did you see anything?" he asked.

"No," she replied, and he felt the tension of her body relax. "No, there's nothing. And since you have come back, Dick, I am no longer afraid." She looked up at him with a smile, and tightened her clasp upon his arm with a pretty air of ownership. "My Dick!" she said, and laughed.

The door-handle rattled, and Violet proved that she had lost her fear.

"That's Miss Ralston," she said. "Let us go out," and she slipped out of the window quickly. As quickly Linforth followed her. She was waiting for him in the darkness.

"Dick," she said in a whisper, and she caught him close to her.

"Violet."

He looked up to the dark, clear, starlit sky and down to the sweet and gentle face held up towards his. That night and in this Indian garden, it seemed to him that his faith was proven and made good. With the sense of failure heavy upon his soul, he yet found here a woman whose trust was not diminished by any failure, who still looked to him with confidence and drew comfort and strength from his presence, even as he did from hers. Alone in the drawing-room she had been afraid; outside here in the garden she had no fear, and no room in her mind for any thought of fear.

"When you spoke about your window to-night, Violet," he said gently, "although I was alarmed for you, although I was troubled that you should have cause for alarm—"

"I saw that," said Violet with a smile.

"Yet I never spoke."

"Your eyes, your face spoke. Oh, my dear, I watch you," and she drew in a breath. "I am a little afraid of you." She did not laugh. There was nothing provocative in her accent. She spoke with simplicity and truth, now as often, what was set down to her for a coquetry by those who disliked her. Linforth was in no doubt, however. Mistake her as he did, he judged her in this respect more truly than the worldly-wise. She had at the bottom of her heart a great fear of her lover, a fear that she might lose him, a fear that he might hold her in scorn, if he knew her only half as well as she knew herself.

"I don't want you to be afraid of me," he said, quietly. "There is no reason for it."

"You are hard to others if they come in your way," she replied, and Linforth stopped. Yes, that was true. There was his mother in the house under the Sussex Downs. He had got his way. He was on the Frontier. The Road now would surely go on. It would be a strange thing if he did not manage to get some portion of that work entrusted to his hands. He had got his way, but he had been hard, undoubtedly.

A. E. W. Mason

"It is quite true," he answered. "But I have had my lesson. You need not fear that I shall be anything but very gentle towards you."

"In your thoughts?" she asked quickly. "That you will be gentle in word and in deed—yes, of that I am sure. But will you think gently of me—always? That is a different thing."

"Of course," he answered with a laugh.

But Violet Oliver was in no mood lightly to be put off.

"Promise me that!" she cried in a low and most passionate voice. Her lips trembled as she pleaded; her dark eyes besought him, shining starrily. "Oh, promise that you will think of me gently—that if ever you are inclined to be hard and to judge me harshly, you will remember these two nights in the dark garden at Peshawur."

"I shall not forget them," said Linforth, and there was no longer any levity in his tones. He spoke gravely, and more than gravely. There was a note of anxiety, as though he were troubled.

"I promise," he said.

"Thank you," said Violet simply; "for I know that you will keep the promise."

"Yes, but you speak"—and the note of trouble was still more audible in Linforth's voice—"you speak as if you and I were going to part to-morrow morning for the rest of our lives."

"No," Violet cried quickly and rather sharply. Then she moved on a step or two.

"I interrupted you," she said. "You were saying that when I spoke about my window, although you were troubled on my account—"

"I felt at the same time some relief," Linforth continued.

"Relief?" she asked.

"Yes; for on my return from Ajmere this morning I noticed a change in you." He felt at once Violet's hand shake upon his arm as she started; but she did not interrupt him by a word.

"I noticed it at once when we met for the first time since we had talked together in the garden, for the first time since your hands had lain in mine and your lips touched mine. And afterwards it was still there."

"What change?" Violet asked. But she asked the question in a stifled voice and with her face averted from him.

"There was a constraint, an embarrassment," he said. "How can I explain it? I felt it rather than noticed it by visible signs. It seemed to me that you avoided being alone with me. I had a dread that you regretted the evening in the garden, that you were sorry we had agreed to live our lives together."

Violet did not protest. She did not turn to him with any denial in her eyes. She walked on by his side with her face still turned away from his, and for a little while she walked in silence. Then, as if compelled, she suddenly stopped and turned. She spoke, too, as if compelled, with a kind of desperation in her voice.

"Yes, you were right," she cried. "Oh, Dick, you were right. There was constraint, there was embarrassment. I will tell you the reason—now."

"I know it," said Dick with a smile.

Violet stared at him for a moment. She perceived his contentment. He was now quite unharassed by fear. There was no disappointment, no anger against her. She shook her head and said slowly:

"You can't know it."

"I do."

"Tell me the reason then."

"You were frightened by this business of the window."

Violet made a movement. She was in the mood to contradict him. But he went on, and so the mood passed.

"It was only natural. Here were you in a frontier town, a wild town on the borders of a wild country. A window bolted at dinner-time and unlocked at bedtime—it was easy to find something sinister in that. You did not like to speak of it, lest it should trouble your hosts. Yet it weighed on you. It occupied your thoughts."

"And to that you put down my embarrassment?" she asked quietly. They had come again to the window of the drawing-room.

"Yes, I do," he answered.

She looked at him strangely for a few moments. But the compulsion which she had felt upon her a moment ago to speak was gone. She no longer sought to contradict him. Without a word she slipped into the drawing-room.

CHAPTER XXVIII

THE THIEF

Violet Oliver was harassed that night as she had never before been harassed at any moment of her easy life. She fled to her room. She stood in front of her mirror gazing helplessly at the reflection of her troubled face.

"What shall I do?" she cried piteously. "What shall I do?"

And it was not until some minutes had passed that she gave a thought to whether her window on this night was bolted or not.

She moved quickly across the room and drew the curtains apart. This time the bolt was shot. But she did not turn back to her room. She let the curtains fall behind her and leaned her forehead against the glass. There was a moon to-night, and the quiet garden stretched in front of her a place of black shadows and white light. Whether a thief lurked in those shadows and watched from them she did not now consider. The rattle of a rifle from a sentry near at hand gave her confidence; and all her trouble lay in the house behind her.

She opened her window and stepped out. "I tried to speak, but he would not listen. Oh, why did I ever come here?" she

A. E. W. Mason

cried. "It would have been so easy not to have come."

But even while she cried out her regrets, they were not all the truth. There was still alive within her the longing to follow the difficult way—the way of fire and stones, as it would be for her—if only she could! She had made a beginning that night. Yes, she had made a beginning though nothing had come of it. That was not her fault, she assured herself. She had tried to speak. But could she keep it up? She turned and twisted; she was caught in a trap. Passion had trapped her unawares.

She went back to the room and bolted the window. Then again she stood in front of her mirror and gazed at herself in thought.

Suddenly her face changed. She looked up; an idea took shape in her mind. "Theft," Ralston had said. Thus had he explained the unbolted window. She must lock up what jewels she had. She must be sure to do that. Violet Oliver looked towards the window and shivered. It was very silent in the room. Fear seized hold of her. It was a big room, and furtively she peered into the corners lest already hidden behind some curtain the thief should be there.

But always her eyes returned to the window. If she only dared! She ran to her trunks. From one of them she took out from its deep hiding-place a small jewel-case, a jewel-case very like to that one which a few months ago she had sealed up in her tent and addressed to Kohara. She left it on her dressing-table. She did not open it. Then she looked about her again. It would be the easy way—if only she dared! It would be an easier way than trying again to tell her lover what she would have told him to-night, had he only been willing to listen.

She stood and listened, with parted lips. It seemed to her that even in this lighted room people, unseen people, breathed about her. Then, with a little sob in her throat, she ran to the window and shot back the bolt. She undressed hurriedly, placed a candle by her bedside and turned out the electric lights. As soon as she was in bed she blew out the candle. She lay in the darkness, shivering with fear, regretting what she had done. Every now and then a board cracked in the corridor outside the room, as though beneath a stealthy footstep. And once inside the room the door of a wardrobe sprang open. She would have cried out, but terror paralysed her throat; and the next moment she heard the tread of the sentry outside her window. The sound reassured her. There was safety in the heavy regularity of the steps. It was a soldier who was passing, a drilled, trustworthy soldier. "Trustworthy" was the word which the Commissioner had used. And lulled by the soldier's presence in the garden Violet Oliver fell asleep.

But she waked before dawn. The room was still in darkness. The moon had sunk. Not a ray of light penetrated from behind the curtains. She lay for a little while in bed, listening, wondering whether that window had been opened. A queer longing came upon her—a longing to thrust back the curtains, so that—if anything happened—she might see. That would be better than lying here in the dark, knowing nothing, seeing nothing, fearing everything. If she pulled back the curtains, there would be a panel of dim light visible, however dark the night.

The longing became a necessity. She could not lie there. She sprang out of bed, and hurried across towards the window. She had not stopped to light her candle and she held her hands outstretched in front of her. Suddenly, as she was half-way across the room, her hands touched something soft.

A. E. W. Mason

She drew them back with a gasp of fright and stood stone-still, stone-cold. She had touched a human face. Already the thief was in the room. She stood without a cry, without a movement, while her heart leaped and fluttered within her bosom. She knew in that moment the extremity of mortal fear.

A loud scratch sounded sharply in the room. A match spurted into flame, and above the match there sprang into view, framed in the blackness of the room, a wild and menacing dark face. The eyes glittered at her, and suddenly a hand was raised as if to strike. And at the gesture Violet Oliver found her voice.

She screamed, a loud shrill scream of terror, and even as she screamed, in the very midst of her terror, she saw that the hand was lowered, and that the threatening face smiled. Then the match went out and darkness cloaked her and cloaked the thief again. She heard a quick stealthy movement, and once more her scream rang out. It seemed to her ages before any answer came, before she heard the sound of hurrying footsteps in the corridors. There was a loud rapping upon her door. She ran to it. She heard Ralston's voice.

"What is it? Open! Open!" and then in the garden the report of a rifle rang loud.

She turned up the lights, flung a dressing-gown about her shoulders and opened the door. Ralston was in the passage, behind him she saw lights strangely wavering and other faces. These too wavered strangely. From very far away, she heard Ralston's voice once more.

"What is it? What is it?"

And then she fell forward against him and sank in a swoon

upon the floor.

Ralston lifted her on to her bed and summoned her maid. He went out of the house and made inquiries of the guard. The sentry's story was explicit and not to be shaken by any cross-examination. He had patrolled that side of the house in which Mrs. Oliver's room lay, all night. He had seen nothing. At one o'clock in the morning the moon sank and the night became very dark. It was about three when a few minutes after passing beneath the verandah, and just as he had turned the corner of the house, he heard a shrill scream from Mrs. Oliver's room. He ran back at once, and as he ran he heard a second scream. He saw no one, but he heard a rustling and cracking in the bushes as though a fugitive plunged through. He fired in the direction of the noise and then ran with all speed to the spot. He found no one, but the bushes were broken.

Ralston went back into the house and knocked at Mrs. Oliver's door. The maid opened it.

"How is Mrs. Oliver?" he asked, and he heard Violet herself reply faintly from the room:

"I am better, thank you. I was a little frightened, that's all."

"No wonder," said Ralston, and he spoke again to the maid. "Has anything gone? Has anything been stolen? There was a jewel-case upon the dressing-table. I saw it."

The maid looked at him curiously, before she answered. "Nothing has been touched."

Then, with a glance towards the bed, the maid stooped quickly to a trunk which stood against the wall close by the door and then slipped out of the room, closing the door behind her. The corridors were now lighted up, as though it were still evening and the household had not yet gone to bed. Ralston saw that the maid held a bundle in her hands.

"I do not think," she said in a whisper, "that the thief came to steal any thing." She laid some emphasis upon the word.

Ralston took the bundle from her hands and stared at it.

"Good God!" he muttered. He was astonished and more than astonished. There was something of horror in his low exclamation. He looked at the maid. She was a woman of forty. She had the look of a capable woman. She was certainly quite self-possessed.

"Does your mistress know of this?" he asked.

The maid shook her head.

"No, sir. I saw it upon the floor before she came to. I hid it between the trunk and the wall." She spoke with an ear to the door of the room in which Violet lay, and in a low voice.

"Good!" said Ralston. "You had better tell her nothing of it for the present. It would only frighten her"; as he ended he heard Violet Oliver call out:

"Adela! Adela!"

"Mrs. Oliver wants me," said the maid, as she slipped back into the bedroom.

Ralston walked slowly back down the corridor into the great hall. He was carrying the bundle in his hands and his face was very grave. He saw Dick Linforth in the hall, and before he spoke he looked upwards to the gallery which ran round it. Even when he had assured himself that there was no one listening, he spoke in a low voice.

"Do you see this, Linforth?"

He held out the bundle. There was a thick cloth, a sort of pad of cotton, and some thin strong cords.

"These were found in Mrs. Oliver's room."

He laid the things upon the table and Linforth turned them over, startled as Ralston had been.

"I don't understand," he said.

"They were left behind," said Ralston.

"By the thief?"

"If he was a thief"; and again Linforth said:

"I don't understand."

But there was now more of anger, more of horror in his voice, than surprise; and as he spoke he took up the pad of cotton wool.

"You do understand," said Ralston, quietly.

Linforth's fingers worked. That pad of cotton seemed to him more sinister than even the cords.

"For her!" he cried, in a quiet but dangerous voice. "For Violet," and at that moment neither noticed his utterance of her Christian name. "Let me only find the man who entered her room."

Ralston looked steadily at Linforth.

"Have you any suspicion as to who the man is?" he asked.

There was a momentary silence in that quiet hall. Both men stood looking at each other.

"It can't be," said Linforth, at length. But he spoke rather to himself than to Ralston. "It can't be."

Ralston did not press the question.

"It's the insolence of the attempt which angers me," he said. "We must wait until Mrs. Oliver can tell us what happened, what she saw. Meanwhile, she knows nothing of those things. There is no need that she should know."

He left Linforth standing in the hall and went up the stairs. When he reached the gallery, he leaned over quietly and looked down.

Linforth was still standing by the table, fingering the cotton-pad.

Ralston heard him say again in a voice which was doubtful now rather than incredulous:

"It can't be he! He would not dare!"

But no name was uttered.

CHAPTER XXIX

MRS. OLIVER RIDES THROUGH PESHAWUR

Violet Oliver told her story later during that day. But there was a certain hesitation in her manner which puzzled Ralston, at all events, amongst her audience.

"When you went to your room," he asked, "did you find the window again unbolted?"

"No," she replied. "It was really my fault last night. I felt the heat oppressive. I opened the window myself and went out on to the verandah. When I came back I think that I did not bolt it."

"You forgot?" asked Ralston in surprise.

But this was not the only surprising element in the story.

"When you touched the man, he did not close with you, he made no effort to silence you," Ralston said. "That is strange enough. But that he should strike a match, that he should let you see his face quite clearly—that's what I don't understand. It looks, Mrs. Oliver, as if he almost wanted you to recognise him."

A. E. W. Mason

Ralston turned in his chair sharply towards her. "Did you recognise him?" he asked.

"Yes," Violet Oliver replied. "At least I think I did. I think that I had seen him before."

Here at all events it was clear that she was concealing nothing. She was obviously as puzzled as Ralston was himself.

"Where had you seen him?" he asked, and the answer increased his astonishment.

"In Calcutta," she answered. "It was the same man or one very like him. I saw him on three successive evenings in the Maidan when I was driving there."

"In Calcutta?" cried Ralston. "Some months ago, then?"

"Yes."

"How did you come to notice him in the Maidan?" Mrs. Oliver shivered slightly as she answered:

"He seemed to be watching me. I thought so at the time. It made me uncomfortable. Now I am sure. He *was* watching me," and she suddenly came forward a step.

"I should like to go away to-day if you and your sister won't mind," she pleaded.

Ralston's forehead clouded.

"Of course, I quite understand," he said, "and if you wish to go we can't prevent you. But you leave us rather helpless, don't you?—as you alone can identify the man. Besides, you leave yourself too in danger."

"But I shall go far away," she urged. "As it is I am going back to England in a month."

"Yes," Ralston objected. "But you have not yet started, and if the man followed you from Calcutta to Peshawur, he may follow you from Peshawur to Bombay."

Mrs. Oliver drew back with a start of terror and Ralston instantly took back his words.

"Of course, we will take care of you on your way south. You may rely on that," he said with a smile. "But if you could bring yourself to stay here for a day or two I should be much obliged. You see, it is impossible to fix the man's identity from a description, and it is really important that he should be caught."

"Yes, I understand," said Violet Oliver, and she reluctantly consented to stay.

"Thank you," said Ralston, and he looked at her with a smile. "There is one more thing which I should like you to do. I should like you to ride out with me this afternoon through Peshawur. The story of last night will already be known in the bazaars. Of that you may be very sure. And it would be a good thing if you were seen to ride through the city quite unconcerned."

Violet Oliver drew back from the ordeal which Ralston so calmly proposed to her.

"I shall be with you," he said. "There will be no danger—or at all events no danger that Englishwomen are unprepared to face in this country."

A. E. W. Mason

The appeal to her courage served Ralston's turn. Violet raised her head with a little jerk of pride.

"Certainly I will ride with you this afternoon through Peshawur," she said; and she went out of the room and left Ralston alone.

He sat at his desk trying to puzzle out the enigma of the night. The more he thought upon it, the further he seemed from any solution. There was the perplexing behaviour of Mrs. Oliver herself. She had been troubled, greatly troubled, to find her window unbolted on two successive nights after she had taken care to bolt it. Yet on the third night she actually unbolts it herself and leaving it unbolted puts out her light and goes to bed. It seemed incredible that she should so utterly have forgotten her fears. But still more bewildering even than her forgetfulness was the conduct of the intruder.

Upon that point he took Linforth into his counsels.

"I can't make head or tail of it," he cried. "Here the fellow is in the dark room with his cords and the thick cloth and the pad. Mrs. Oliver touches him. He knows that his presence is revealed to her. She is within reach. And she stands paralysed by fear, unable to cry out. Yet he does nothing, except light a match and give her a chance to recognise his face. He does not seize her, he does not stifle her voice, as he could have done—yes, as he could have done, before she could have uttered a cry. He strikes a match and shows her his face."

"So that he might see hers," said Linforth. Ralston shook his head. He was not satisfied with that explanation. But Linforth had no other to offer. "Have you any clue to the man?"

"None," said Ralston.

He rode out with Mrs. Oliver that afternoon down from his house to the Gate of the City. Two men of his levies rode at a distance of twenty paces behind them. But these were his invariable escort. He took no unusual precautions. There were no extra police in the streets. He went out with his guest at his side for an afternoon ride as if nothing whatever had occurred. Mrs. Oliver played her part well. She rode with her head erect and her eyes glancing boldly over the crowded streets. Curious glances were directed at her, but she met them without agitation. Ralston observed her with a growing admiration.

"Thank you," he said warmly. "I know this can hardly be a pleasant experience for you. But it is good for these people here to know that nothing they can do will make any difference—no not enough to alter the mere routine of our lives. Let us go forward."

They turned to the left at the head of the main thoroughfare, and passed at a walk, now through the open spaces where the booths were erected, now through winding narrow streets between high houses. Violet Oliver, though she held her head high and her eyes were steady, rode with a fluttering heart. In front of them, about them, and behind them the crowd of people thronged, tribesmen from the hills, Mohammedans and Hindus of the city; from the upper windows the lawyers and merchants looked down upon them; and Violet held all of them in horror.

The occurrence of last night had inflicted upon her a heavier shock than either Ralston imagined or she herself had been aware until she had ridden into the town. The dark wild face suddenly springing into view above the lighted match was as vivid and terrible to her still, as a nightmare to a child. She

A. E. W. Mason

was afraid that at any moment she might see that face again in the throng of faces. Her heart sickened with dread at the thought, and even though she should not see him, at every step she looked upon twenty of his like—kinsmen, perhaps, brothers in blood and race. She shrank from them in repulsion and she shrank from them in fear. Every nerve of her body seemed to cry out against the folly of this ride.

What were they two and the two levies behind them against the throng? Four at the most against thousands at the least.

She touched Ralston timidly on the arm.

"Might we go home now?" she asked in a voice which trembled; and he looked suddenly and anxiously into her face.

"Certainly," he said, and he wheeled his horse round, keeping close to her as she wheeled hers.

"It is all right," he said, and his voice took on an unusual friendliness. "We have not far to go. It was brave of you to have come, and I am very grateful. We ask much of the Englishwomen in India, and because they never fail us, we are apt to ask too much. I asked too much of you." Violet responded to the flick at her national pride. She drew herself up and straightened her back.

"No," she said, and she actually counterfeited a smile. "No. It's all right."

"I asked more than I had a right to ask," he continued remorsefully. "I am sorry. I have lived too much amongst men. That's my trouble. One becomes inconsiderate to women. It's ignorance, not want of good-will. Look!" To distract her thoughts he began to point her out houses and people which were of interest.

"Do you see that sign there, 'Bahadur Gobind, Barrister-at-Law, Cambridge B.A.,' on the first floor over the cookshop? Yes, he is the genuine article. He went to Cambridge and took his degree and here he is back again. Take him for all in all, he is the most seditious man in the city. Meanly seditious. It only runs to writing letters over a pseudonym in the native papers. Now look up. Do you see that very respectable white-bearded gentleman on the balcony of his house? Well, his daughter-in-law disappeared one day when her husband was away from home—disappeared altogether. It had been a great grief to the old gentleman that she had borne no son to inherit the family fortune. So naturally people began to talk. She was found subsequently under the floor of the house, and it cost that respectable old gentleman twenty thousand rupees to get himself acquitted."

Ralston pulled himself up with a jerk, realising that this was not the most appropriate story which he could have told to a lady with the overstrained nerves of Mrs. Oliver.

He turned to her with a fresh apology upon his lips. But the apology was never spoken.

"What's the matter, Mrs. Oliver?" he asked.

She had not heard the story of the respectable old gentleman. That was clear. They were riding through an open oblong space of ground dotted with trees. There were shops down the middle, two rows backing upon a stream, and shops again at the sides. Mrs. Oliver was gazing with a concentrated look across the space and the people who crowded it towards an opening of an alley between two houses. But fixed though her gaze was, there was no longer any fear in her eyes. Rather they expressed a keen interest, a strong curiosity.

A. E. W. Mason

Ralston's eyes followed the direction of her gaze. At the corner of the alley there was a shop wherein a man sat rounding a stick of wood with a primitive lathe. He made the lathe revolve by working a stringed bow with his right hand, while his left hand worked the chisel and his right foot directed it. His limbs were making three different motions with an absence of effort which needed much practice, and for a moment Ralston wondered whether it was the ingenuity of the workman which had attracted her. But in a moment he saw that he was wrong.

There were two men standing in the mouth of the alley, both dressed in white from head to foot. One stood a little behind with the hood of his cloak drawn forward over his head, so that it was impossible to discern his face. The other stood forward, a tall slim man with the elegance and the grace of youth. It was at this man Violet Oliver was looking.

Ralston looked again at her, and as he looked the colour rose into her cheeks; there came a look of sympathy, perhaps of pity, into her eyes. Almost her lips began to smile. Ralston turned his head again towards the alley, and he started in his saddle. The young man had raised his head. He was gazing fixedly towards them. His features were revealed and Ralston knew them well.

He turned quickly to Mrs. Oliver.

"You know that man?"

The colour deepened upon her face.

"It is the Prince of Chiltistan."

"But you know him?" Ralston insisted.

"I have met him in London," said Violet Oliver.

So Shere Ali was in Peshawur, when he should have been in Chiltistan! "Why?"

Ralston put the question to himself and looked to his companion for the answer. The colour upon her face, the interest, the sympathy of her eyes gave him the answer. This was the woman, then, whose image stood before Shere Ali's memories and hindered him from marrying one of his own race! Just with that sympathy and that keen interest does a woman look upon the man who loves her and whose love she does not return. Moreover, there was Linforth's hesitation. Linforth had admitted there was an Englishwoman for whom Shere Ali cared, had admitted it reluctantly, had extenuated her thoughtlessness, had pleaded for her. Oh, without a doubt Mrs. Oliver was the woman!

There flashed before Ralston's eyes the picture of Linforth standing in the hall, turning over the cords and the cotton pad and the thick cloth. Ralston looked down again upon him from the gallery and heard his voice, saying in a whisper:

"It can't be he! It can't be he!"

What would Linforth say when he knew that Shere Ali was lurking in Peshawur?

Ralston was still gazing at Shere Ali when the man behind the Prince made a movement. He flung back the hood from his face, and disclosing his features looked boldly towards the riders.

A cry rang out at Ralston's side, a woman's cry. He turned in his saddle and saw Violet Oliver. The colour had suddenly fled from her cheeks. They were blanched. The sympathy

A. E. W. Mason

had gone from her eyes, and in its place, stark terror looked out from them. She swayed in her saddle.

"Do you see that man?" she cried, pointing with her hand. "The man behind the Prince. The man who has thrown back his cloak."

"Yes, yes, I see him," answered Ralston impatiently.

"It was he who crept into my room last night."

"You are sure?"

"Could I forget? Could I forget?" she cried; and at that moment, the man touched Shere Ali on the sleeve, and they both fled out of sight into the alley.

There was no doubt left in Ralston's mind. It was Shere Ali who had planned the abduction of Mrs. Oliver. It was his companion who had failed to carry it out. Ralston turned to the levies behind him.

"Quick! Into that valley! Fetch me those two men who were standing there!"

The two levies pressed their horses through the crowd, but the alley was empty when they came to it.

CHAPTER XXX

THE NEEDED IMPLEMENT

Ralston rode home with an uncomfortable recollection of the little dinner-party in Calcutta at which Hatch had told his story of the Englishwoman in Mecca. Had that story fired Shere Ali? The time for questions had passed; but none the less this particular one would force itself into the front of his mind.

"I would have done better never to have meddled," he said to himself remorsefully—even while he gave his orders for the apprehension of Shere Ali and his companion. For he did not allow his remorse to hamper his action; he set a strong guard at the gates of the city, and gave orders that within the gates the city should be methodically searched quarter by quarter.

"I want them both laid by the heels," he said; "but, above all, the Prince. Let there be no mistake. I want Shere Ali lodged in the gaol here before nightfall"; and Linforth's voice broke in rapidly upon his words.

"Can I do anything to help? What can I do?"

Ralston looked sharply up from his desk. There had been a noticeable eagerness, a noticeable anger in Linforth's voice.

A. E. W. Mason

"You?" said Ralston quietly. "*You* want to help? You were Shere Ali's friend."

Ralston smiled as he spoke, but there was no hint of irony in either words or smile. It was a smile rather of tolerance, and almost of regret—the smile of a man who was well accustomed to seeing the flowers and decorative things of life wither over-quickly, and yet was still alert and not indifferent to the change. His work for the moment was done. He leaned back thoughtfully in his chair. He no longer looked at Linforth. His one quick glance had shown him enough.

"So it's all over, eh?" he said, as he played with his paper-knife. "Summer mornings on the Cherwell. Travels in the Dauphine. The Meije and the Aiguilles d'Arves. Oh, I know." Linforth moved as he stood at the side of Ralston's desk, but the set look upon his face did not change. And Ralston went on. There came a kind of gentle mockery into his voice. "The shared ambitions, the concerted plans—gone, and not even a regret for them left, eh? *Tempi passati!* Pretty sad, too, when you come to think of it."

But Linforth made no answer to Ralston's probings. Violet Oliver's instincts had taught her the truth, which Ralston was now learning. Linforth could be very hard. There was nothing left of the friendship which through many years had played so large a part in his life. A woman had intervened, and Linforth had shut the door upon it, had sealed his mind against its memories, and his heart against its claims. The evening at La Grave in the Dauphine had borne its fruit. Linforth stood there white with anger against Shere Ali, hot to join in the chase. Ralston understood that if ever he should need a man to hunt down that quarry through peril and privations, here at his hand was the man on whom he could rely.

Linforth's eager voice broke in again.

"What can I do to help?"

Ralston looked up once more.

"Nothing—for the moment. If Shere Ali is captured in Peshawur—nothing at all."

"But if he escapes."

Ralston shrugged his shoulders. Then he filled his pipe and lit it.

"If he escapes—why, then, your turn may come. I make no promises," he added quickly, as Linforth, by a movement, betrayed his satisfaction. "It is not, indeed, in my power to promise. But there may come work for you—difficult work, dangerous work, prolonged work. For this outrage can't go unpunished. In any case," he ended with a smile, "the Road goes on."

He turned again to his office-table, and Linforth went out of the room.

The task which Ralston had in view for Linforth came by a long step nearer that night. For all night the search went on throughout the city, and the searchers were still empty-handed in the morning. Ahmed Ismail had laid his plans too cunningly. Shere Ali was to be compromised, not captured. There was to be a price upon his head, but the head was not to fall. And while the search went on from quarter to quarter of Peshawur, the Prince and his attendant were already out in the darkness upon the hills.

Ralston telegraphed to the station on the Malakand Pass, to the fort at Jamrud, even to Landi Khotal, at the far end of the Khyber Pass, but Shere Ali had not travelled along any one of the roads those positions commanded.

"I had little hope indeed that he would," said Ralston with a shrug of the shoulders. "He has given us the slip. We shall not catch up with him now."

He was standing with Linforth at the mouth of the well which irrigated his garden. The water was drawn up after the Persian plan. A wooden vertical wheel wound up the bucket, and this wheel was made to revolve by a horizontal wheel with the spokes projecting beyond the rim and fitting into similar spokes upon the vertical wheel. A bullock, with a bandage over its eyes, was harnessed to the horizontal wheel, and paced slowly round and round, turning it; while a boy sat on the bullock's back and beat it with a stick. Both men stood and listened to the groaning and creaking of the wheels for a few moments, and then Linforth said:

"So, after all, you mean to let him go?"

"No, indeed," answered Ralston. "Only now we shall have to fetch him out of Chiltistan."

"Will they give him up?"

Ralston shook his head.

"No." He turned to Linforth with a smile. "I once heard the Political Officer described as the man who stands between the soldier and his medal. Well, I have tried to stand just in that spot as far as Chiltistan is concerned. But I have not succeeded. The soldier will get his medal in Chiltistan this year. I have had telegrams this morning from Lahore. A punitive force has been gathered at Nowshera. The preparations have been going on quietly for a few weeks. It will start in a few days. I shall go with it as Political Officer."

"You will take me?" Linforth asked eagerly.

"Yes," Ralston answered. "I mean to take you. I told you yesterday there might be service for you."

"In Chiltistan?"

"Or beyond," replied Ralston. "Shere Ali may give us the slip again."

He was thinking of the arid rocky borders of Turkestan, where flight would be easy and where capture would be most difficult. It was to that work that Ralston, looking far ahead, had in his mind dedicated young Linforth, knowing well that he would count its difficulties light in the ardour of his pursuit. Anger would spur him, and the Road should be held out as his reward. Ralston listened again to the groaning of the water-wheel, and watched the hooded bullock circle round and round with patient unvarying pace, and the little boy on its back making no difference whatever with a long stick.

"Look!" he said. "There's an emblem of the Indian administration. The wheels creak and groan, the bullock goes on round and round with a bandage over its eyes, and the little boy on its back cuts a fine important figure and looks as if he were doing ever so much, and somehow the water comes up—that's the great thing, the water is fetched up somehow and the land watered. When I am inclined to be despondent, I come and look at my water-wheel." He turned away and walked back to the house with his hands folded behind his back and his head bent forward.

"You are despondent now?" Linforth asked.

"Yes," replied Ralston, with a rare and sudden outburst of

A. E. W. Mason

confession. "You, perhaps, will hardly understand. You are young. You have a career to make. You have particular ambitions. This trouble in Chiltistan is your opportunity. But it's my sorrow—it's almost my failure." He turned his face towards Linforth with a whimsical smile. "I have tried to stand between the soldier and his medal. I wanted to extend our political influence there—yes. Because that makes for peace, and it makes for good government. The tribes lose their fear that their independence will be assailed, they come in time to the Political Officer for advice, they lay their private quarrels and feuds before him for arbitration. That has happened in many valleys, and I had always a hope that though Chiltistan has a ruling Prince, the same sort of thing might in time happen there. Yes, even at the cost of the Road," and again his very taking smile illumined for a moment his worn face. "But that hope is gone now. A force will go up and demand Shere Ali. Shere Ali will not be given up. Even were the demand not made, it would make no difference. He will not be many days in Chiltistan before Chiltistan is in arms. Already I have sent a messenger up to the Resident, telling him to come down."

"And then?" asked Linforth.

Ralston shrugged his shoulders.

"More or less fighting, more or less loss, a few villages burnt, and the only inevitable end. We shall either take over the country or set up another Prince."

"Set up another Prince?" exclaimed Linforth in a startled voice. "In that case—"

Ralston broke in upon him with a laugh.

"Oh, man of one idea, in any case the Road will go on to the foot of the Hindu Kush. That's the price which Chiltistan must pay as security for future peace—the military road through Kohara to the foot of the Hindu Kush."

Linforth's face cleared, and he said cheerfully:

"It's strange that Shere Ali doesn't realise that himself."

The cheerfulness of his voice, as much as his words, caused Ralston to stop and turn upon his companion in a moment of exasperation.

"Perhaps he does." he exclaimed, and then he proceeded to pay a tribute to the young Prince of Chiltistan which took Linforth fairly by surprise.

"Don't you understand—you who know him, you who grew up with him, you who were his friend? He's a man. I know these hill-people, and like every other Englishman who has served among them, I love them—knowing their faults. Shere Ali has the faults of the Pathan, or some of them. He has their vanity; he has, if you like, their fanaticism. But he's a man. He's flattered and petted like a lap-dog, he's played with like a toy. Well, he's neither a lap-dog nor a toy, and he takes the flattery and the petting seriously. He thinks it's *meant*, and he behaves accordingly. What, then? The toy is thrown down on the ground, the lap-dog is kicked into the corner. But he's not a lap-dog, he's not a toy. He's a man. He has a man's resentments, a man's wounded heart, a man's determination not to submit to flattery one moment and humiliation the next. So he strikes. He tries to take the white, soft, pretty thing which has been dangled before his eyes and snatched away—he tries to take her by force and fails. He goes back to his own people, and strikes. Do you blame him? Would you rather he sat down and grumbled and bragged of his successes, and took to drink, as more than one down south has done? Perhaps so. It would be more comfortable if he did. But which of the pictures do you admire? Which of the two is the better man? For me, the man who strikes— even if I have to go up into his country and exact the penalty afterwards. Shere Ali is one of the best of the Princes. But he has been badly treated and so he must suffer."

Ralston repeated his conclusion with a savage irony. "That's the whole truth. He's one of the best of them. Therefore he doesn't take bad treatment with a servile gratitude. Therefore he must suffer still more. But the fault in the beginning was not his."

Thus it fell to Ralston to explain, twenty-six years later, the saying of a long-forgotten Political Officer which had seemed so dark to Colonel Dewes when it was uttered in the little fort in Chiltistan. There was a special danger for the best in the upbringing of the Indian princes in England.

Linforth flushed as he listened to the tirade, but he made no answer. Ralston looked at him keenly, wondering with a queer amusement whether he had not blunted the keen edge of that tool which he was keeping at his side because he foresaw the need of it. But there was no sign of any softening upon Linforth's face. He could be hard, but on the other hand, when he gave his faith he gave it without reserve. Almost every word which Ralston had spoken had seemed to him an aspersion upon Violet Oliver. He said nothing, for he had learned to keep silence. But his anger was hotter than ever against Shere Ali, since but for Shere Ali the aspersions would never have been cast.

CHAPTER XXXI

AN OLD TOMB AND A NEW SHRINE

The messenger whom Ralston sent with a sealed letter to the Resident at Kohara left Peshawur in the afternoon and travelled up the road by way of Dir and the Lowari Pass. He travelled quickly, spending little of his time at the rest-houses on the way, and yet arrived no sooner on that account. It was not he at all who brought his news to Kohara. Neither letter nor messenger, indeed, ever reached the Resident's door, although Captain Phillips learned something of the letter's contents a day before the messenger was due. A queer, and to use his own epithet, a dramatic stroke of fortune aided him at a very critical moment.

It happened in this way. While Captain Phillips was smoking a cheroot as he sat over his correspondence in the morning, a servant from the great Palace on the hill brought to him a letter in the Khan's own handwriting. It was a flowery letter and invoked many blessings upon the Khan's faithful friend and brother, and wound up with a single sentence, like a lady's postscript, in which the whole object of the letter was contained. Would his Excellency the Captain, in spite of his overwhelming duties, of which the Khan was well aware, since they all tended to the great benefit and prosperity of his State, be kind enough to pay a visit to the Khan that day?

A. E. W. Mason

"What's the old rascal up to now?" thought Captain Phillips. He replied, with less ornament and fewer flourishes, that he would come after breakfast; and mounting his horse at the appointed time he rode down through the wide street of Kohara and up the hill at the end, on the terraced slopes of which climbed the gardens and mud walls of the Palace. He was led at once into the big reception-room with the painted walls and the silver-gilt chairs, where the Khan had once received his son with a loaded rifle across his knees. The Khan was now seated with his courtiers about him, and was carving the rind of a pomegranate into patterns, like a man with his thoughts far away. But he welcomed Captain Phillips with alacrity and at once dismissed his Court.

Captain Phillips settled down patiently in his chair. He was well aware of the course the interview would take. The Khan would talk away without any apparent aim for an hour or two hours, passing carelessly from subject to subject, and then suddenly the important question would be asked, the important subject mooted. On this occasion, however, the Khan came with unusual rapidity to his point. A few inquiries as to the Colonel's health, a short oration on the backwardness of the crops, a lengthier one upon his fidelity to and friendship for the British Government and the miserable return ever made to him for it, and then came a question ludicrously inapposite and put with the solemn *naivet,* of a child.

"I suppose you know," said the Khan, tugging at his great grey beard, "that my grandfather married a fairy for one of his wives?"

It was on the strength of such abrupt questions that strangers were apt to think that the Khan had fallen into his second childhood before his time. But the Resident knew his man. He was aware that the Khan was watching for his answer. He sat up in his chair and answered politely:

"So, your Highness, I have heard."

"Yes, it is true," continued the Khan. "Moreover, the fairy bore him a daughter who is still alive, though very old."

"So there is still a fairy in the family," replied Captain Phillips pleasantly, while he wondered what in the world the Khan was driving at. "Yes, indeed, I know that. For only a week ago I was asked by a poor man up the valley to secure your Highness's intercession. It seems that he is much plagued by a fairy who has taken possession of his house, and since your Highness is related to the fairies, he would be very grateful if you would persuade his fairy to go away."

"I know," said the Khan gravely. "The case has already been brought to me. The fellow *will* open closed boxes in his house, and the fairy resents it."

"Then your Highness has exorcised the fairy?"

"No; I have forbidden him to open boxes in his house," said the Khan; and then, with a smile, "But it was not of him we were speaking, but of the fairy in my family."

He leaned forward and his voice shook.

"She sends me warnings, Captain Sahib. Two nights ago, by the flat stone where the fairies dance, she heard them—the voices of an innumerable multitude in the air talking the Chilti tongue—talking of trouble to come in the near days."

He spoke with burning eyes fixed upon the Resident and with his fingers playing nervously in and out among the hairs of his beard. Whether the Khan really believed the story of

A. E. W. Mason

the fairies—there is nothing more usual than a belief in fairies in the countries bordered by the snow-peaks of the Hindu Kush—or whether he used the story as a blind to conceal the real source of his fear, the Resident could not decide. But what he did know was this: The Khan of Chiltistan was desperately afraid. A whole programme of reform was sketched out for the Captain's hearing.

"I have been a good friend to the English, Captain Sahib. I have kept my Mullahs and my people quiet all these years. There are things which might be better, as your Excellency has courteously pointed out to me, and the words have never been forgotten. The taxes no doubt are very burdensome, and it may be the caravans from Bokhara and Central Asia should pay less to the treasury as they pass through Chiltistan, and perhaps I do unjustly in buying what I want from them at my own price." Thus he delicately described the system of barefaced robbery which he practised on the traders who passed southwards to India through Chiltistan. "But these things can be altered. Moreover," and here he spoke with an air of distinguished virtue, "I propose to sell no more of my people into slavery—No, and to give none of them, not even the youngest, as presents to my friends. It is quite true of course that the wood which I sell to the merchants of Peshawur is cut and brought down by forced labour, but next year I am thinking of paying. I have been a good friend to the English all my life, Colonel Sahib."

Captain Phillips had heard promises of the kind before and accounted them at their true value. But he had never heard them delivered with so earnest a protestation. And he rode away from the Palace with the disturbing conviction that there was something new in the wind of which he did not know.

He rode up the valley, pondering what that something new

might be. Hillside and plain were ablaze with autumn colours. The fruit in the orchards—peaches, apples, and grapes—was ripe, and on the river bank the gold of the willows glowed among thickets of red rose. High up on the hills, field rose above field, supported by stone walls. In the bosom of the valley groups of great walnut-trees marked where the villages stood.

Captain Phillips rode through the villages. Everywhere he was met with smiling faces and courteous salutes; but he drew no comfort from them. The Chilti would smile pleasantly while he was fitting his knife in under your fifth rib. Only once did Phillips receive a hint that something was amiss, but the hint was so elusive that it did no more than quicken his uneasiness.

He was riding over grass, and came silently upon a man whose back was turned to him.

"So, Dadu," he said quietly, "you must not open closed boxes any more in your house."

The man jumped round. He was not merely surprised, he was startled.

"Your Excellency rides up the valley?" he cried, and almost he barred the way.

"Why not, Dadu?"

Dadu's face became impassive.

"It is as your Excellency wills. It is a good day for a ride," said Dadu; and Captain Phillips rode on.

It might of course have been that the man had been startled

A. E. W. Mason

merely by the unexpected voice behind him; and the question which had leaped from his mouth might have meant nothing at all. Captain Phillips turned round in his saddle. Dadu was still standing where he had left him, and was following the rider with his eyes.

"I wonder if there is anything up the valley which I ought to know about?" Captain Phillips said to himself, and he rode forward now with a watchful eye. The hills began to close in; the bosom of the valley to narrow. Nine miles from Kohara it became a defile through which the river roared between low precipitous cliffs. Above the cliffs on each side a level of stony ground, which here and there had been cleared and cultivated, stretched to the mountain walls. At one point a great fan of debris spread out from a side valley. Across this fan the track mounted, and then once more the valley widened out. On the river's edge a roofless ruin of a building, with a garden run wild at one end of it, stood apart. A few hundred yards beyond there was a village buried among bushes, and then a deep nullah cut clean across the valley. It was a lonely and a desolate spot. Yet Captain Phillips never rode across the fan of shale and came within sight of it but his imagination began to people it with living figures and a surge of wild events. He reined in his horse as he came to the brow of the hill, and sat for a moment looking downwards. Then he rode very quickly a few yards down the hill. Before, he and his horse had been standing out clear against the sky. Now, against the background of grey and brown he would be an unnoticeable figure.

He halted again, but this time his eyes, instead of roving over the valley, were fixed intently upon one particular spot. Under the wall of the great ruined building he had seen something move. He made sure now of what the something was. There were half a dozen horses—no, seven—seven horses tethered apart from each other, and not a syce for any one of them. Captain Phillips felt his blood quicken. The Khan's protestations and Dadu's startled question, had primed him to expectation. Cautiously he rode down into the valley, and suspense grew upon him as he rode. It was a still, windless day, and noise carried far. The only sound he heard was the sound of the stones rattling under the hoofs of his horse. But in a little while he reached turf and level ground and so rode forward in silence. When he was within a couple of hundred yards of the ruin he halted and tied up his horse in a grove of trees. Thence he walked across an open space, passed beneath the remnant of a gateway into a court and, crossing the court, threaded his way through a network of narrow alleys between crumbling mud walls. As he advanced the sound of a voice reached his ears—a deep monotonous voice, which spoke with a kind of rhythm. The words Phillips could not distinguish, but there was no need that he should. The intonation, the flow of the sentences, told him clearly enough that somewhere beyond was a man praying. And then he stopped, for other voices broke suddenly in with loud and, as it seemed to Phillips, with fierce appeals. But the appeals died away, the one voice again took up the prayer, and again Phillips stepped forward.

At the end of the alley he came to a doorway in a high wall. There was no door. He stood on the threshold of the doorway and looked in. He looked into a court open to the sky, and the seven horses and the monotonous voice were explained to him. There were seven young men—nobles of Chiltistan, as Phillips knew from their *chogas* of velvet and Chinese silk—gathered in the court. They were kneeling with their backs towards him and the doorway, so that not one of them had noticed his approach. They were facing a small rough-hewn obelisk of stone which stood at the head of a low mound of earth at the far end of the court. Six of them were grouped in a sort of semi-circle, and the seventh, a man clad from head to foot in green robes, knelt a little in advance and

A. E. W. Mason

alone. But from none of the seven nobles did the voice proceed. In front of them all knelt an old man in the brown homespun of the people. Phillips, from the doorway, could see his great beard wagging as he prayed, and knew him for one of the incendiary priests of Chiltistan.

The prayer was one with which Phillips was familiar: The Day was at hand; the infidels would be scattered as chaff; the God of Mahommed was besought to send the innumerable company of his angels and to make his faithful people invulnerable to wounds. Phillips could have gone on with the prayer himself, had the Mullah failed. But it was not the prayer which held him rooted to the spot, but the setting of the prayer.

The scene was in itself strange and significant enough. These seven gaily robed youths assembled secretly in a lonely and desolate ruin nine miles from Kohara had come thither not merely for prayer. The prayer would be but the seal upon a compact, the blessing upon an undertaking where life and death were the issues. But there was something more; and that something more gave to the scene in Phillips' eyes a very startling irony. He knew well how quickly in these countries the actual record of events is confused, and how quickly any tomb, or any monument becomes a shrine before which "the faithful" will bow and make their prayer. But that here of all places, and before this tomb of all tombs, the God of the Mahommedans should be invoked—this was life turning playwright with a vengeance. It needed just one more detail to complete the picture and the next moment that detail was provided. For Phillips moved.

His boot rattled upon a loose stone. The prayer ceased, the worshippers rose abruptly to their feet and turned as one man towards the doorway. Phillips saw, face to face, the youth robed in green, who had knelt at the head of his companions.

It was Shere Ali, the Prince of Chiltistan.

Phillips advanced at once into the centre of the group. He was wise enough not to hold out his hand lest it should be refused. But he spoke as though he had taken leave of Shere Ali only yesterday.

"So your Highness has returned?"

"Yes," replied Shere Ali, and he spoke in the same indifferent tone.

But both men knew, however unconcernedly they spoke, that Shere Ali's return was to be momentous in the history of Chiltistan. Shere Ali's father knew it too, that troubled man in the Palace above Kohara.

"When did you reach Kohara?" Phillips asked.

"I have not yet been to Kohara. I ride down from here this afternoon."

Shere Ali smiled as he spoke, and the smile said more than the words. There was a challenge, a defiance in it, which were unmistakable. But Phillips chose to interpret the words quite simply.

"Shall we go together?" he said, and then he looked towards the doorway. The others had gathered there, the six young men and the priest. They were armed and more than one had his hand ready upon his swordhilt. "But you have friends, I see," he added grimly. He began to wonder whether he would himself ride back to Kohara that afternoon.

"Yes," replied Shere Ali quietly, "I have friends in Chiltistan," and he laid a stress upon the name of his country, as though he wished to show to Captain Phillips that he recognised no friends outside its borders.

Again Phillips' thoughts were swept to the irony, the tragic irony of the scene in which he now was called to play a part.

"Does your Highness know this spot?" he asked suddenly. Then he pointed to the tomb and the rude obelisk. "Does your Highness know whose bones are laid at the foot of that monument?"

Shere Ali shrugged his shoulders.

"Within these walls, in one of these roofless rooms, you were born," said Phillips, "and that grave before which you prayed is the grave of a man named Luffe, who defended this fort in those days."

"It is not," replied Shere Ali. "It is the tomb of a saint," and he called to the mullah for corroboration of his words.

"It is the tomb of Luffe. He fell in this courtyard, struck down not by a bullet, but by overwork and the strain of the siege. I know. I have the story from an old soldier whom I met in Cashmere this summer and who served here under Luffe. Luffe fell in this court, and when he died was buried here."

Shere Ali, in spite of himself was beginning to listen to Captain Phillips' words.

"Who was the soldier?" he asked.

"Colonel Dewes."

Shere Ali nodded his head as though he had expected the

name. Then he said as he turned away:

"What is Luffe to me? What should I know of Luffe?"

"This," said Phillips, and he spoke in so arresting a voice that Shere Ali turned again to listen to him. "When Luffe was dying, he uttered an appeal—he bequeathed it to India, as his last service; and the appeal was that you should not be sent to England, that neither Eton nor Oxford should know you, that you should remain in your own country."

The Resident had Shere Ali's attention now.

"He said that?" cried the Prince in a startled voice. Then he pointed his finger to the grave. "The man lying there said that?"

"Yes."

"And no one listened, I suppose?" said Shere Ali bitterly.

"Or listened too late," said Phillips. "Like Dewes, who only since he met you in Calcutta one day upon the racecourse, seems dimly to have understood the words the dead man spoke."

Shere Ali was silent. He stood looking at the grave and the obelisk with a gentler face than he had shown before.

"Why did he not wish it?" he asked at length.

"He said that it would mean unhappiness for you; that it might mean ruin for Chiltistan."

"Did he say that?" said Shere Ali slowly, and there was something of awe in his voice. Then he recovered himself and cried defiantly. "Yet in one point he was wrong. It will not mean ruin for Chiltistan."

So far he had spoken in English. Now he turned quickly towards his friends and spoke in his own tongue.

"It is time. We will go," and to Captain Phillips he said, "You shall ride back with me to Kohara. I will leave you at the doorway of the Residency." And these words, too, he spoke in his own tongue.

There rose a clamour among the seven who waited in the doorway, and loudest of all rose the voice of the mullah, protesting against Shere Ali's promise.

"My word is given," said the Prince, and he turned with a smile to Captain Phillips. "In memory of my friend,"—he pointed to the grave—"For it seems I had a friend once amongst the white people. In memory of my friend, I give you your life."

CHAPTER XXXII

SURPRISES FOR CAPTAIN PHILLIPS

The young nobles ceased from their outcry. They went sullenly out and mounted their horses under the ruined wall of the old fort. But as they mounted they whispered together with quick glances towards Captain Phillips. The Resident intercepted the glance and had little doubt as to the subject of the whispering.

"I am in the deuce of a tight place," he reflected; "it's seven to one against my ever reaching Kohara, and the one's a doubtful quantity."

He looked at Shere Ali, who seemed quite undisturbed by the prospect of mutiny amongst his followers. His face had hardened a little. That was all.

"And your horse?" Shere Ali asked.

Captain Phillips pointed towards the clump of trees where he had tied it up.

"Will you fetch it?" said Shere Ali, and as Phillips walked off, he turned towards the nobles and the old mullah who stood amongst them. Phillips heard his voice, as he began to speak, and was surprised by a masterful quiet ring in it. "The doubtful quantity seems to have grown into a man," he thought, and the thought gained strength when he rode his horse back from the clump of trees towards the group. Shere Ali met him gravely.

"You will ride on my right hand," he said. "You need have no fear."

The seven nobles clustered behind, and the party rode at a walk over the fan of shale and through the defile into the broad valley of Kohara. Shere Ali did not speak. He rode on with a set and brooding face, and the Resident fell once more to pondering the queer scene of which he had been the witness. Even at that moment when his life was in the balance his thoughts would play with it, so complete a piece of artistry it seemed. There was the tomb itself—an earth grave and a rough obelisk without so much as a name or a date upon it set up at its head by some past Resident at Kohara. It was appropriate and seemly to the man without friends, or family, or wife, but to whom the Frontier had been all these. He would have wished for no more himself, since vanity had played so small a part in his career. He had been the great Force upon the Frontier, keeping the Queen's peace by the strength of his character and the sagacity of his mind. Yet before his grave, invoking him as an unknown saint, the nobles of Chiltistan had knelt to pray for the destruction of such as he and the overthrow of the power which he had lived to represent. And all because his advice had been neglected.

Captain Phillips was roused out of his reflections as the cavalcade approached a village. For out of that village and from the fields about it, the men, armed for the most part with good rifles, poured towards them with cries of homage. They joined the cavalcade, marched with it past their homes, and did not turn back. Only the women and the children were left behind. And at the next village and at the next the same thing happened. The cavalcade began to swell into a small army, an army of men well equipped for war; and at the head of the gathering force Shere Ali rode with an impassive face, never speaking but to check a man from time to time who brandished a weapon at the Resident.

"Your Highness has counted the cost?" Captain Phillips asked. "There will be but the one end to it."

Shere Ali turned to the Resident, and though his face did not change from its brooding calm, a fire burned darkly in his eyes.

"From Afghanistan to Thibet the frontier will rise," he said proudly.

Captain Phillips shook his head.

"From Afghanistan to Thibet the Frontier will wait, as it always waits. It will wait to see what happens in Chiltistan."

But though he spoke boldly, he had little comfort from his thoughts. The rising had been well concerted. Those who flocked to Shere Ali were not only the villagers of the Kohara valley. There were shepherds from the hills, wild men from the far corners of Chiltistan. Already the small army could be counted with the hundred for its unit. To-morrow the hundred would be a thousand. Moreover, for once in a way there was no divided counsel. Jealousy and intrigue were not, it seemed, to do their usual work in Chiltistan. There was only one master, and he of unquestioned authority. Else how came it that Captain Phillips rode amidst that great and frenzied throng, unhurt and almost unthreatened?

Down the valley the roof-tops of Kohara began to show amongst the trees. The high palace on the hill with its latticed windows bulked against the evening sky. The sound of many drums was borne to the Resident's ears. The Residency stood a mile and a half from the town in a great garden. A high wall enclosed it, but it was a house, not a fortress; and Phillips had at his command but a few levies to defend it. One of them stood by the gate. He kept his ground as Shere Ali and his force approached. The only movement which he made was to stand at attention, and as Shere Ali halted at the entrance, he saluted. But it was Captain Phillips whom he saluted, and not the Prince of Chiltistan. Shere Ali spoke with the same quiet note of confident authority which had surprised Captain Phillips before, to the seven nobles at his back. Then he turned to the Resident.

"I will ride with you to your door," he said.

The two men passed alone through the gateway and along a broad path which divided the forecourt to the steps of the house. And not a man of all that crowd which followed Shere Ali to Kohara pressed in behind them. Captain Phillips looked back as much in surprise as in relief. But there was no surprise on the face of Shere Ali. He, it was plain, expected obedience.

"Upon my word," cried Phillips in a burst of admiration, "you have got your fellows well in hand."

"I?" said Shere Ali. "I am nothing. What could I do who a week ago was still a stranger to my people? I am a voice, nothing more. But the God of my people speaks through me"; and as he spoke these last words, his voice suddenly rose to a shrill trembling note, his face suddenly quivered with excitement.

Captain Phillips stared. "The man's in earnest," he muttered to himself. "He actually believes it."

It was the second time that Captain Phillips had been surprised within five minutes, and on this occasion the surprise came upon him with a shock. How it had come about—that was all dark to Captain Phillips. But the result was clear. The few words spoken as they had been spoken revealed the fact. The veneer of Shere Ali's English training had gone. Shere Ali had reverted. His own people had claimed him.

"And I guessed nothing of this," the Resident reflected bitterly. Signs of trouble he had noticed in abundance, but this one crucial fact which made trouble a certain and unavoidable thing—that had utterly escaped him. His thoughts went back to the nameless tomb in the courtyard of the fort.

"Luffe would have known," he thought in a very bitter humility. "Nay, he did know. He foresaw."

There was yet a third surprise in store for Captain Phillips. As the two men rode up the broad path, he had noticed that the door of the house was standing open, as it usually did. Now, however, he saw it swing to—very slowly, very noiselessly. He was surprised, for he knew the door to be a strong heavy door of walnut wood, not likely to swing to even in a wind. And there was no wind. Besides, if it had swung to of its own accord, it would have slammed. Its weight would have made it slam. Whereas it was not quite closed. As he reined in his horse at the steps, he saw that there was a chink between the door and the door-post.

"There's someone behind that door," he said to himself, and he glanced quietly at Shere Ali. It would be quite in keeping with the Chilti character for Shere Ali politely to escort him home knowing well that an assassin waited behind the door; and it was with a smile of some irony that he listened to Shere Ali taking his leave.

"You will be safe, so long as you stay within your grounds. I will place a guard about the house. I do not make war against my country's guests. And in a few days I will send an escort and set you and your attendants free from hurt beyond our borders. But"—and his voice lost its courtesy—"take care you admit no one, and give shelter to no one."

The menace of Shere Ali's tone roused Captain Phillips. "I take no orders from your Highness," he said firmly. "Your Highness may not have noticed that," and he pointed upwards to where on a high flagstaff in front of the house the English flag hung against the pole.

"I give your Excellency no orders," replied Shere Ali. "But on the other hand I give you a warning. Shelter so much as one man and that flag will not save you. I should not be able to hold in my men."

Shere Ali turned and rode back to the gates. Captain Phillips dismounted, and calling forward a reluctant groom, gave him his horse. Then he suddenly flung back the door. But there was no resistance. The door swung in and clattered against the wall. Phillips looked into the hall, but the dusk was gathering in the garden. He looked into a place of twilight and shadows. He grasped his riding-crop a little more firmly in his hand and strode through the doorway. In a dark corner something moved.

"Ah! would you!" cried Captain Phillips, turning sharply on the instant. He raised his crop above his head and then a crouching figure fell at his feet and embraced his knees; and a trembling voice of fear cried:

"Save me! Your Excellency will not give me up! I have been a good friend to the English!"

For the second time the Khan of Chiltistan had sought refuge from his own people. Captain Phillips looked round.

"Hush," he whispered in a startled voice. "Let me shut the door!"

CHAPTER XXXIII

IN THE RESIDENCY

Captain Phillips with a sharp gesture ordered the Khan back to the shadowy corner from which he had sprung out. Then he shut the door and, with the shutting of the door, the darkness deepened suddenly in the hall. He shot the bolt and put up the chain. It rattled in his ears with a startling loudness. Then he stood without speech or movement. Outside he heard Shere Ali's voice ring clear, and the army of tribesmen clattered past towards the town. The rattle of their weapons, the hum of their voices diminished. Captain Phillips took his handkerchief from his pocket and wiped his forehead. He had the sensations of a man reprieved.

"But it's only a reprieve," he thought. "There will be no commutation."

He turned again towards the dark corner.

"How did you come?" he asked in a low voice.

"By the orchard at the back of the house."

"Did no one see you?"

"I hid in the orchard until I saw the red coat of one of your servants. I called to him and he let me in secretly. But no one else saw me."

"No one in the city?"

"I came barefoot in a rough cloak with the hood drawn over my face," said the Khan. "No one paid any heed to me. There was much noise and running to and fro, and polishing of weapons. I crept out into the hill-side at the back and so came down into your orchard."

Captain Phillips shrugged his shoulders. He opened a door and led the Khan into a room which looked out upon the orchard.

"Well, we will do what we can," he said, "but it's very little. They will guess immediately that you are here of course."

"Once before—" faltered the Khan, and Phillips broke in upon him impatiently.

"Yes, once before. But it's not the same thing. This is a house, not a fort, and I have only a handful of men to defend it; and I am not Luffe." Then his voice sharpened. "Why didn't you listen to him? All this is your fault—yours and Dewes', who didn't understand, and held his tongue."

The Khan was mystified by the words, but Phillips did not take the trouble to explain. He knew something of the Chilti character. They would have put up with the taxes, with the selling into slavery, with all the other abominations of the Khan's rule. They would have listened to the exhortations of the mullahs without anything coming of it, so long as no leader appeared. They were great accepters of facts as they were. Let the brother or son or nephew murder the ruling

Khan and sit in his place, they accepted his rule without any struggles of conscience. But let a man rise to lead them, then they would bethink them of the exhortations of their priests and of their own particular sufferings and flock to his standard. And the man had risen—just because twenty-five years ago the Khan would not listen to Luffe.

"It's too late, however, for explanations," he said, and he clapped his hands together for a servant. In a few moments the light of a lamp gleamed in the hall through the doorway. Phillips went quickly out of the room, closing the door behind him.

"Fasten the shutters first," he said to the servant in the hall. "Then bring the lamp in."

The servant obeyed, but when he brought the lamp into the room, and saw the Khan of Chiltistan standing at the table with no more dignity of dress or, indeed, of bearing than any beggar in the kingdom, he nearly let the lamp fall.

"His Highness will stay in this house," said Phillips, "but his presence must not be spoken of. Will you tell Poulteney Sahib that I would like to speak to him?" The servant bowed his forehead to the palms of his hand and turned away upon his errand. But Poulteney Sahib was already at the door. He was the subaltern in command of the half company of Sikhs which served Captain Phillips for an escort and a guard.

"You have heard the news I suppose," said Phillips.

"Yes," replied Poulteney. He was a wiry dark youth, with a little black moustache and a brisk manner of speech. "I was out on the hill after chikkor when my shikari saw Shere Ali and his crowd coming down the valley. He knew all about it and gave me a general idea of the situation. It seems the whole country's rising. I should have been here before, but it seemed advisable to wait until it was dark. I crawled in between a couple of guard-posts. There is already a watch kept on the house," and then he stopped abruptly. He had caught sight of the Khan in the background. He had much ado not to whistle in his surprise. But he refrained and merely bowed.

"It seems to be a complicated situation," he said to Captain Phillips. "Does Shere Ali know?" and he glanced towards the Khan.

"Not yet," replied Phillips grimly. "But I don't think it will be long before he does."

"And then there will be ructions," Poulteney remarked softly. "Yes, there will be ructions of a highly-coloured and interesting description."

"We must do what we can," said Phillips with a shrug of his shoulders. "It isn't much, of course," and for the next two hours the twenty-five Sikhs were kept busy. The doors were barricaded, the shutters closed upon the windows and loop-holed, and provisions were brought in from the outhouses.

"It is lucky we had sense enough to lay in a store of food," said Phillips.

The Sikhs were divided into watches and given their appointed places. Cartridges were doled out to them, and the rest of the ammunition was placed in a stone cellar.

"That's all that we can do," said Phillips. "So we may as well dine."

They dined with the Khan, speaking little and with ears on

the alert, in a room at the back of the house. At any moment the summons might come to surrender the Khan. They waited for a blow upon the door, the sound of the firing of a rifle or a loud voice calling upon them from the darkness. But all they heard was the interminable babble of the Khan, as he sat at the table shivering with fear and unable to eat a morsel of his food.

"You won't give me up!... I have been a good friend to the English.... All my life I have been a good friend to the English."

"We will do what we can," said Phillips, and he rose from the table and went up on to the roof. He lay down behind the low parapet and looked over towards the town. The house was a poor place to defend. At the back beyond the orchard the hill-side rose and commanded the roof. On the east of the house a stream ran by to the great river in the centre of the valley. But the bank of the stream was a steep slippery bank of clay, and less than a hundred yards down a small water-mill on the opposite side overlooked it. The Chiltis had only to station a few riflemen in the water-mill and not a man would be able to climb down that bank and fetch water for the Residency. On the west stood the stables and the storehouses, and the barracks of the Sikhs, a square of buildings which would afford fine cover for an attacking force. Only in front within the walls of the forecourt was there any open space which the house commanded. It was certainly a difficult—nay, a hopeless—place to defend.

But Captain Phillips, as he lay behind the parapet, began to be puzzled. Why did not the attack begin? He looked over to the city. It was a place of tossing lights and wild clamours. The noise of it was carried on the night wind to Phillips' ears. But about the Residency there was quietude and darkness. Here and there a red fire glowed where the guards were posted; now and then a shower of sparks leaped up into the air as a fresh log was thrown upon the ashes; and a bright flame would glisten on the barrel of a rifle and make ruddy the dark faces of the watchmen. But there were no preparations for an attack.

Phillips looked across the city. On the hill the Palace was alive with moving lights—lights that flashed from room to room as though men searched hurriedly.

"Surely they must already have guessed," he murmured to himself. The moving lights in the high windows of the Palace held his eyes—so swiftly they flitted from room to room, so frenzied seemed the hurry of the search—and then to his astonishment one after another they began to die out. It could not be that the searchers were content with the failure of their search, that the Palace was composing itself to sleep. In the city the clamour had died down; little by little it sank to darkness. There came a freshness in the air. Though there were many hours still before daylight, the night drew on towards morning. What could it mean, he wondered? Why was the Residency left in peace?

And as he wondered, he heard a scuffling noise upon the roof behind him. He turned his head and Poulteney crawled to his side.

"Will you come down?" the subaltern asked; "I don't know what to do."

Phillips at once crept back to the trap-door. The two men descended, and Poulteney led the way into the little room at the back of the house where they had dined. There was no longer a light in the room; and they stood for awhile in the darkness listening.

A. E. W. Mason

"Where is the Khan?" whispered Phillips.

"I fixed up one of the cellars for him," Poulteney replied in the same tone, and as he ended there came suddenly a rattle of gravel upon the shutter of the window. It was thrown cautiously, but even so it startled Phillips almost into a cry.

"That's it," whispered Poulteney. "There is someone in the orchard. That's the third time the gravel has rattled on the shutter. What shall I do?"

"Have you got your revolver?" asked Phillips.

"Yes."

"Then stand by."

Phillips carefully and noiselessly opened the shutter for an inch or two.

"Who's that?" he asked in a low voice; he asked the question in Pushtu, and in Pushtu a voice no louder than his own replied:

"I want to speak to Poulteney Sahib."

A startled exclamation broke from the subaltern. "It's my shikari," he said, and thrusting open the shutter he leaned out.

"Well, what news do you bring?" he asked; and at the answer Captain Phillips for the first time since he had entered into his twilit hall had a throb of hope. The expeditionary troops from Nowshera, advancing by forced marches, were already close to the borders of Chiltistan. News had been brought to the Palace that evening. Shere Ali had started with every man he could collect to take up the position where he meant to give battle.

"I must hurry or I shall be late," said the shikari, and he crawled away through the orchard.

Phillips closed the shutter again and lit the lamp. The news seemed too good to be true. But the morning broke over a city of women and old men. Only the watchmen remained at their posts about the Residency grounds.

CHAPTER XXXIV

ONE OF THE LITTLE WARS

The campaign which Shere Ali directed on the borders of Chiltistan is now matter of history, and may be read of, by whoso wills, in the Blue-books and despatches of the time. Those documents, with their paragraphs and diaries and bare records of facts, have a dry-as-dust look about them which their contents very often belie. And the reader will not rise from the story of this little war without carrying away an impression of wild fury and reckless valour which will long retain its colours in his mind. Moreover, there was more than fury to distinguish it. Shere Ali turned against his enemies the lessons which they had taught him; and a military skill was displayed which delayed the result and thereby endangered the position of the British troops. For though at the first the neighbouring tribes and states, the little village republics which abound in those parts, waited upon the event as Phillips had foretold, nevertheless as the days passed, and the event still hung in the balance, they took heart of grace and gathered behind the troops to destroy their communications and cut off their supplies.

Dick Linforth wrote three letters to his mother, who was living over again the suspense and terror which had fallen to her lot a quarter of a century ago. The first letter was brought to the house under the Sussex Downs at twilight on an evening of late autumn, and as she recognized the writing for her son's a sudden weakness overcame her, and her hand so shook that she could hardly tear off the envelope.

"I am unhurt," he wrote at the beginning of the letter, and tears of gratitude ran down her cheeks as she read the words. "Shere Ali," he continued, "occupied a traditional position of defence in a narrow valley. The Kohara river ran between steep cliffs through the bed of the valley, and, as usual, above the cliffs on each side there were cultivated maidans or plateaus. Over the right-hand maidan, the road—*our* road—ran to a fortified village. Behind the village, a deep gorge, or nullah, as we call them in these parts, descending from a side glacier high up at the back of the hills on our right, cut clean across the valley, like a great gash. The sides of the nullah were extraordinarily precipitous, and on the edge furthest from us stone sangars were already built as a second line of defence. Shere Ali occupied the village in front of the nullah, and we encamped six miles down the valley, meaning to attack in the morning. But the Chiltis abandoned their traditional method of fighting behind walls and standing on the defence. A shot rang out on the outskirts of our camp at three o'clock in the morning, and in a moment they were upon us. It was reckoned that there were fifteen thousand of them engaged from first to last in this battle, whereas we were under two thousand combatants. We had seven hundred of the Imperial Service troops, four companies of Gurkhas, three hundred men of the Punjab Infantry, three companies of the Oxfordshires, besides cavalry, mountain batteries and Irregulars. The attack was unexpected. We bestrode the road, but Shere Ali brought his men in by an old disused Buddhist road, running over the hills on our right hand, and in the darkness he forced his way through our lines into a little village in the heart of our position. He seized the bazaar and held it all that day, a few

A. E. W. Mason

houses built of stone and with stones upon the roof which made them proof against our shells. Meanwhile the slopes on both sides of the valley were thronged with Chiltis. They were armed with jezails and good rifles stolen from our troops, and they had some old cannon—sher bachas as they are called. Altogether they caused us great loss, and towards evening things began to look critical. They had fortified and barricaded the bazaar, and kept up a constant fire from it. At last a sapper named Manders, with half a dozen Gurkhas behind him, ran across the open space, and while the Gurkhas shot through the loop holes and kept the fire down, Manders fixed his gun cotton at the bottom of the door and lighted the fuse. He was shot twice, once in the leg, once in the shoulder, but he managed to crawl along the wall of the houses out of reach of the explosion, and the door was blown in. We drove them out of that house and finally cleared the bazaar after some desperate fighting. Shere Ali was in the thick of it. He was dressed from head to foot in green, and was a conspicuous mark. But he escaped unhurt. The enemy drew off for the night, and we lay down as we were, dog-tired and with no fires to cook any food. They came on again in the morning, clouds of them, but we held them back with the gatlings and the maxims, and towards evening they again retired. To-day nothing has happened except the arrival of an envoy with an arrogant letter from Shere Ali, asking why we are straying inside the borders of his country 'like camels without nose-rings.' We shall show him why to-morrow. For to-morrow we attack the fort on the maidan. Good-night, mother. I am very tired." And the last sentence took away from Sybil Linforth all the comfort the letter had brought her. Dick had begun very well. He could have chosen no better words to meet her eyes at the commencement than those three, "I am unhurt." But he could have chosen no worse with which to end it. For they had ended the last letter which her husband had written to her, and her mind flew back to that day, and was filled with fore-bodings.

But by the next mail came another letter in his hand, describing how the fort had been carried at the point of the bayonet, and Shere Ali driven back behind the nullah. This, however, was the strongest position of all, and the most difficult to force. The road which wound down behind the fort into the bed of the nullah and zigzagged up again on the far side had been broken away, the cliffs were unscaleable, and the stone sangars on the brow proof against shell and bullet. Shere Ali's force was disposed behind these stone breastworks right across the valley on both sides of the river. For three weeks the British force sat in front of this position, now trying to force it by the river-bed, now under cover of night trying to repair the broken road. But the Chiltis kept good watch, and at the least sound of a pick in the gulf below avalanches of rocks and stones would be hurled down the cliff-sides. Moreover, wherever the cliffs seemed likely to afford a means of ascent Shere Ali had directed the water-channels, and since the nights were frosty these points were draped with ice as smooth as glass. Finally, however, Mrs. Linforth received a third letter which set her heart beating with pride, and for the moment turned all her fears to joy.

"The war is over," it began. "The position was turned this morning. The Chiltis are in full flight towards Kohara with the cavalry upon their heels. They are throwing away their arms as they run, so that they may be thought not to have taken part in the fight. We follow to-morrow. It is not yet known whether Shere Ali is alive or dead and, mother, it was I—yes, I your son, who found out the road by which the position could be turned. I had crept up the nullah time after time towards the glacier at its head, thinking that if ever the position was to be taken it must be turned at that end. At last I thought that I had made out a way up the cliffs. There were some gullies and a ledge and then some rocks which seemed practicable, and which would lead one out on the brow of the cliff just between the two last sangars on the enemy's left. I

A. E. W. Mason

didn't write a word about it to you before. I was so afraid I might be wrong. I got leave and used to creep up the nullah in the darkness to the tongue of the glacier with a little telescope and lie hidden all day behind a boulder working out the way, until darkness came again and allowed me to get back to camp. At last I felt sure, and I suggested the plan to Ralston the Political Officer, who carried it to the General-in-Command. The General himself came out with me, and I pointed out to him that the cliffs were so steep just beneath the sangars that we might take the men who garrisoned them by surprise, and that in any case they could not fire upon us, while sharpshooters from the cliffs on our side of the nullah could hinder the enemy from leaving their sangars and rolling down stones. I was given permission to try and a hundred Gurkhas to try with. We left camp that night at half-past seven, and crept up the nullah with our blankets to the foot of the climb, and there we waited till the morning."

The years of training to which Linforth had bent himself with a definite aim began, in a word, to produce their results. In the early morning he led the way up the steep face of cliffs, and the Gurkhas followed. One of the sharpshooters lying ready on the British side of the nullah said that they looked for all the world like a black train of ants. There were thirteen hundred feet of rock to be scaled, and for nine hundred of it they climbed undetected. Then from a sangar lower down the line where the cliffs of the nullah curved outwards they were seen and the alarm was given. But for awhile the defenders of the threatened position did not understand the danger, and when they did a hail of bullets kept them in their shelters. Linforth followed by his Gurkhas was seen to reach the top of the cliffs and charge the sangars from the rear. The defenders were driven out and bayoneted, the sangars seized, and the Chilti force enfolded while reinforcements clambered in support. "In three hours the position, which for eighteen days had resisted every attack and held the British force immobile, was in our hands. The way is clear in front of us. Manders is recommended for the Victoria Cross. I believe that I am for the D.S.O. And above all the Road goes on!"

Thus characteristically the letter was concluded. Linforth wrote it with a flush of pride and a great joy. He had no doubt now that he would be appointed to the Road. Congratulations were showered upon him. Down upon the plains, Violet would hear of his achievement and perhaps claim proudly and joyfully some share in it herself. His heart leaped at the thought. The world was going very well for Dick Linforth that night. But that is only one side of the picture. Linforth had no thoughts to spare upon Shere Ali. If he had had a thought, it would not have been one of pity. Yet that unhappy Prince, with despair and humiliation gnawing at his heart, broken now beyond all hope, stricken in his fortune as sorely as in his love, was fleeing with a few devoted followers through the darkness. He passed through Kohara at daybreak of the second morning after the battle had been lost, and stopping only to change horses, galloped off to the north.

Two hours later Captain Phillips mounted on to the roof of his house and saw that the guards were no longer at their posts.

A. E. W. Mason

CHAPTER XXXV

A LETTER FROM VIOLET

Within a week the Khan was back in his Palace, the smoke rose once more above the roof-tops of Kohara, and a smiling shikari presented himself before Poulteney Sahib in the grounds of the Residency.

"It was a good fight, Sahib," he declared, grinning from ear to ear at the recollection of the battles. "A very good fight. We nearly won. I was in the bazaar all that day. Yes, it was a near thing. We made a mistake about those cliffs, we did not think they could be climbed. It was a good fight, but it is over. Now when will your Excellency go shooting? I have heard of some markhor on the hill."

Poulteney Sahib stared, speechless with indignation. Then he burst out laughing:

"You old rascal! You dare to come here and ask me to take you out when I go shooting, and only a week ago you were fighting against us."

"But the fight is all over, Excellency," the Shikari explained. "Now all is as it was and we will go out after the markhor." The idea that any ill-feeling could remain after so good a fight was one quite beyond the shikari's conception. "Besides," he said, "it was I who threw the gravel at your Excellency's windows."

"Why, that's true," said Poulteney, and a window was thrown up behind him. Ralston's head appeared at the window.

"You had better take him," the Chief Commissioner said. "Go out with him for a couple of days," and when the shikari had retired, he explained the reason of his advice.

"That fellow will talk to you, and you might find out which way Shere Ali went. He wasn't among the dead, so far as we can discover, and I think he has been headed off from Afghanistan. But it is important that we should know. So long as he is free, there will always be possibilities of trouble."

In every direction, indeed, inquiries were being made. But for the moment Shere Ali had got clear away. Meanwhile the Khan waited anxiously in the Palace to know what was going to happen to him; and he waited in some anxiety. It fell to Ralston to inform him in durbar in the presence of his nobles and the chief officers of the British force that the Government of India had determined to grant him a pension and a residence rent-free at Jellundur.

"The Government of India will rule Chiltistan," said Ralston. "The word has been spoken."

He went out from the Palace and down the hill towards the place where the British forces were encamped just outside the city. When he came to the tents, he asked for Mr. Linforth, and was conducted through the lines. He found Linforth sitting alone within his tent on his camp chair, and knew from his attitude that some evil thing had befallen him. Linforth rose and offered Ralston his chair, and as he did so

A. E. W. Mason

a letter fluttered from his lap to the ground. There were two sheets, and Linforth stooped quickly and picked them up.

"Don't move," said Ralston. "This will do for me," and he sat down upon the edge of the camp bed. Linforth sat down again on his chair and, as though he were almost unaware of Ralston's presence, he smoothed out upon his knee the sheets of the letter. Ralston could not but observe that they were crumpled and creased, as though they had been clenched and twisted in Linforth's hand. Then Linforth raised his head, and suddenly thrust the letter into his pocket.

"I beg your pardon," he said, and he spoke in a spiritless voice. "The post has just come in. I received a letter which— interested me. Is there anything I can do?"

"Yes," said Ralston. "We have sure news at last. Shere Ali has fled to the north. The opportunity you asked for at Peshawur has come."

Linforth was silent for a little while. Then he said slowly:

"I see. I am to go in pursuit?"

"Yes!"

It seemed that Linforth's animosity against Shere Ali had died out. Ralston watched him keenly from the bed. Something had blunted the edge of the tool just when the time had come to use it. He threw an extra earnestness into his voice.

"You have got to do more than go in pursuit of him. You have got to find him. You have got to bring him back as your prisoner."

Linforth nodded his head.

"He has gone north, you say?"

"Yes. Somewhere in Central Asia you will find him," and as Linforth looked up startled, Ralston continued calmly, "Yes, it's a large order, I know, but it's not quite so large as it looks. The trade-routes, the only possible roads, are not so very many. No man can keep his comings and goings secret for very long in that country. You will soon get wind of him, and when you do you must never let him shake you off."

"Very well," said Linforth, listlessly. "When do I start?"

Ralston plunged into the details of the expedition and told him the number of men he was to take with him.

"You had better go first into Chinese Turkestan," he said. "There are a number of Hindu merchants settled there—we will give you letters to them. Some of them will be able to put you on the track of Shere Ali. You will have to round him up into a corner, I expect. And whatever you do, head him off Russian territory. For we want him. We want him brought back into Kohara. It will have a great effect on this country. It will show them that the Sirkar can even pick a man out of the bazaars of Central Asia if he is rash enough to stand up against it in revolt."

"That will be rather humiliating for Shere Ali," said Linforth, after a short pause; and Ralston sat up on the bed. What in the world, he wondered, could Linforth have read in his letter, so to change him? He was actually sympathising with Shere Ali—he who had been hottest in his anger.

"Shere Ali should have thought of that before," Ralston said sharply, and he rose to his feet. "I rely upon you, Linforth. It

A. E. W. Mason

may take you a year. It may take you only a few months. But I rely upon you to bring Shere Ali back. And when you do," he added, with a smile, "there's the road waiting for you."

But for once even that promise failed to stir Dick Linforth into enthusiasm.

"I will do my best," he said quietly; and with that Ralston left him.

Linforth sat down in his chair and once more took out the crumpled letter. He had walked with the Gods of late, like one immune from earthly troubles. But his bad hour had been awaiting him. The letter was signed Violet. He read it through again, and this was what he read:

"This is the most difficult letter I have ever written. For I don't feel that I can make you understand at all just how things are. But somehow or other I do feel that this is going to hurt you frightfully, and, oh, Dick, do forgive me. But if it will console or help at all, know this," and the words were underlined—as indeed were many words in Violet Oliver's letters—"that I never was good enough for you and you are well rid of me. I told you what I was, didn't I, Dick?—a foolish lover of beautiful things. I tried to tell you the whole truth that last evening in the garden at Peshawur, but you wouldn't let me, Dick. And I must tell you now. I never sent the pearl necklace back, Dick, although I told you that I did. I meant to send it back the night when I parted from the Prince. I packed it up and put it ready. But—oh, Dick, how can I tell you?—I had had an imitation one made just like it for safety, and in the night I got up and changed them. I couldn't part with it—I sent back the false one. Now you know me, Dick! But even now perhaps you don't. You remember the night in Peshawur, the terrible night? Mr. Ralston wondered why, after complaining that my window was unbolted, I unbolted it myself. Let me tell you, Dick! Mr. Ralston said that 'theft' was the explanation. Well, after I tried to tell you in the garden and you would not listen, I thought of what he had said. I thought it would be such an easy way out of it, if the thief should come in when I was asleep and steal the necklace and go away again before I woke up. I don't know how I brought myself to do it. It was you, Dick! I had just left you, I was full of thoughts of you. So I slipped back the bolt myself. But you see, Dick, what I am. Although I wanted to send that necklace back, I couldn't, I *simply couldn't*, and it's the same with other things. I would be very, very glad to know that I could be happy with you, dear, and live your life. But I know that I couldn't, that it wouldn't last, that I should be longing for other things, foolish things and vanities. Again, Dick, you are well rid of a silly vain woman, and I wish you all happiness in that riddance. I never would have made you a good wife. Nor will I make any man a good wife. I have not the sense of a dog. I know it, too! That's the sad part of it all, Dick. Forgive me, and thanks, a thousand thanks, for the honour you ever did me in wanting me at all." Then followed—it seemed to Linforth—a cry. "Won't you forgive me, dear, dear Dick!" and after these words her name, "Violet."

But even so the letter was not ended. A postscript was added:

"I shall always think of the little dreams we had together of our future, and regret that I couldn't know them. That will always be in my mind. Remember that! Perhaps some day we will meet. Oh, Dick, good-bye!"

Dick sat with that letter before his eyes for a long while. Violet had told him that he could be hard, but he was not hard to her. He could read between the lines, he understood the struggle which she had had with herself, he recognised the suffering which the letter had caused her. He was touched to pity, to a greater humanity. He had shown it in his forecasts of the humiliation which would befall Shere Ali when he was brought back a prisoner to Kohara. Linforth, in a word, had shed what was left of his boyhood. He had come to recognise that life was never all black and all white. He tore up the letter into tiny fragments. It required no answer.

"Everything is just wrong," he said to himself, gently, as he thought over Shere Ali, Violet, himself. "Everything is just not what it might have been."

And a few days later he started northwards for Turkestan.

CHAPTER XXXVI

"THE LITTLE LESS—"

Three years passed before Linforth returned on leave to England. He landed at Marseilles towards the end of September, travelled to his home, and a fortnight later came up from Sussex for a few days to London. It was the beginning of the autumn season. People were returning to town. Theatres were re-opening with new plays; and a fellow-officer, who had a couple of stalls for the first production of a comedy about which public curiosity was whetted, meeting Linforth in the hall of his club, suggested that they should go together.

"I shall be glad," said Linforth. "I always go to the play with the keenest of pleasure. The tuning-up of the orchestra and the rising of the curtain are events to me. And, to be honest, I have never been to a first night before. Let us do the thing handsomely and dine together before we go. It will be my last excitement in London for another three or four years, I expect."

The two young men dined together accordingly at one of the great restaurants. Linforth, fresh from the deep valleys of Chiltistan, was elated by the lights, the neighbourhood of people delicately dressed, and the subdued throb of music

A. E. W. Mason

from muted violins.

"I am the little boy at the bright shop window," he said with a laugh, while his eyes wandered round the room. "I look in through the glass from the pavement outside, and—"

His voice halted and stopped; and when he resumed he spoke without his former gaiety. Indeed, the change of note was more perceptible than the brief pause. His friend conjectured that the words which Linforth now used were not those which he had intended to speak a moment ago.

"—and," he said slowly, "I wonder what sort of fairyland it is actually to live and breathe in?"

While he spoke, his eyes were seeking an answer to his question, and seeking it in one particular quarter. A few tables away, and behind Linforth's friend and a little to his right, sat Violet Oliver. She was with a party of six or eight people, of whom Linforth took no note. He had eyes only for her. Bitterness had long since ceased to colour his thoughts of Violet Oliver. And though he had not forgotten, there was no longer any living pain in his memories. So much had intervened since he had walked with her in the rose-garden at Peshawur—so many new experiences, so much compulsion of hard endeavour. When his recollections went back to the rose-garden at Peshawur, as at rare times they would, he was only conscious at the worst that his life was rather dull when tested by the high aspirations of his youth. There was less music in it than he had thought to hear. Instead of swinging in a soldier's march to the sound of drums and bugles down the road, it walked sedately. To use his own phrase, every-thing was—*just not*. There was no more in it than that. And indeed at the first it was almost an effort for him to realise that between him and this woman whom he now actually saw, after three years, there had once existed a bond of passion. But, as he continued to look, the memories took substance, and he began to wonder whether in her fairyland it was "just not," too. She had what she had wanted—that was clear. A collar of pearls, fastened with a diamond bow, encircled her throat. A great diamond flashed upon her bosom. Was she satisfied? Did no memory of the short week during which she had longed to tread the road of fire and stones, the road of high endeavour, trouble her content?

Linforth was curious. She was not paying much heed to the talk about the table. She took no part in it, but sat with her head a little raised, her eyes dreamily fixed upon nothing in particular. But Linforth remembered with a smile that there was no inference to be drawn from that not unusual attitude of hers. It did not follow that she was bored or filled with discontent. She might simply be oblivious. A remark made about her by some forgotten person who had asked a question and received no answer came back to Linforth and called a smile to his face. "You might imagine that Violet Oliver is thinking of the angels. She is probably considering whether she should run upstairs and powder her nose."

Linforth began to look for other signs; and it seemed to him that the world had gone well with her. She had a kind of settled look, almost a sleekness, as though anxiety never came near to her pillow. She had married, surely, and married well. The jewels she wore were evidence, and Linforth began to speculate which of the party was her husband. They were young people who were gathered at the table. In her liking for young people about her she had not changed. Of the men no one was noticeable, but Violet Oliver, as he remembered, would hardly have chosen a noticeable man. She would have chosen someone with great wealth and no ambitions, one who was young enough to ask nothing more from the world than Violet Oliver, who would not, in a word, trouble her with a career. She might have chosen anyone of her companions. And then her eyes travelled round the room and met his.

For a moment she gazed at him, not seeing him at all. In a moment or two consciousness came to her. Her brows went up in astonishment. Then she smiled and waved her hand to him across the room—gaily, without a trace of embarrassment, without even the colour rising to her cheeks. Thus might one greet a casual friend of yesterday. Linforth bethought him, with a sudden sting of bitterness which surprised him by its sharpness, of the postscript in the last of the few letters she had written to him. That letter was still vivid enough in his memories for him to be able to see the pages, to recognise the writing, and read the sentences.

"I shall always think of the little dreams we had together of our future, and regret that I couldn't know them. That will always be in my mind. Remember that!"

How much of that postscript remained true, he wondered, after these three years. Very little, it seemed. Linforth fell to speculating, with an increasing interest, as to which of the men at her table she had mated with. Was it the tall youth with the commonplace good looks opposite to her? Linforth detected now a certain flashiness in his well grooming which he had not noticed before. Or was it the fat insignificant young man three seats away from her?

A rather gross young person, Linforth thought him—the offspring of some provincial tradesman who had retired with a fortune and made a gentleman of his son.

"Well, no doubt he has the dibs," Linforth found himself saying with an unexpected irritation, as he contemplated the possible husband. And his friend broke in upon his thoughts.

"If you are going to eat any dinner, Linforth, it might be as well to begin; we shall have to go very shortly."

Linforth fell to accordingly. His appetite was not impaired, he was happy to notice, but, on the whole, he wished he had not seen Violet Oliver. This was his last night in London. She might so easily have come to-morrow instead, when he would already have departed from the town. It was a pity.

He did not look towards her table any more, but the moment her party rose he was nevertheless aware of its movement. He was conscious that she passed through the restaurant towards the lobby at no great distance from himself. He was aware, though he did not raise his head, that she was looking at him.

Five minutes afterwards the waiter brought to him a folded piece of paper. He opened it and read:

"Dick, won't you speak to me at all? I am waiting.— VIOLET."

Linforth looked up at his friend.

"There is someone I must go and speak to," he said. "I won't be five minutes."

He rose from the table and walked out of the restaurant. His heart was beating rather fast, but it was surely curiosity which produced that effect. Curiosity to know whether with her things were—just not, too. He passed across the hall and up the steps. On the top of the steps she was waiting for him. She had her cloak upon her shoulders, and in the background the gross young man waited for her without interposing—the very image of a docile husband.

A. E. W. Mason

"Dick," she said quickly, as she held out her hand to him, "I did so want to talk to you. I have to rush off to a theatre. So I sent in for you. Why wouldn't you speak to me?"

That he should have any reason to avoid her she seemed calmly and completely unconscious. And so unembarrassed was her manner that even with her voice in his ears and her face before him, delicate and pretty as of old, Dick almost believed that never had he spoken of love to her, and never had she answered him.

"You are married?" he asked.

Violet nodded her head. She did not, however, introduce her husband. She took no notice of him whatever. She did not mention her new name.

"And you?" she asked.

Linforth laughed rather harshly.

"No."

Perhaps the harshness of the laugh troubled her. Her forehead puckered. She dropped her eyes from his face.

"But you will," she said in a low voice.

Linforth did not answer, and in a moment or two she raised her head again. The trouble had gone from her face. She smiled brightly.

"And the Road?" she asked. She had just remembered it. She had almost an air of triumph in remembering it. All these old memories were so dim. But at the awkward difficult moment, by an inspiration she had remembered the great long-cherished aim of Dick Linforth's life. The Road! Dick wondered whether she remembered too that there had been a time when for a few days she had thought to have a share herself in the making of that road which was to leave India safe.

"It goes on," he said quietly. "It has passed Kohara. It has passed the fort where Luffe died. But I beg your pardon. Luffe belongs to the past, too, very much to the past—more even than I do."

Violet paid no heed to the sarcasm. She had not heard it. She was thinking of something else. It seemed that she had something to say, but found the utterance difficult. Once or twice she looked up at Dick Linforth and looked down again and played with the fringe of her cloak. In the background the docile husband moved restlessly.

"There's a question I should like to ask," she said quickly, and then stopped.

Linforth helped her out.

"Perhaps I can guess the question."

"It's about—" she began, and Linforth nodded his head.

"Shere Ali?" he said.

"Yes," replied Violet.

Linforth hesitated, looking at his companion. How much should he tell her, he asked himself? The whole truth? If he did, would it trouble her? He wondered. He had no wish to hurt her. He began warily:

A. E. W. Mason

"After the campaign was over in Chiltistan I was sent after him."

"Yes. I heard that before I left India," she replied.

"I hunted him," and it seemed to Linforth that she flinched. "There's no other word, I am afraid. I hunted him—for months, from the borders of Tibet to the borders of Russia. In the end I caught him."

"I heard that, too," she said.

"I came up with him one morning, in a desert of stones. He was with three of his followers. The only three who had been loyal to him. They had camped as best they could under the shelter of a boulder. It was very cold. They had no coverings and little food. The place was as desolate as you could imagine—a wilderness of boulders and stones stretching away to the round of the sky, level as the palm of your hand, with a ragged tree growing up here and there. If we had not come up with them that day I think they would have died."

He spoke with his eyes upon Violet, ready to modify his words at the first evidence of pain. She gave that evidence as he ended. She drew her cloak closer about her and shivered.

"What did he say?" she asked.

"To me? Nothing. We spoke only formally. All the way back to India we behaved as strangers. It was easier for both of us. I brought him down through Chiltistan and Kohara into India. I brought him down—along the Road which at Eton we had planned to carry on together. Down that road we came together—I the captor, he the prisoner."

Again Violet flinched.

"And where is he now?" she asked in a low voice.

Suddenly Linforth turned round and looked down the steps, across the hall to the glass walls of the restaurant.

"Did he ever come here with you?" he asked. "Did he ever dine with you there amongst the lights and the merry-makers and the music?"

"Yes," she answered.

Linforth laughed, and again there was a note of bitterness in the laughter.

"How long ago it seems! Shere Ali will dine here no more. He is in Burma. He was deported to Burma."

He told her no more than that. There was no need that she should know that Shere Ali, broken-hearted, ruined and despairing, was drinking himself to death with the riffraff of Rangoon, or with such of it as would listen to his abuse of the white women and his slanders upon their honesty. The contrast between Shere Ali's fate and the hopes with which he had set out was shocking enough. Yet even in his case so very little had turned the scale. Between the fulfilment of his hopes and the great failure what was there? If he had been sent to Ajmere instead of to England, if he and Linforth had not crossed the Meije to La Grave in Dauphine, if a necklace of pearls he had offered had not been accepted—very likely at this very moment he might be reigning in Chiltistan, trusted and supported by the Indian Government, a helpful friend gratefully recognised. To Linforth's thinking it was only "just not" with Shere Ali, too.

Linforth saw his companion coming towards him from the restaurant. He held out his hand.

A. E. W. Mason

"I have got to go," he said.

"I too," replied Violet. But she detained him. "I want to tell you," she said hurriedly. "Long ago—in Peshawur—do you remember? I told you there was someone else—a better mate for you than I was. I meant it, Dick, but you wouldn't listen. There is still the someone else. I am going to tell you her name. She has never said a word to me—but—but I am sure. It may sound mean of me to give her away—but I am not really doing that. I should be very happy, Dick, if it were possible. It's Phyllis Casson. She has never married. She is living with her father at Camberley." And before he could answer she had hurried away.

But Linforth was to see her again that night. For when he had taken his seat in the stalls of the theatre he saw her and her husband in a box. He gathered from the remarks of those about him that her jewels were a regular feature upon the first nights of new plays. He looked at her now and then during the intervals of the acts. A few people entered her box and spoke to her for a little while. Linforth conjectured that she had dropped a little out of the world in which he had known her. Yet she was contented. On the whole that seemed certain. She was satisfied with her life. To attend the first productions of plays, to sit in the restaurants, to hear her jewels remarked upon—her life had narrowed sleekly down to that, and she was content. But there had been other possibilities for Violet Oliver.

Linforth walked back from the theatre to his club. He looked into a room and saw an old gentleman dozing alone amongst his newspapers.

"I suppose I shall come to that," he said grimly. "It doesn't look over cheerful as a way of spending the evening of one's days," and he was suddenly seized with the temptation to go home and take the first train in the morning for Camberley. He turned the plan over in his mind for a moment, and then swung away from it in self-disgust. He retained a general reverence for women, and to seek marriage without bringing love to light him in the search was not within his capacity.

"That wouldn't be fair," he said to himself—"even if Violet's tale were true." For with his reverence he had retained his modesty. The next morning he took the train into Sussex instead, and was welcomed by Sybil Linforth to the house under the Downs. In the warmth of that welcome, at all events, there was nothing that was just not.

ABOUT THE AUTHOR

 **Alfred Edward Woodley Mason** (7 May 1865 Dulwich, London - 22 November 1948 London) was a British author.

He studied at Dulwich College and graduated from Trinity College, Oxford in 1888.

His first novel, A Romance of Wastdale, was published in 1895. He is the author of more than twenty books, among them The Four Feathers, originally published in London in 1902. His next successful work was At The Villa Rose (1910), where he introduced his French detective, Hanaud.

Mason was elected as a Liberal Member of Parliament for Coventry in the 1906 general election. He served only a single term in Parliament, retiring at the next general election in January 1910.

Mason rose to the rank of major during the First World War serving with The Manchester Regiment and the Royal Marine Light Infantry. His military career included work in naval intelligence, serving in Spain and Mexico, where he set up counter-espionage networks on behalf of the British government.

He died in 1948 while working on a non-fiction book about Admiral Robert Blake.

Choose from Thousands of 1stWorldLibrary Classics By

A. M. Barnard
Ada Leverson
Adolphus William Ward
Aesop
Agatha Christie
Alexander Aaronsohn
Alexander Kielland
Alexandre Dumas
Alfred Gatty
Alfred Ollivant
Alice Duer Miller
Alice Turner Curtis
Alice Dunbar
Allen Chapman
Alleyne Ireland
Ambrose Bierce
Amelia E. Barr
Amory H. Bradford
Andrew Lang
Andrew McFarland Davis
Andy Adams
Angela Brazil
Anna Alice Chapin
Anna Sewell
Annie Besant
Annie Hamilton Donnell
Annie Payson Call
Annie Roe Carr
Annonaymous
Anton Chekhov
Archibald Lee Fletcher
Arnold Bennett
Arthur C. Benson
Arthur Conan Doyle
Arthur M. Winfield
Arthur Ransome
Arthur Schnitzler
Arthur Train
Atticus
B.H. Baden-Powell
B. M. Bower
B. C. Chatterjee
Baroness Emmuska Orczy
Baroness Orczy
Basil King
Bayard Taylor
Ben Macomber
Bertha Muzzy Bower
Bjornstjerne Bjornson

Booth Tarkington
Boyd Cable
Bram Stoker
C. Collodi
C. E. Orr
C. M. Ingleby
Carolyn Wells
Catherine Parr Traill
Charles A. Eastman
Charles Amory Beach
Charles Dickens
Charles Dudley Warner
Charles Farrar Browne
Charles Ives
Charles Kingsley
Charles Klein
Charles Hanson Towne
Charles Lathrop Pack
Charles Romyn Dake
Charles Whibley
Charles Willing Beale
Charlotte M. Braeme
Charlotte M. Yonge
Charlotte Perkins Stetson
Clair W. Hayes
Clarence Day Jr.
Clarence E. Mulford
Clemence Housman
Confucius
Coningsby Dawson
Cornelis DeWitt Wilcox
Cyril Burleigh
D. H. Lawrence
Daniel Defoe
David Garnett
Dinah Craik
Don Carlos Janes
Donald Keyhoe
Dorothy Kilner
Dougan Clark
Douglas Fairbanks
E. Nesbit
E. P. Roe
E. Phillips Oppenheim
E. S. Brooks
Earl Barnes
Edgar Rice Burroughs
Edith Van Dyne
Edith Wharton

Edward Everett Hale
Edward J. O'Biren
Edward S. Ellis
Edwin L. Arnold
Eleanor Atkins
Eleanor Hallowell Abbott
Eliot Gregory
Elizabeth Gaskell
Elizabeth McCracken
Elizabeth Von Arnim
Ellem Key
Emerson Hough
Emilie F. Carlen
Emily Bronte
Emily Dickinson
Enid Bagnold
Enilor Macartney Lane
Erasmus W. Jones
Ernie Howard Pie
Ethel May Dell
Ethel Turner
Ethel Watts Mumford
Eugene Sue
Eugenie Foa
Eugene Wood
Eustace Hale Ball
Evelyn Everett-green
Everard Cotes
F. H. Cheley
F. J. Cross
F. Marion Crawford
Fannie E. Newberry
Federick Austin Ogg
Ferdinand Ossendowski
Fergus Hume
Florence A. Kilpatrick
Fremont B. Deering
Francis Bacon
Francis Darwin
Frances Hodgson Burnett
Frances Parkinson Keyes
Frank Gee Patchin
Frank Harris
Frank Jewett Mather
Frank L. Packard
Frank V. Webster
Frederic Stewart Isham
Frederick Trevor Hill
Frederick Winslow Taylor

Friedrich Kerst
Friedrich Nietzsche
Fyodor Dostoyevsky
G.A. Henty
G.K. Chesterton
Gabrielle E. Jackson
Garrett P. Serviss
Gaston Leroux
George A. Warren
George Ade
Geroge Bernard Shaw
George Cary Eggleston
George Durston
George Ebers
George Eliot
George Gissing
George MacDonald
George Meredith
George Orwell
George Sylvester Viereck
George Tucker
George W. Cable
George Wharton James
Gertrude Atherton
Gordon Casserly
Grace E. King
Grace Gallatin
Grace Greenwood
Grant Allen
Guillermo A. Sherwell
Gulielma Zollinger
Gustav Flaubert
H. A. Cody
H. B. Irving
H.C. Bailey
H. G. Wells
H. H. Munro
H. Irving Hancock
H. R. Naylor
H. Rider Haggard
H. W. C. Davis
Haldeman Julius
Hall Caine
Hamilton Wright Mabie
Hans Christian Andersen
Harold Avery
Harold McGrath
Harriet Beecher Stowe
Harry Castlemon
Harry Coghill
Harry Houidini

Hayden Carruth
Helent Hunt Jackson
Helen Nicolay
Hendrik Conscience
Hendy David Thoreau
Henri Barbusse
Henrik Ibsen
Henry Adams
Henry Ford
Henry Frost
Henry James
Henry Jones Ford
Henry Seton Merriman
Henry W Longfellow
Herbert A. Giles
Herbert Carter
Herbert N. Casson
Herman Hesse
Hildegard G. Frey
Homer
Honore De Balzac
Horace B. Day
Horace Walpole
Horatio Alger Jr.
Howard Pyle
Howard R. Garis
Hugh Lofting
Hugh Walpole
Humphry Ward
Ian Maclaren
Inez Haynes Gillmore
Irving Bacheller
Isabel Cecilia Williams
Isabel Hornibrook
Israel Abrahams
Ivan Turgenev
J.G.Austin
J. Henri Fabre
J. M. Barrie
J. M. Walsh
J. Macdonald Oxley
J. R. Miller
J. S. Fletcher
J. S. Knowles
J. Storer Clouston
J. W. Duffield
Jack London
Jacob Abbott
James Allen
James Andrews
James Baldwin

James Branch Cabell
James DeMille
James Joyce
James Lane Allen
James Lane Allen
James Oliver Curwood
James Oppenheim
James Otis
James R. Driscoll
Jane Abbott
Jane Austen
Jane L. Stewart
Janet Aldridge
Jens Peter Jacobsen
Jerome K. Jerome
Jessie Graham Flower
John Buchan
John Burroughs
John Cournos
John F. Kennedy
John Gay
John Glasworthy
John Habberton
John Joy Bell
John Kendrick Bangs
John Milton
John Philip Sousa
John Taintor Foote
Jonas Lauritz Idemil Lie
Jonathan Swift
Joseph A. Altsheler
Joseph Carey
Joseph Conrad
Joseph E. Badger Jr
Joseph Hergesheimer
Joseph Jacobs
Jules Vernes
Julian Hawthrone
Julie A Lippmann
Justin Huntly McCarthy
Kakuzo Okakura
Karle Wilson Baker
Kate Chopin
Kenneth Grahame
Kenneth McGaffey
Kate Langley Bosher
Kate Langley Bosher
Katherine Cecil Thurston
Katherine Stokes
L. A. Abbot
L. T. Meade

L. Frank Baum
Latta Griswold
Laura Dent Crane
Laura Lee Hope
Laurence Housman
Lawrence Beasley
Leo Tolstoy
Leonid Andreyev
Lewis Carroll
Lewis Sperry Chafer
Lilian Bell
Lloyd Osbourne
Louis Hughes
Louis Joseph Vance
Louis Tracy
Louisa May Alcott
Lucy Fitch Perkins
Lucy Maud Montgomery
Luther Benson
Lydia Miller Middleton
Lyndon Orr
M. Corvus
M. H. Adams
Margaret E. Sangster
Margret Howth
Margaret Vandercook
Margaret W. Hungerford
Margret Penrose
Maria Edgeworth
Maria Thompson Daviess
Mariano Azuela
Marion Polk Angellotti
Mark Overton
Mark Twain
Mary Austin
Mary Catherine Crowley
Mary Cole
Mary Hastings Bradley
Mary Roberts Rinehart
Mary Rowlandson
M. Wollstonecraft Shelley
Maud Lindsay
Max Beerbohm
Myra Kelly
Nathaniel Hawthrone
Nicolo Machiavelli
O. F. Walton
Oscar Wilde

Owen Johnson
P.G. Wodehouse
Paul and Mabel Thorne
Paul G. Tomlinson
Paul Severing
Percy Brebner
Percy Keese Fitzhugh
Peter B. Kyne
Plato
Quincy Allen
R. Derby Holmes
R. L. Stevenson
R. S. Ball
Rabindranath Tagore
Rahul Alvares
Ralph Bonehill
Ralph Henry Barbour
Ralph Victor
Ralph Waldo Emmerson
Rene Descartes
Ray Cummings
Rex Beach
Rex E. Beach
Richard Harding Davis
Richard Jefferies
Richard Le Gallienne
Robert Barr
Robert Frost
Robert Gordon Anderson
Robert L. Drake
Robert Lansing
Robert Lynd
Robert Michael Ballantyne
Robert W. Chambers
Rosa Nouchette Carey
Rudyard Kipling
Saint Augustine
Samuel B. Allison
Samuel Hopkins Adams
Sarah Bernhardt
Sarah C. Hallowell
Selma Lagerlof
Sherwood Anderson
Sigmund Freud
Standish O'Grady
Stanley Weyman
Stella Benson
Stella M. Francis

Stephen Crane
Stewart Edward White
Stijn Streuvels
Swami Abhedananda
Swami Parmananda
T. S. Ackland
T. S. Arthur
The Princess Der Ling
Thomas A. Janvier
Thomas A Kempis
Thomas Anderton
Thomas Bailey Aldrich
Thomas Bulfinch
Thomas De Quincey
Thomas Dixon
Thomas H. Huxley
Thomas Hardy
Thomas More
Thornton W. Burgess
U. S. Grant
Upton Sinclair
Valentine Williams
Various Authors
Vaughan Kester
Victor Appleton
Victor G. Durham
Victoria Cross
Virginia Woolf
Wadsworth Camp
Walter Camp
Walter Scott
Washington Irving
Wilbur Lawton
Wilkie Collins
Willa Cather
Willard F. Baker
William Dean Howells
William le Queux
W. Makepeace Thackeray
William W. Walter
William Shakespeare
Winston Churchill
Yei Theodora Ozaki
Yogi Ramacharaka
Young E. Allison
Zane Grey